ADDRESSING THE NEEDS OF WOUNDED MILITARY VETERANS: AN INTRODUCTION TO THE SPECIAL ISSUE

Rosemarie Scolaro Moser[1] and George A. Zitnay[2]

[1]RSM Psychology Center, LLC, Lawrenceville, NJ and [2]Defense and Veterans Brain Injury Center, Loretto, PA, USA

Wounded military veterans and their families are often frustrated by the lack of adequate assessment, treatment, and support they deserve due to an overburdened, constrained military health care system (Scott, 2005). Furthermore, they currently have limited or no access to state of the art modalities, tools, and treatments that are already available in the private sector. With traumatic brain injury (TBI) being called the signature injury in the "global war on terrorism" (Okie, 2005), blast-related injuries and extended deployments are contributing to an unprecedented number of warriors suffering from TBI and psychological conditions (Schneiderman, Braver, & Kang, 2008), the most controversial of which may be post-traumatic stress disorder (PTSD) (Bontke, 1996).

Operation Enduring Freedom (OEF) and Operation Iraqi Freedom (OIF) have become settings for what until recent history has been a less-prevalent form of TBI, specifically blast-related mild TBI. Although the effects of shock waves on internal organs (spalling, implosion, acceleration/deceleration, and pressure differential) have been well documented (Treadwell, 1989), we are now faced with attempting to understand the specific effects of blasts on the most vital internal organ: the brain. These effects whether cognitive and/or emotional in presentation are often an enigma. There are few clear answers to the myriad questions regarding the epidemiology and causation of the co-morbidity of mild TBI and PTSD (see Hoge et al., 2008). This state of affairs has challenged scientists and health care professionals to think outside of the box, beyond the current state of research and treatment, toward innovative, creative, and empirically based methods of assessment, treatment, and care, with the goal of disentangling the complexity of TBI and PTSD. Collaborative efforts, reaching beyond the military to the greater community, have been proposed to best address the TBI/PTSD dilemma (McCrea et al., 2007). This special issue of *The Clinical Neuropsychologist* tackles some of these pressing concerns.

Address correspondence to: Rosemarie Scolaro Moser, Ph.D., Director, RSM Psychology Center, LLC, Room 110, Bldg 5, 3131 Princeton Pike, Lawrenceville, NJ 08648, USA. E-mail: moserRS@comcast.net

© 2009 Psychology Press, an imprint of the Taylor & Francis group, an Informa business

With such concerns in mind, the International Conference on Behavioral Health and Traumatic Brain Injury convened on October 12–15, 2008 in Paterson, New Jersey. The conference was the brainchild of United States Representative Bill Pascrell Jr (NJ-08), who serves as the Co-Chair of the Congressional Task Force on Traumatic Brain Injury, in collaboration with Dr. George Zitnay, Co-Founder of the Defense and Veterans Brain Injury Center-Johnstown. Both gentlemen have been dedicated to advancing science, technology, and health care services for those individuals suffering from brain injury. This conference focused on our returning military veterans who are recovering from traumatic brain injury and post-traumatic stress disorder.

In addition to Congressman Pascrell and the Congressional Task Force on TBI, other major contributors joined in hosting this conference, including the Defense and Veterans Brain Injury Center (DVBIC), a component of the Department of Defense, Defense Centers of Excellence for Psychological Health and TBI (DCoE PH/TBI), St. Joseph's Regional Medical Center, located in Paterson, New Jersey, which graciously provided the site and accommodations, the National Brain Injury Research, Treatment, and Training Foundation (NBIRTT), the International Brain Research Foundation IBRF), the Henry H. Kessler Foundation, the University of Missouri HealthCare/Missouri Rehabilitation Center, and Pearson Assessment, among others. In sum, over 100 international scientists, health care professionals and administrators, military personnel, epidemiologists, policy analysts, legal experts, legislators, community supporters, veterans, and family members participated in the conference, which served as an interdisciplinary "think tank," addressing the current and future needs of our wounded veterans. Importantly, although the major impetus for the conference was to propel science and the advancement of services for injured veterans, the topics, discussion, and outcome could ultimately impact all those who suffer from TBI and/or PTSD.

Together, through working group assignments, the conference participants contributed to the *Report of the International Conference* that was presented to Congress on March 12, 2008, with specific recommendations for action and funding. That Congressional presentation featured U.S. Army First Lieutenant Brian Brennan and his family from New Jersey. Lt. Brennan was severely wounded when the patrol he was leading in Afghanistan in March 2008 was hit by two improvised explosive devices (IEDs), resulting in three casualties. Lt. Brennan was discovered in cardiac arrest, unconscious, and requiring bilateral partial leg amputations, with multiple internal organ and bone injuries, resulting in numerous surgeries, infections, and medical complications. Importantly, Lt. Brennan was brought stateside on Mother's Day, with a severe disorder of consciousness.

His mother, Mrs. Joanne Brennan, president of a medical and hospital practice consulting and management firm, has recounted her family's story many times. Lt. Brennan is a testament to the resilience and marvels of the human brain. He has defied the odds since he was born, as it was predicted that he would not survive birth; then it was predicted that he would not live more than 30 days after his birth; and then it was predicted that he would suffer significant brain injury and cerebral palsy if he did survive. Instead, with his mother's perseverance and family's resources, he learned to walk by age 3, attended school never needing special education services, was the high school football hero, and successfully graduated college at The Citadel where he was the head platoon leader for his senior class. After only 3 months of deployment in OEF, he was severely injured on a tour of duty. Despite his family members' round-the-clock vigil and attempts to rouse him, they were told that he would likely never awaken from his vegetative state. Remarkably, on June 10, or day 23 as referred to by Mrs. Brennan, General David Howell Petraeus visited Lt. Brennan, and talked to him at length, yet he remained unresponsive. But just as the General was leaving the hospital room, the General spoke the motto of Lt. Brennan's military division, "Currahee." *Currahee* is the Cherokee word for "Stands alone." Amazingly, Lt. Brennan awoke, sat at attention, and became extremely emotional. Coincidence? Non-invasive brain stimulation?

Since then, Lt. Brennan religiously attends rehabilitation services five days per week at Walter Reed Medical Center and returns home on weekends to his own specially constructed independent apartment. He does not consider himself a hero and will deny such a reference as he "was just doing my job." He is able to drive a car with his leg prostheses, and has as his goal to live as normal a life as possible. He publicly admits that he continues to struggle with the flashbacks and panic of PTSD and that his brain injury is his biggest challenge, especially his attention and concentration, which continue to improve. Nevertheless, his brain recovery has again defied the odds.

At the congressional presentation on March 12, 2009, Lt. Brennan's parents urged U.S. Congress to look deep into their "hearts" and "pockets" to support research and services for these young military service members and their families, to find cures for brain injury and severe disorders of consciousness, and to reach out to rural families, and those with limited financial resources who cannot secure the needed medical interventions. The Brennans are just one of many families that are searching for answers to the mysteries of brain injury and recovery, and that are looking to scientists—to us—to find solutions as soon as possible.

This special issue of *The Clinical Neuropsychologist* was created as a product of the International Conference. For this journal issue we have gathered a selection of topics related to the conference, with papers authored by some of the conference's speakers and participants. We believe that the topics touch on some of the most salient, as well as controversial, issues that we now face as researchers, scientists, and clinicians.

We are honored that this issue includes an *Introduction to the Report of the International Conference* by Congressman Pascrell, followed by the *Report of the International Conference*. The Report is endorsed by its numerous, multidisciplinary authors, many of whom represent the field of neuropsychology. These authors and conference participants should be commended for volunteering up to 4 days of on-site time and expertise, working collaborative, wrestling with seemingly discrepant viewpoints about assessment, research, and treatment, and ultimately demonstrating their commitment to the needs of our wounded military veterans.

As guest editors of this special issue, we wish to acknowledge the instrumental support of the military sector in executing the International Conference which brought together our many scientists, researchers, health care professionals, and other participants. Specifically, we wish to acknowledge the participation of Brigadier General Loree K. Sutton, MD, National Director of the DCoE PH/TBI, and Colonel Michael Jaffee, MD, Director of the DVBIC, whose enthusiastic contributions, presentations, and interactions affirmed the relevancy of the conference's mission.

We wish to thank Pearson for its strong commitment to the mission of the conference by facilitating the production of this special issue through its sponsorship. We also wish to thank the numerous other sponsors and supporters who donated not only funds, but time and in-kind contributions, which are too numerous to note here.

Importantly, we are most pleased to acknowledge the generosity and assistance of Drs. Russell Bauer and Jerry Sweet, editors of *The Clinical Neuropsychologist*, whose unequivocal support and assistance in bringing this special issue to fruition are greatly appreciated. Their commitment to the needs of our wounded warriors and to the dissemination of the *Report of the International Conference* via journal publication has been invaluable.

Ultimately we hope that venues such as the International Conference and this special journal issue will enlighten Congress, our community leaders, and all those who serve our injured military veterans. We also hope that scientists and researchers will be encouraged to seek new and effective evidenced-based assessments and treatments. We cannot underestimate the immediate need to improve the standard of care and outcomes for those suffering from TBI and/or PTSD.

REFERENCES

Bontke, C. F. (1996). Do patients with mild brain injuries have posttraumatic stress disorder, too? *Journal of Head Trauma Rehabilitation, 11*(1), 95–102.

Hoge, C. W., McGurk, D., Thomas, J. L., Cox, A. L., Engle, C. C., & Castro, C. A. (2008). Mild traumatic brain injury in U.S. soldiers returning from Iraq. *The New England Journal of Medicine, 358*, 453–463.

McCrea, M., Pliskin, N., Barth, J., Cox, D., Fink, J., French, L., et al. (2007). Official position of the Military TBI Task Force on the role of neuropsychology and rehabilitation psychology in the evaluation, management and research of military veterans with traumatic brain injury. Pre-publication executive summary. *American Academy of Clinical Neuropsychology, October*, 2007.

Okie, S. (2005). Traumatic brain injury in the war zone. *New England Journal of Medicine, 352*, 2043–2047.

Scott, L. (2005). Mental health cases threaten to swamp VA. *Fort Lewis Ranger, April 21–27*, 3.

Schneiderman, A. I., Braver, E. R., & Kang, H. K. (2008). Undersatnding sequelae of injury mechanisms and mild traumatic brain injury incurred during the conflicts in Iraq and Afghanistan: Persistent postconcussive symptoms and posttraumatic stress disorder. *American Journal of Epidemiology, 167*, 1446–1452.

Treadwell, I. (1989). Effects of blast on the human body. *Nursing RSA, March 4*(3), 32–36.

INTRODUCTION TO THE REPORT OF THE INTERNATIONAL CONFERENCE ON BEHAVIORAL HEALTH AND TRAUMATIC BRAIN INJURY

Congressman Bill Pascrell, Jr. (NJ-08)
Co-Chair, Congressional Brain Injury Task Force

On October 12–15, 2008, The International Conference on Behavioral Health and Traumatic Brain Injury, sponsored by the Congressional Brain Injury Task Force, brought together some of the world's greatest minds in traumatic brain injury (TBI) and behavioral health at St. Joseph's Regional Medical Center in my hometown of Paterson, New Jersey, to generate the report that is before you. The Task Force works tirelessly to ensure that individuals have access to reliable information, effective prevention strategies, and, if injured, comprehensive and appropriate treatments. The Task Force is able to accomplish this mission by bringing together great minds like the authors of this report in a collaborative, multi-disciplinary manner that includes both military and civilian perspectives.

The recommendations in this report are vital now more than ever. I believe that we stand at an auspicious convergence of public awareness, unprecedented necessity, and scientific discovery in moving forward to address TBI and behavioral health conditions like post-traumatic stress disorder (PTSD). Furthermore, the advancements and breakthroughs that we make on the battlefield will help us to better respond to injuries on our football fields and playgrounds.

Public awareness of TBI is at its peak. In the United States, 1.4 million new civilian TBI cases occur each year; and an estimated 320,000 soldiers deployed to Iraq and Afghanistan may have sustained a brain injury while in the line of duty. These are numbers with which the public has become increasingly familiar over the past several years as this important issue has made its way into the media. ABC reporter Bob Woodruff gave the American public a face and a story to attach to TBI when he was injured by a roadside bomb while reporting from Iraq in 2006.

Fortunately, Bob Woodruff received the world-class care for which the Department of Defense had been renowned for years. However, there were weaknesses in the Defense health care system, and many injured soldiers weren't receiving the level of care that they deserved. This was met with public outcry. Since that time, the military has made great strides to better prevent, identify, and treat TBIs and behavioral health issues among our brave men and women in uniform, but there is still room for progress and the public remains interested and invested in the implementation of these improvements.

Furthermore, there is an unprecedented necessity for relevant policies and effective treatments to address TBI and behavioral health. The numbers of individuals returning from Iraq and Afghanistan with brain injuries and PTSD have undoubtedly strained our Defense and Veterans health care systems. At an estimated combined societal cost of $7 billion, there is no doubt that these individuals impact our community systems and resources. The RAND Corporation recently estimated that over a quarter of soldiers with TBI may also have PTSD or depression—suggesting an enigmatic relationship between the two. These factors necessitate more collaboration between the civilian and military sectors; more resources to address the growing number of impacted individuals streaming back into our communities; and more research into the causes, interactions, and treatments of these conditions.

Finally, scientific discovery in TBI and behavioral health is at a precipitous moment. Science has achieved more in these conditions in the last 5 years than in the last 500, but relatively little is still known about some of the long-term effects of TBI and the interaction between psychological health conditions and brain injury. Fortunately, the discoveries that have been made in science have changed perceptions about these conditions and removed some of the stigma, which has served as a real barrier to care for many, especially our armed service members. But we still have a long way to go.

I look forward to working with my colleagues in Congress, the authors of this report, and the Administration to quickly implement effective policies to realize the level of care that our wounded warriors deserve.

THE HONORABLE WILLIAM J. PASCRELL, JR.
United States House of Representatives
Co-Chair and Founder, Congressional Brain Injury Task Force

THE 2008 INTERNATIONAL CONFERENCE ON BEHAVIORAL HEALTH AND TRAUMATIC BRAIN INJURY

REPORT TO CONGRESS ON IMPROVING THE CARE OF WOUNDED WARRIORS *NOW*

Traumatic brain injury is often called the "signature injury" in the war on global terrorism. Blast-related injuries and extended deployments are contributing to an unprecedented number of warriors suffering from traumatic brain injury (TBI) and post-traumatic stress disorder (PTSD).

The Rand Corporation, Department of Defense (DoD), and the Centers for Disease Control and Prevention all report that the long-term effects and consequences of TBI and PTSD will cost billions of dollars in care, treatment, and rehabilitation unless action is immediately taken. Of the 1.64 million U.S. troops deployed in the war on terrorism, approximately 360,000 are estimated to have suffered a TBI and another 300,000 suffer from PTSD. The Rand Report estimates that PTSD-related and major depression-related costs could range from $4.0 to $6.2 billion over 2 years (in 2007 dollars). TBI costs per patient range from a 1-year cost of $25,000 in mild cases to $408,000 in severe cases. The total cost for TBI-related health issues is estimated to be in the billions of dollars and does not include the lost productivity of our wounded veterans nor quality of life issues for them and their families.

The Congressional Brain Injury Task Force, chaired by Bill Pascrell and Todd Platts, recognizing the importance of TBI and PTSD, hosted an international gathering of experts and family members to prepare recommendations to mitigate the long-term consequences of this serious public health problem. The Congressional Brain Injury Task Force will take the recommendations included here, to DoD for decisive action and to Congress to enact appropriate legislation and provide needed funding.

The rationale for *The International Conference on Behavioral Health and Traumatic Brain Injury* was to ensure that Congressional funding would directly support targeted research, treatments, and clinical services recommended by experts and family members.

On October 12 through October 15, 2008, *The International Conference on Behavioral Health and Traumatic Brain Injury* was held at St. Joseph's Regional Medical Center in Paterson, New Jersey. The conference's primary sponsors included the DoD, the Defense and Veterans Brain Injury Center (DVBIC), the Congressional Brain Injury Task Force, St. Joseph's Regional Medical Center, the International Brain Research Foundation, Kessler Medical Rehabilitation Research and Education Corporation, and the Henry H. Kessler Foundation. Additional support was also derived from numerous other organizations.

Over 100 international experts in neuroscience, medical research, neuro-rehabilitation, behavioral health, treatment, ethics, and training joined with family members and wounded warriors to prepare recommendations for the DoD and Congress to address the complex issues of TBI and PTSD.

Priority *State of the Art* recommendations to the DoD and Congress were made within the following five content areas:

(1) Research
(2) Education
(3) Assessment
(4) Family
(5) Treatment

The conference allowed experts to collaboratively review the current cutting edge biomedical literature, best health care practices, available family support and resources, and up to date technology. After one and a half days of scientific and medical presentations, conference participants were divided into five work groups, based on the content areas, to discuss the most pressing issues, prioritize needs, and to develop specific recommendations.

The following recommendations were formally presented by these work groups for funding and budgeting consideration, and for programmatic and research development.

I. RESEARCH
Goals

To significantly improve treatment choices for all levels (mild to severe) of traumatic brain injury and PTSD, thus leading to improved outcomes and prevention of secondary conditions, such as chronic anxiety, major depression, substance abuse, suicide, occupational/social difficulties, and homelessness; and to increase targeted funding to further brain trauma research.

Recommendations

(a) Support collaborative research on *Neuro-Protection*, to be facilitated by the DVBIC and DCoE (Defense Centers of Excellence), in conjunction with universities, research institutes, and VA hospitals.
(b) Support pre-clinical and clinical research that defines the pathophysiology and natural history of blast injury.
(c) Support research that generates improved methods that are multimodal evidence-based for the identification of neurological and psychological injuries, and for the diagnosis and quantification of the effects of such injuries, so as to better facilitate return to duty.
(d) Support research on brain repair and recovery of function after TBI, so as to improve understanding of the molecular, genetic, and environmental mechanisms by which the brain recovers.

(e) Support research to identify and address individual differences in vulnerability, resilience, response to injury, psychological stress, and treatment effectiveness.

II. EDUCATION
Goal

To assure that every member of the military, the National Guard, Reserve, and their family members have easy access, with multilingual translation, to usable and timely information and resources regarding TBI and Psychological Health.

Recommendations

(a) Initiate a Public Service Awareness (PSA) campaign with a visible national spokesperson, utilizing television, multimedia applications, and advanced technology such as newer Internet-based vehicles, blogs, YouTube, and social networking sites.
(b) Direct the DoD, through DVBIC and the DCoE, to establish one centralized national helpline call system.
(c) Direct the DoD, through the DCoE, to establish a fixed-point of referral for wounded warriors and their families that will serve as a Coordinating Center for the tri-services, which will also be accessible through the national helpline.
(d) Expand the current care coordination program across the country, employing both the DVBIC network and private sector providers, with centralized access through the fixed-point referral Coordinating Center. Increase the efficiency and penetration of care by utilizing video teleconferencing and other electronic communication platforms and vehicles.
(e) Promote the development of a Federal Interagency Task Force to gather and disseminate information and educational material that has been developed by both the public and private sectors.
(f) Direct DoD and VA to collaborate directly with State TBI programs and State Veterans Departments to provide a seamless network of information and resources for the military, veterans, the National Guard, Reserves, and their families.
(g) Develop and execute a standardized TBI/Psychological Health education module that will be required for training all health care personnel in the tri-services, National Guard, and Reserves.
(h) Have DVBIC/DCoE create a high-tech traveling Mobile Library to improve awareness and to address the educational and resource needs of wounded warriors, their families, and health care personnel in rural areas that have limited Internet access.

III. ASSESSMENT
Goal

To provide in-theatre testing and post-injury assessment that is scientifically based, validated, and well-standardized to improve the accurate and timely identification of injury.

Recommendations

(a) Establish an automated web-centric, scientifically based assessment tool to be used in theatre, by all services, to determine if a warrior may return to duties after exposure to a blast or to other events that may cause TBI or psychological problems. In addition, assessment tools should be developed for use across the care continuum from the acute stage through to community re-entry. The development of assessment tools must be performed by a group of recognized experts in the area of testing and assessment of TBI/Psychological Health and who possess reasonable and relevant experience in this area of expertise.
(b) Fund the development of a standardized assessment battery for TBI and PTSD that is symptom-based and that can be utilized after the exposure event. This battery will include bio-psycho-social measures to guide treatment and management. This battery should be socially and culturally sensitive and consider multi-language contexts. The battery should include:

  (1) A database that is accessible through the Internet for all levels of medical care; and
  (2) Assessment components that incorporate neuropsychological/neurocognitive evaluation, imaging findings (both structural and functional), biometrics, effort and motivational factors, and social functioning.
  (3) The value of pre-deployment assessment should be explored.

IV. FAMILY
Goal

To provide family members with resources to ease their stress, to increase their understanding, to help them support their wounded loved ones.

Recommendations

(a) Expand the Congressionally mandated Family Caregiver Program. Establish a "Family to Family" rural network support system so that families can efficiently access important information and resources available from the Veterans Administration (VA), DoD, and the private sector. This network should utilize state of the art information technology platforms such as video teleconferencing, blogs, and other Internet vehicles.
(b) Create a new technology-based simulated mentor/coach system for immediate use by wounded warriors and their families. This simulated coaching system

should be interactive, contain answers to frequently asked questions, include the use of a national spokesperson serving as the "coach," and be kept up-to-date. This "Sim Coach" system can use a gaming system-like format that is user friendly. A pilot study to determine the feasibility and effectiveness of such a tool should first be conducted.

(c) Provide funding for temporary housing and transportation so that family members may actively and closely participate in the rehabilitation of their wounded warriors.

(d) Develop specially designed cognitively appropriate, educational materials for children of wounded warriors to help them understand what has happened to their wounded family members. Utilize age-appropriate, attractive electronic technologies and fund the comprehensive dissemination of these materials.

(e) Develop educational brochures and materials for families that feature clear and insightful information about ethical decision making, care and treatment options, informed consent, and participation in research protocols.

(f) Educate families about the value of journaling and recording medical events and questions/answers regarding healthcare concerns, especially during the acute phase of care.

(g) Develop a respite care program for family caregivers of active military and veterans with brain injury that includes counseling and guidance services.

V. TREATMENT

Goal

To establish and provide the most up to date standard of care for all severity levels of injury.

Recommendations

(a) Direct the NIH/DoD to convene a "Consensus Conference" to clearly define mild TBI (mTBI) and PTSD and to establish specific standards for treatment. Definitions and treatment standards should be evidence based and incorporate a thorough review of available treatment programs and outcome measures. The Consensus Conference must strive to equitably involve all stakeholders.

(b) Direct the DoD, through the DVBIC/DCoE, to contract with groups of scientific experts and skilled practitioners to create, disseminate, and employ comprehensive, integrated, individualized treatment algorithms aimed at preventing secondary complications from TBI and stress-related disorders.

(c) Direct the DoD/DCoE to develop, implement, and validate an integrated psycho-educational model to prevent the later development of persistent neuro-behavioral complications that can lead to family discord, divorce, substance abuse, homelessness, or suicide.

(d) Fund the establishment of six DCoE geographically dispersed TBI/PTSD treatment, research, care coordination, and educational centers utilizing the existing infrastructure of Centers of Excellence in TBI. These centers should incorporate both rural and urban area locations. Rigorous program evaluation

of these centers must be conducted. These centers must utilize state of the art telemedicine and information technology applications.
(e) One of the six centers must be a consortium of the leading centers, foundations, and universities capable of providing state of the art research, treatment, neurorehabilitation, and training for wounded warriors and veterans with severe traumatic brain injury. The consortium must be directed and managed by experienced leaders in the field and utilize the latest scientific research and technology currently available. This center will establish the standard of care for this population.
(f) Support further translational, clinical research of specific electrical, metabolic, chemical neuroimaging studies of brain states that would be utilized to develop neuromarkers targeted to specific newly developed treatment non-invasive interventions.

CONCLUSION

This international group of experts and family members, who are the authors of this report, firmly believe that genuine progress will result, and patient outcomes will significantly improve if the above recommendations are expeditiously funded and implemented. The over-arching goal is to provide our wounded warriors and their families with what they deserve: the best health care and support services that our state of the art science and medicine has to offer. And in doing so, we will create a standard of excellence in military health care, research, and training that will serve as an exemplary model for the rest of world. To achieve this over-arching goal, it is imperative that the DoD reorganize the Office of Health Affairs to respond more quickly and decisively to the emergent needs of wounded warriors and to implement the latest advances in research and cutting edge technology in the most timely manner. We strongly urge that the DCoE for TBI be placed within the Office of the Secretary of Defense in order to successfully execute these recommendations.

We recommend that Congress appropriate $350 million to implement these recommendations and to maintain comprehensive oversight of that funding, to assure that these dollars will be used as intended.

We, the undersigned, support the recommendations of this report and request immediate Congressional and Department of Defense consideration and action.

Judith Avner, Esq.
Brain Injury Association of New York State

William B. Barr, PhD
New York University, NY

Jeffrey T. Barth, PhD
University of Virginia Medical School, VA

Dennis Benigno
Coalition for Brain Injury Research, Clifton, NJ

Jean E. Bérubé, Esq.
Government Relations Consultant, Washington, DC

Joseph Bleiberg, PhD
National Rehabilitation Hospital, Washington, DC

Frank J. Brady
Medical Missions for Children, Paterson, NJ

Lucia W. Braga, PhD
SARAH Network of Rehabilitation Hospitals, Brazil

Shane S. Bush, PhD
Long Island Neuropsychology, PC, NY

Virgilio Caraballo
Rehabilitation Specialists, Fair Lawn, NJ

George Carnevale, PhD
St. Joseph's Regional Medical Center, Paterson, NJ

Marie Cavallo, PhD
Brain Injury Association of New York
NY Center for Comprehensive Cognitive Rehabilitation

Anne-Lise Christensen, PhD
University of Copenhagen, Denmark

Rory A. Cooper, PhD
University of Pittsburgh Healthcare System, PA

Anthony D'Ambrosio, MD
St. Joseph's Regional Medical Center, Paterson, NJ

Philip A. DeFina, PhD
International Brain Research Foundation, Inc., Edison, NJ

John DeLuca, PhD
Kessler Foundation Research Center, West Orange, NJ

Barbara Demuth, RN, MSN
CERMUSA, St. Francis University, Loretto, PA

Dirk DeRidder, MD, PhD
Antwerp University Hospital, Belgium

William A. Ditto, MSW
National Association of State Head Injury Administrators

Ruben J. Echemendia, PhD
National Academy of Neuropsychology

Eileen Elias, M.Ed
JBS International, Inc., Washington, DC

Monika Eller, OTR
Kessler Institute for Rehabilitation Center, Chester, NJ

Brace Feldbusch
Wounded Warrior Project, Johnstown, PA

Charlene Feldbusch
Wounded Warrior Project, Johnstown, PA

Sgt. (ret.) Jeremy Feldbusch
Wounded Warrior Project. Johnstown, PA

Jonathan Fellus, MD
Kessler Institute for Rehabilitation, West Orange, NJ

Patricia Fitzgerald, PT, PhD, MPT
CERMUSA, St. Francis University, Loretto, PA

Martin B. Foil, III
Hinds' Feet Farm, Huntersville, NC

Bruce M. Gans, MD
Kessler Institute for Rehabilitation, West Orange, NJ

Barbara Geiger-Parker
Brain Injury Association of New Jersey

Thomas Grady
Brain Injury Association of New Jersey

Jay Gunkelman
Q-Metrx, Inc., Burbank, CA
International Brain Research Foundation, Inc.

Robin Hedeman, OTR, MHA
Kessler Institute for Rehabilitation, West Orange, NJ

David Hovda, PhD
Brain Injury Research Center, University of California, Los Angeles, CA

Grant L. Iverson, PhD
University of British Columbia, Canada

Andy S. Jagoda, MD
Mt. Sinai School of Medicine, NY, NY

Melissa Kagarise, MMS, DHSc, PA-C
CERMUSA, St. Francis University, Loretto, PA

Tanya Kaushik, PsyD
Headminder, Inc., NY, NY

Yuri Kropotov, PhD
Russian Academy of Sciences, St. Petersburg, Russia

Andrew Maas, MD, PhD
University Hospital Antwerp, Belgium

Kay Malek, PT, PhD, MS
St. Francis University, Loretto, PA

Thomas A. Martin, PsyD
Missouri Rehabilitation Center, University of Missouri, Mt. Vernon, MO

Robert J. McCaffrey, PhD
University of Albany, State University of New York, NY

Thomas McCallister, MD
Dartmouth Medical College, Hanover, NH

Michael McCrea, PhD
ProHealth Care, Waukesha Memorial Hospital, Waukesha WI

William McDonald
St. Joseph's Regional Medical Center, Paterson, NJ

Maria McNish, MS
Kessler Institute for Rehabilitation, West Orange, NJ

Rosemarie Scolaro Moser, PhD
RSM Psychology Center, LLC, Lawrenceville, NJ

St. Francis Medical Center, Trenton, NJ

Claudio I. Perino, PhD
University of Torino, Torino, Italy

Charles Prestigiacomo, MD
UMDNJ Neurological Institute of New Jersey

Theresa Rankin
Brain Injury Services, Inc.
WETA BrainLine, Arlington, VA

Ali Rezai, MD
Cleveland Clinic, Cleveland OH

Jay Roberts, MA
CERMUSA, St. Francis University, Loretto, PA

Bradley G. Sewick, PhD
American Board of Professional Neuropsychology

Charles P. Steiner, ME
Cleveland Clinic, Cleveland, OH

James Thompson, PhD
International Brain Research Foundation, Inc., Edison, NJ

Kent Tonkin, MA
CERMUSA, St. Francis University, Loretto, PA

Carl Valenziano, MD
St. Joseph's Regional Medical Center, Paterson, NJ

Nathan D. Zasler, MD
Concussion Care Centre of Virginia, Tree of Life Services, Inc.
International Brain Injury Association

George A. Zitnay, PhD
University of Pittsburgh, Johnstown, PA
Co-Founder, Defense and Veterans Brain Injury Center

A BRIEF OVERVIEW OF TRAUMATIC BRAIN INJURY (TBI) AND POST-TRAUMATIC STRESS DISORDER (PTSD) WITHIN THE DEPARTMENT OF DEFENSE

Col. Michael S. Jaffee and Kimberly S. Meyer

Defense and Veterans Brain Injury Center, Washington, DC, USA

The current conflicts in the Middle East have yielded increasing awareness of the acute and chronic effect of traumatic brain injury (TBI) and post-traumatic stress disorder (PTSD). The increasing frequency of exposure to blast and multiple deployments potentially impact the probability that a service member may sustain one of these injuries. The 2008 International Conference on Behavioral Health and Traumatic Brain Injury united experts in the fields of behavioral health and traumatic brain injury to address these significant health concerns. This article summarizes current Department of Defense (DoD) initiatives related to TBI and PTSD.

Keywords: Traumatic brain injury (TBI); Post-traumatic stress disorder (PTSD); Department of Defense.

INTRODUCTION

The current conflicts in the Middle East have yielded increasing awareness of the acute and chronic effects of traumatic brain injury (TBI) and post-traumatic stress disorder (PTSD). The RAND Report (Tanelian & Jaycox, 2008) and Centers for Disease Control and Prevention estimate that TBI and PTSD treatment and rehabilitation will cost billions of dollars, without factoring in loss of productivity, wages and quality of life. The increasing frequency of exposure to blast, combined with multiple deployments, potentially impact the probability that service member may sustain one of these injuries.

INCIDENCE

TBI and concussion rates among service members returning from Operation Iraqi Freedom (OIF) have been reported at 22% (Terrio et al., 2009). However, the rate of persistent symptoms has been reported as significantly lower (8%). The co-morbidity of TBI and PTSD in combat injuries has been well described. Recent studies demonstrate that up to 44% of service members with self-reported concussion may meet diagnostic criteria for PTSD when evaluated 3–4 months after returning from deployment (Hoge et al., 2008). In this sample, with the exception of headache, symptoms were non-specific to either diagnosis.

Address correspondence to: Dr. Michael S. Jaffee, Defense and Veterans Brain Injury Center, Washington, DC 20012, USA. E-mail: Michael.jaffee@amedd.army.mil

© 2009 Psychology Press, an imprint of the Taylor & Francis group, an Informa business

Another study reported PTSD rates of 5–10% in patients at all severity levels of TBI (Bombardier et al., 2006). However, subgroup analysis has demonstrated higher rates of PTSD in patients with complicated mild traumatic brain injury (mTBI). The correlation between TBI and PTSD has been further illustrated in a retrospective review of those injured in the Oklahoma City Bombing (Walilko et al., in press). Similarly, these observations that PTSD rates may be higher in patients with TBI, compared to those with other injuries, have also been noted in OIF/OEF (Operation Enduring Freedom) combat injuries (Hoge et al., 2008) and suggest some important pathophysiological overlaps. Controversy regarding the effects of post-traumatic amnesia on the development of PTSD remains.

The use of advanced body armor has increased the survivability of today's wounded warrior. Fewer penetrating brain, abdominal, and thoracic injuries are sustained compared to previous conflicts (Gondusky & Reiter, 2005; Patel et al., 2004). This, coupled with rapid air evacuation, has led to decreased mortality from combat-related polytrauma (Grissom & Farmer, 2005). For instance, severely injured service members are airlifted to military hospitals where they undergo life-saving surgeries almost immediately (Peoples, Gerlinger, Craig, & Berlingame, 2005). Once stabilized, the patient can then be transferred briefly to Landstuhl Regional Medical Center (LRMC), the secure trauma center outside of the combat zone for further stabilization with subsequent evacuation to the United States in as few as 48–72 hours. These polytrauma survivors often exhibit comorbid TBI or PTSD (Clark, Bair, Buckenmaier, Gironda, & Walker, 2007; Mora et al., 2009).

Aggressive efforts at improving TBI surveillance have been instituted within the DoD. The Defense and Veterans Brain Injury Center (DVBIC), in collaboration with the Armed Forces Health Surveillance Center and representatives from each branch of service, has revised and upgraded surveillance methods to ensure accurate reporting. This includes the identification of the standard International Coding of Disease-9 (ICD-9) for traumatic brain injury and the development of a database that allows capture of 25 variables, including demographics and injury severity, on each patient with TBI. TBI severity is assigned based on the duration of loss of consciousness, post-traumatic amnesia, and alteration of consciousness. Imaging findings are also considered when determining injury severity. This classification is congruent with definitions of prominent organizations such as the American Academy of Rehabilitation Medicine, American Academy of Neurology and others.

PATHOPHYSIOLOGY OF BLAST-RELATED INJURY

Blast injury may cause physiological effects on the brain by one of four mechanisms (DoDD policy 6025.21E, 2006). Primary blast injury is postulated to cause axonal injury as a result of rapid shifts in kinetic energy that lead from blast-induced over-pressurization waves to negative pressure waves. Secondary blast injury results from environmental objects that are set in motion by blast energy. Blast energy may also displace a person into an environmental structure, thereby leading to tertiary blast injury. Finally, release of heat pulses and noxious fumes may contribute to quaternary blast injury. In addition to causing TBI, witnessing an explosion and its after-effects may also contribute to the development of anxiety and other stress-related reactions, including PTSD. There is ongoing research to better characterize the effects of blast on the brain. Currently it is accepted that there is likely little or no difference in blunt and blast-related brain injury. A recent study by Belanger, Kretzmer, Yoash-Gantz, Pickett, and Tupler (2009) demonstrated no significant difference in neuropsychological function in those with blast-related injury compared to those with blunt trauma. However, preliminary data from acute TBI diffusion tensor imaging studies suggest that there are pathological differences between blunt and blast-related TBI.

CURRENT DoD INITIATIVES

Recognizing the importance of early diagnosis and treatment of TBI, the DoD has implemented screening processes throughout the course of combat operations. If exposed to significant blast or other traumatic events, service members are immediately screened to determine if an alteration in consciousness occurred. If so, further cognitive evaluation is performed utilizing the Military Acute Concussion Evaluation (MACE). The MACE consists of two components: the history, which serves to identify the presence of a traumatic event and subsequent alteration or loss of consciousness, and a cognitive evaluation, the Standardized Assessment of Concussion (SAC) (McCrea, Kelly, & Randolph, 2000). Those diagnosed with concussion through this process are managed locally when possible and referred to higher echelon centers for management of complex or persistent symptoms. Key to successful management is providing educational materials that describe the natural course of the injury and normalize symptoms (Mittenberg, Tremont, Zielinski, Fichera, & Rayls, 1996; Ponsford et al., 2002). Combat stress counseling may also be initiated as psychological stressors may impact cognitive performance and symptom reporting (DoD, 2008). Additional mandatory screening is completed at post-deployment with the incorporation of an adaptation of the Brief TBI Screen (BTBIS; Schwab et al., 2007) into the Post-Deployment Health Assessment (PDHA). The purpose of this process is to identify those who may have sustained an injury that was not identified nor treated acutely.

Since May 2008 baseline neurocognitive testing, utilizing the Automated Neuropsychological Assessment Metrics (ANAM; Reeves, Kane, Winter, & Elsmore, 2005) has been performed on service members preparing for deployment. Specifically, the ANAM TBI military battery includes code substitution, simple reaction time, matching to sample, procedural reaction times, and mathematical processing to evaluate neural processing, memory, and learning measured during a 15-minute computerized assessment. It is intended that these results can then be used to assess fitness for duty following injury by comparing individual baselines to post-injury scores. It is postulated that comparison to one's own baseline can be a more sensitive indicator of an individual's post concussion cognitive function than comparison to a normative data set.

Many of the above DoD initiatives were recently endorsed in the Institute of Medicine's (IOM) report *Long-term Consequences of Traumatic Brain Injury* (2008). Specifically, actions recommended by the report included:

- Continue utilization of the Brief Traumatic Brain injury Screen and MACE
- Conduct longitudinal studies of blast-related TBI

- Conduct research on blast-related neurotrauma
- Develop the Veteran's Health Registry
- Perform pre-deployment neurocognitive testing.

The DoD has established TBI treatment centers based on resource availability. Severe and penetrating injuries are transferred to Walter Reed Army Medical Center or National Naval Medical Center. The exception to this occurs in cases of a polytrauma patient with significant burn injuries. These patients are managed at Brook Army Medical Center. Moderate TBI can be treated at any of these facilities as well as Eisenhower Army Medical Center. Every effort is made to manage uncomplicated concussion in the primary care setting. However, if necessary, referrals can be made to designated TBI centers for those individuals requiring more intensive evaluation and management.

As TBI training is minimal in most medical training programs, clinical practice guidelines (CPG) for the evaluation and management of concussion have been developed by literature review and consensus of Tri-service and civilian experts in order to aid primary care providers as they encounter this patient population. The stateside practice guidelines for TBI are based on symptom complexes that follow Cicerone's Neurobehavioral Symptom Inventory (Cicerone & Kalmar, 1995). Appropriate assessment and management recommendations for commonly occurring concussive symptom complexes are provided to primary care providers. Similarly, algorithms of care have been developed for use in the deployed setting. The deployed setting CPG provides recommendations for care based on the unique aspects and resource limitations of the combat setting. A more rigorous, scientific review of the literature has been undertaken by the Veteran's Affairs (VA)/DoD evidence-based work group, which yielded the recently released Management of Concussion/Mild Traumatic Brain Injury CPG (2009). A key component of these guidelines has been incorporation of education emphasizing expectations of recovery.

Other ongoing DoD initiatives include the development of a Family Caregiver Curriculum (National Defense Authorization Act, 2007) to conduct training for those families who provide care for members and former members of the Armed Forces with TBI, regardless of etiology. This curriculum will incorporate multimedia to ensure the family caregiver has the necessary information and resources to understand TBI and the DoD/VA medical care systems as well as the skills and tools needed to provide care. A website (www.traumaticbraininjuryatoz.org), produced by the United States Air Force Center of Excellence for Medical Multimedia, offers service members and families TBI information and shares stories of the personal journeys of some wounded warriors with TBI. Development of a family-to-family rural support group is also being discussed. Further expansion of the DVBIC care coordination program is underway. This will lead to better follow-up and referral for those with TBI who require ongoing services.

DVBIC, the primary operational TBI component of the Defense Centers of Excellence for Traumatic Brain Injury and Psychological Health, has been instrumental in the development and implementation of many DoD initiatives related to TBI. Together, the 19 network sites of DVBIC contribute TBI research, education, clinical care, and subject-matter expertise throughout the DoD.

The success of this network is largely due to the interdisciplinary approach to project development, which includes neurologists, psychologists, psychiatrists, rehabilitations specialists, civilian sports concussion experts, and military representatives with operational experience.

THE WAY FORWARD

Improvement in the evaluation and management of combat-related TBI and PTSD is dependent on the ongoing research efforts of clinicians and neuroscientists. Individuals and entities within the DoD continue to expand projects and partnerships that will further illuminate the effects of blast injury on the brain as well as outcomes following TBI. The following list represents some of the key efforts that are currently underway:

- 15 Year Longitudinal TBI Study: This is a study mandated by Congress to determine the long-term consequences of combat-related TBI.
- DoD TBI Registry: A research database that records over 200 parameters on each TBI case as part of an ongoing registry project mandated by Congress is being conducted. Current initiatives include collaboration with VA and National Institute of Disability and Rehabilitation Research (NIDRR) model systems.
- MACE Validation Study: This study is to validate the use of the MACE screening tool in an austere environment. The study recently was funded by Congressionally Directed Medical Research Programs (CDMRP) and is currently under review by Human Studies Committees.
- Neuroendocrine studies: Studies are evaluating the hypothalamic-pituitary-adrenal (HPA) axis in blast-related TBI and PTSD to determine the incidence and differences in HPA dysfunction. Previous data from blunt injury demonstrates differences in hormonal function between patients with TBI and PTSD (Resnick, Yehuda, Pitman, & Foy, 1995; Tariverdi et al., 2006).
- Longitudinal Study of mTBI: This study is to evaluate the validity of the screening tool used by the DoD and VA, and to better understand the long-term interactions between TBI and psychological symptoms.
- CDMRP studies are being conducted on the effects of blast waves on biological and central nervous system (CNS) tissue.
- Helmet mounted sensor study: A sensor prototype is being evaluated by Army Medical Research and Materiel Command (MRMC). These sensors will detect blast exposure and aid in TBI risk assessment in service members in high-risk occupations.
- Institute of Soldier Nanotechnology (ISN): DVBIC is collaborating on several projects with (ISN) at Massachusetts Institute of Technology (MIT) to include the development of the most advanced system of computer modeling of blast effects on the brain.
- DVBIC/Armed Forces Institute of Pathology TBI Research Center: Laboratory and infrastructure are set up in conjunction with the Armed Forces Institute of Pathology to focus on translational applications of biophysics and neuropathology. The lab offers advanced imaging to include

7T and 9.4T magnetic resonance imaging (MRI) machines with the ability to perform cutting-edge MR microscopy. The lab has obtained a Coherent Anti-stokes Raman Scattering (CARS) microscope, which will allow for in vivo studies of the effects of blast on the brain. There is only one other such advanced instrument in the federal government at the National Institute of Standards and Technology (NIST). This collaboration has also led to the development of a DoD TBI Brain Bank with the enhancement of whole brain imaging and focused pathological examination using a 40 cm 4.7T Bruker Magnetic Spectrometer (MRS).

- The DoD with the University of Florida, Gainesville are developing a novel MRI associated infrastructure, specifically an MRI compatible split Hopkinson pressure bar. Recent diffusion tensor imaging (DTI) studies are showing different patterns in blast injuries compared to impact injuries.

Although there is much being discovered about TBI and PTSD, considerable work remains to be completed. As we make our way forward into the future, further research is needed to better clarify the interface between these comorbid conditions, and to better understand the assessment and management of post-concussive and psychological symptoms. The focus of the 2008 International Conference on Behavioral Health and Traumatic Brain Injury was instrumental in identifying gaps in knowledge that should be addressed and in continuing to develop collaborations that will allow us to best serve this population of wounded military service members. The DoD is committed to scientific advances that generate the best standards of evidence-based care for our wounded warriors. DVBIC is proud to have co-sponsored this landmark conference, which included state-of-the-science reviews and the expertise of international scientists, which ultimately targeted specific areas for future research.

REFERENCES

Belanger, H. G., Kretzmer, T., Yoash-Gantz, R., Pickett, T., & Tupler, L. A. (2009). Cognitive sequlae of blast-related versus other mechanisms of brain trauma. *Journal of International Neuropsychological Society*, *15*(1), 1–8.

Bombardier, C. H., Fann, J. R., Temkin, N., Esselman, P. C., Pelzer., E., Keough, M., et al. (2006). Post-traumatic stress disorder symptoms during the first six months after traumatic brain injury. *Journal of Neuropsychiatry & Clinical Neurosciences*, *18*, 501–508.

Cicerone, K. D., & Kalmar, K. (1995). Structure of subjective complaints after mild traumatic brain injury. *Journal of Head Trauma Rehabilitation*, *10*(3), 1–17.

Clark, M. E., Bair, M. J., Buckenmaier, C. C., Gironda, R. J., & Walker, R. L. (2007). Pain and combat injuries in soldiers returning from Operation Enduring Freedom and Operation Iraqi Freedom: Implications for research and practice. *Journal of Rehabilitation, Research and Development*, *44*(2), 179–194.

De Mittenberg, W., Tremont, G., Zielinski, R. E., Fichera, S., & Rayls, K. R. (1996). Cognitive-behavioral prevention of postconcussion syndrome. *Archives of Clinical Neuropsychology*, *11*(2), 139–145.

Department of Defense. (2006). *DoDD 6025.21E: Medical research program for the prevention, mitigation and treatment of blast injuries.* Retrieved August 23, 2009, from www.dtic.mil/whs/directives/corres/pdf/603521p.pdf

Department of Defense. (2008). *Evaluation and management of mTBI/concussion in the deployed setting (clinical practice guideline)*. Retrieved August 24, 2009, from http://dvbic.gbkdev.com/images/pdfs/Providers/Deployed_setting_CPG_10OCT08.aspx

Gondusky, J. S., & Reiter, M. P. (2005). Protecting military convoys in Iraq: An examination of battle injuries sustained by a mechanized battalion during Operation Iraqi Freedom II. *Military Medicine, 170*(6), 546–549.

Grissom, T. E., & Farmer, J. C. (2005). The provision of sophisticated critical care beyond the hospital: Lessons from physiology and military experiences that apply to civil disaster medical response. *Critical Care Medicine, 33*(1 Suppl), S13–21.

Hoge, C. W., McGurk, D., Thomas, J. L., Cox, A. L., Engel, C. C., & Castro, C. A. (2008). Mild traumatic brain injury in US soldiers returning from Iraq. *New England Journal of Medicine, 358*(5), 453–463.

Institute of Medicine (IOM). (2008). *Long-term consequences of traumatic brain injury (TBI) report*. Washington, DC: National Academies Press.

Management of Concussion/Mild TBI Work Group. (2009). *VA/DoD clinical practice guideline for management of concussion/mild traumatic brain injury*. Department of Veterans Affairs/Department of Defense. Available at: www.warrelatedillness.va.gov/provider/tbi/VADoD-CPG-concussion-mTBI.pdf

McCrea, M., Kelly, J. P., & Randolph, C. (2000. *Standardized Assessment of Concussion (SAC): Manual for administration, scoring and interpretation, 3rd ed*. Waukesha, WI: Comprehensive Neuropsychological Services.

Mora, A. G., Ritenour, A. E., Wade, C. E., Holcomb, J. B., Blackbourne, L. H., & Gaylord, K. M. (2009). Post-traumatic stress disorder in combat casualties with burns sustaining primary blast and concussive injuries. *Journal of Trauma, 66*(4 Suppl), S178–185.

Patel, T. H., Wenner, K. A., Price, S. A., Weber, M. A., Leveridge, A., & McAtee, S. J. (2004). A U.S. Army forward surgical team's experience in Operation Iraqi Freedom. *Journal of Trauma, 57*(2), 201–207.

Peoples, G. E., Gerlinger, T., Craig, R., & Burlingame, B. (2005). The 274th Forward Surgical Team experience during Operation Enduring Freedom. *Military Medicine, 170*(6), 451–459.

Ponsford, J., Wilmott, C., Rothwell, A., Cameron, P., Kelly, A. M., Nelms, R., & Curran, C. (2002). Impact of early intervention on outcome following mild head injury in adults. *Journal of Neurology, Neurosurgery, & Psychiatry, 73*(3), 330–332.

Reeves, D., Kane, R., Winter, K., & Elsmore, T. (2004). *Development and validation of the Automated Neuropsychological Assessment Metrics (ANAM®) for deployment health monitoring applications*. [Annual Report to Congress: Federally Sponsored Research on Gulf War Veterans' Illnesses for 2004. DoD Project #DoD-147, 1998–2004]. Washington, DC: Department of Veterans Affairs, Deployment Health Working Group Research Subcommittee.

Resnick, H. S., Yehuda, R., Pitman, R. K., & Foy, D. W. (1995). Effects of previous trauma on acute plasma cortical level following rape. *American Journal of Psychiatry, 152*(11), 1675–1677.

Schwab, K. A., Ivins, B., Cramer, G., Johnson, W., Sluss-Tiller, M., Kiley, K., et al. (2007). Screening for traumatic brain injury in troops returning from deployment in Afghanistan and Iraq: Initial investigation of the usefulness of a short screening tool for traumatic brain injury. *Journal of Head Trauma Rehabilitation, 22*(6), 377–389.

Tanelian, T. I., & Jaycox, L. H. (Eds.). (2008). *Invisible wounds of war: Psychological and cognitive injuries, their consequences, and services to assist recovery*. Pittsburgh, PA: RAND Corporation.

Tariverdi, F., Senyurek, H., Unluhizarici, K., Selcuklu, A., Casanueva, F. F., & Kelestimur, F. (2006). High risk of hypopituitarism after traumatic brain injury: A prospective investigation of anterior pituitary function in the acute phase and 12 months after trauma. *Journal of Clinical Endocrinology and Metabolism, 91*(6), 2105–2111.

Terrio, H., Brenner, L. A., Ivins, B. J., Cho, J. M., Helmick, K., Schwab, K., et al. (2009). Traumatic brain injury screening: Preliminary findings in a US Army Brigade Combat Team. *Journal of Head Trauma Rehabilitation, 24*(1), 14–23.

Walilko, T., North, C., Young, L. A., Lux, W. E., Warden, D. L., Jaffee, M. S., et al. (In press). Head injury as a PTSD predictor among Oklahoma City Bombing Survivors. *Journal of Head Trauma Rehabilitation.*

CHALLENGES ASSOCIATED WITH POST-DEPLOYMENT SCREENING FOR MILD TRAUMATIC BRAIN INJURY IN MILITARY PERSONNEL

Grant L. Iverson[1], Jean A. Langlois[2], Michael A. McCrea[3,4], and James P. Kelly[5,6]

[1]University of British Columbia & British Columbia Mental Health & Addiction Services, Vancouver, BC, Canada, [2]Office of Research and Development, US Department of Veterans Affairs, Washington, DC, [3]Neuroscience Center, Waukesha Memorial Hospital, Waukesha, Wisconsin, [4]Department of Neurology, Medical College of Wisconsin, Milwaukee, Wisconsin, [5]Departments of Neurosurgery and Physical Medicine and Rehabilitation, University of Colorado Denver School of Medicine, Denver, Colorado, and [6]National Intrepid Center of Excellence, Defense Centers of Excellence for Psychological Health and TBI, US Department of Defense, Washington, DC, USA

There is ongoing debate regarding the epidemiology of mild traumatic brain injury (MTBI) in military personnel. Accurate and timely estimates of the incidence of brain injury and the prevalence of long-term problems associated with brain injuries among active duty service members and veterans are essential for (a) operational planning, and (b) to allocate sufficient resources for rehabilitation and ongoing services and supports. The purpose of this article is to discuss challenges associated with post-deployment screening for MTBI. Multiple screening methods have been used in military, Veterans Affairs, and independent studies, which complicate cross-study comparisons of the resulting epidemiological data. We believe that post-deployment screening is important and necessary—but no screening methodology will be flawless, and false positives and false negatives are inevitable. Additional research is necessary to refine the sequential screening methodology, with the goal of minimizing false negatives during initial post-deployment screening and minimizing false positives during follow-up evaluations.

Keywords: Mild Traumatic Brain Injury; Military; Screening; Epidemiology.

INTRODUCTION

Traumatic brain injuries (TBI) among service members deployed to war zones (Drazen, 2005; Okie, 2005; Tanielian & Jaycox, 2008) are of widespread concern because of their potential to result in long-term disability. At the same time there is ongoing debate regarding the true epidemiology of TBI associated with military

Address correspondence to: Grant Iverson, Ph.D., Department of Psychiatry, University of British Columbia, 2255 Wesbrook Mall, Vancouver, BC, Canada V6T 2A1. E-mail: giverson@interchange.ubc.ca

engagements in Afghanistan and Iraq, Operation Enduring Freedom (OEF) and Operation Iraqi Freedom (OIF), respectively. Accurate and timely estimates of the incidence of TBI and the prevalence of TBI-related disability among active duty service members and veterans after deployment to OEF and OIF are essential for (a) operational planning and (b) allocation of sufficient resources for rehabilitation and long-term services and supports.

The diagnosis of moderate and severe traumatic brain injury is relatively straightforward even in theater because the clinical signs and symptoms, neuroimaging abnormalities, and functional deficits are readily apparent. However, the accurate identification of *mild* traumatic brain injuries (MTBI) can be very challenging because of the more subtle signs of this injury, the paucity of objective abnormalities identified on neuroimaging, the limited diagnostic tools with established sensitivity and specificity that can be administered in an austere environment, and the overlap of concussion symptoms with those of other conditions such as acute stress reaction/post-traumatic stress disorder.

Service members returning from OIF and OEF undergo a range of mandatory health assessments, some of which are referred to as "post-deployment screening" measures intended to specifically assess for a self-reported history of MTBI. These measures have been implemented by the US Department of Defense (DoD), the US Department of Veterans Affairs (VA), and independent researchers (Schwab et al., 2007; Tanielian & Jaycox, 2008). The earliest screening procedure, called the Brief Traumatic Brain Injury Screen (BTBIS), is comprised of three questions (see Table 1). See Tables 2–5 for different versions of the screening measure.

Recent publications reporting data based on these screening measures suggest that between 11.2% and 22.8% of deployed service members screen positive for a possible MTBI (Hoge et al., 2008; Mental Health Advisory Team, V, 2008; Schwab et al., 2007; Tanielian & Jaycox, 2008; Terrio et al., 2009). By extrapolation, it was suggested that of the 1.6 million service members up to that time who have been deployed to Iraq or Afghanistan, an estimated 320,000, have experienced a possible MTBI (Tanielian & Jaycox, 2008). However, limitations in the current screening methodology and variations among the individual screening measures warrant caution in the interpretation and use of these data. For example, an expressed goal of the VA screening was to be over-inclusive.

> When developing its screening tool, VA made some changes to the questions contained in the BTBIS. These changes were based on a review of other TBI screening instruments, published reports of the symptoms that follow a mild TBI, and the experience of MTFs[1] with using modified versions of the BTBIS. The goal of VA's changes was to develop a highly sensitive screening tool that would err on the side of being overly-inclusive in identifying veterans who may be at risk for having a TBI. VA recognized that using a highly sensitive TBI screening tool would result in some veterans who screen positive for possible TBI later being found after follow-up evaluation to not have a TBI. According to VA officials, VA specifically chose to develop a highly sensitive TBI screening tool to reduce the risk of not identifying those veterans who have a TBI.
>
> (Page 21; GAO-08-276)

---

[1] Military Treatment Facilities

Table 1 Original Brief Traumatic Brain Injury Screen (BTBIS)

1. Did you have any injury(ies) during your deployment from any of the following?
(check all that apply):
A. ☐ Fragment
B. ☐ Bullet
C. ☐ Vehicular (any type of vehicle, including airplane)
D. ☐ Fall
E. ☐ Blast (Improvised Explosive Device, RPG, Land mine, Grenade, etc.)
F. ☐ Other specify: _____

2. Did any injury received while you were deployed result in any of the following?
(check all that apply):
A. ☐ Being dazed, confused or "seeing stars"
B. ☐ Not remembering the injury
C. ☐ Losing consciousness (knocked out) for less than a minute
D. ☐ Losing consciousness for 1–20 minutes
E. ☐ Losing consciousness for longer than 20 minutes
F. ☐ Having any symptoms of concussion afterward (such as headache, dizziness, irritability, etc.)
G. ☐ Head Injury
H. ☐ None of the above

3. Are you currently experiencing any of the following problems that you think might be related to a possible head injury or concussion?
(check all that apply):
A. ☐☐ Headaches   E. ☐☐ Ringing in the ears
B. ☐☐ Dizziness   F. ☐☐ Irritability
C. ☐☐ Memory problems   G. ☐☐ Sleep problems
D. ☐☐ Balance problems   H. ☐☐ Other specify:_____

Confirm F and G through clinical interview. Endorsement of A–E meets criteria for positive TBI Screen

The main purpose of this article is to discuss challenges associated with using these screening results as indicators of the numbers of service members who have experienced one or more MTBIs. Moreover, we will comment on the use of the screening measures to estimate the incidence of MTBI and the prevalence of service members and veterans likely to have long-term problems attributable to MTBI.

INTERPRETATION OF MTBI SCREENING DATA

Post-deployment assessments are used to quantify the number of service members who have experienced a deployment-related MTBI. It is important to appreciate that, by design, screening assessments are *not diagnostic tools*. The methodology used for screening results in an irreducible minimum of false positives and false negatives. That is, some service members and veterans will be identified as having experienced a deployment-related MTBI when they did not (false positives), and others will be identified as having not had an MTBI when in fact they did (false negatives). A key goal of any screening program is to minimize the frequency of false positives and false negatives (i.e., Type I and Type II errors, respectively). Figure 1 illustrates possible outcomes from the DoD or VA MTBI screening program.

Table 2 Screening methodology used in the RAND Report (Tanielian & Jaycox, 2008)

A9. Did you have any injuries during your deployment from any of the following? (read list, record all that apply)
1. Fragment
2. Bullet
3. Vehicular (any type of vehicle including airplane)
4. Fall
5. Explosion (IED, RPG, land mine, grenade, etc)
6. Other specify:_____
7. None of the above
8. DK
9. REF

[If A9 = 7,8,9, skip to A11]

A10. Did any injury you received while deployed result in any of the following? (read list, record all that apply)
1. Being dazed, confused, or "seeing stars"
2. Not remembering the injury
3. Losing consciousness (knocked out) for less than a minute
4. Losing consciousness for 1–20 min
5. Losing consciousness for longer than 20 min
6. Having any symptoms of concussion afterward (such as headache, dizziness, irritability, etc)
7. Head injury
8. None of the above
9. DK
10. REF

A11. Are you currently experiencing any of the following problems that you think might be related to a possible head injury or concussion? (read list, record all that apply)
1. Headaches
2. Dizziness
3. Memory problems
4. Balance problems
5. Ringing in the ears
6. Irritability
7. Sleep problems
8. Learning difficulties
9. Concentration problems
10. Excessive fatigue
11. Any other problems I have not mentioned (specify):_____
12. None of the above
13. DK
14. Ref

Used with the permission of the RAND Corporation.

In screening programs aimed at maximizing the likelihood of identifying possible MTBIs, over-identification, and a resulting high rate of false positives, is an inevitable and intended consequence. Although such programs decrease the likelihood that a service member with MTBI will "fall through the cracks," over-identification can be problematic for several reasons. First, it increases the numbers of service members who need detailed follow-up assessments to evaluate possible residual effects from a brain injury, and thus increases the resources needed to conduct post-deployment assessments. Second, it has been suggested that screening

Table 3 Mental Health Advisory Team V Report (MHAT-V)

How many times during this deployment did you have an injury that involved the following:

	Never	One Time	Two Times	Three or Four Times	Five or More Times
Injury to your head					
Being dazed, confused, or "seeing stars"					
Not remembering the injury					
Losing consciousness ("knocked out")					

To screen positive for MTBI, service members had to report having been injured and also report (a) being dazed and confused, (b) not remembering the injury, or (c) losing consciousness.

Table 4 Revised post-deployment screening measure used to identify MTBI in the VA

Section 1: During any of your OEF/OIF deployment(s) did you experience any of the following events? (check all that apply)	Section 2: Did you have any of these symptoms IMMEDIATELY afterwards? (check all that apply)
☐ Blast or Explosion	☐ Losing consciousness/"knocked out"
☐ Vehicular accident/crash (including aircraft)	☐ Being dazed, confused or "seeing stars"
☐ Fragment wound or bullet wound above shoulders	☐ Not remembering the event
	☐ Concussion
☐ Fall	☐ Head injury
Section 3: Did any of the following problems begin or get worse afterwards? (check all that apply)	Section 4: In the past week, have you had any of the symptoms from section 3? (check all that apply)
☐ Memory problems or lapses	☐ Memory problems or lapses
☐ Balance problems or dizziness	☐ Balance problems or dizziness
☐ Sensitivity to bright light	☐ Sensitivity to bright light
☐ Irritability	☐ Irritability
☐ Headaches	☐ Headaches
☐ Sleep problems	☐ Sleep problems

General Accounting Office (2008, p. 16) *Mild traumatic brain injury screening and evaluation implemented for OEF/OIF veterans, but challenges remain.*

itself may have adverse consequences for some service members, especially for false positives. This includes potential harm to the service member and/or family members associated with misattribution of symptoms to "brain injury" versus other possible etiologies. Finally, it complicates surveillance and results in the potential for inaccurate reporting (i.e., over-reporting of the numbers of service members who have experienced a brain injury). However, an often-overlooked *benefit* of including false positives is that symptomatic patients are identified and can be referred for the appropriate care. In conditions with vague and non-specific symptoms it is often necessary to include a multidisciplinary approach to provide effective assessment, treatment, and rehabilitation services (irrespective of the cause or causes of the symptoms).

With regard to the interpretation of screening results for surveillance purposes and reporting of estimates of the numbers of persons who have experienced an

Table 5 DoD Post-Deployment Health Assessment (PDHA)

9.a. During this deployment, did you experience any of the following events? *(Mark all that apply)*
(1) Blast or explosion *(IED, RPG, land mine, grenade, etc.)*
☐ No ☐ ☐ Yes
(2) Vehicular accident/crash *(any vehicle, including aircraft)*
☐ No ☐ ☐ Yes
(3) Fragment wound or bullet wound above your shoulders
☐ No ☐☐ Yes
(4) Fall ☐☐ No ☐☐ Yes
(5) Other event *(for example, a sports injury to your head).*
☐ No ☐ ☐ Yes
Describe:

9.b. Did any of the following happen to you, or were you told happened to you, IMMEDIATELY after any of the event(s) you just noted in question 9.a.? *(Mark all that apply)*
(1) Lost consciousness or got "knocked out"
☐ ☐ No ☐ ☐ Yes
(2) Felt dazed, confused, or "saw stars"
☐☐ No ☐☐ Yes
(3) Didn't remember the event ☐☐ No ☐☐ Yes
(4) Had a concussion ☐☐ No ☐☐ Yes
(5) Had a head injury ☐☐ No ☐☐ Yes

9.c. Did any of the following problems begin or get worse after the event(s) you noted in question 9.a.? *(Mark all that apply)*
(1) Memory problems or lapses
☐ ☐ No ☐ ☐ Yes
(2) Balance problems or dizziness
☐ ☐ No ☐ ☐ Yes
(3) Ringing in the ears ☐ ☐ No ☐ ☐ Yes
(4) Sensitivity to bright light ☐ ☐ No ☐ ☐ Yes
(5) Irritability ☐ ☐ No ☐ ☐ Yes
(6) Headaches ☐ ☐ No ☐ ☐ Yes
(7) Sleep problems ☐ ☐ No ☐ ☐ Yes

9.d. In the past week, have you had any of the symptoms you indicated in 9.c.? *(Mark all that apply)*
(1) Memory problems or lapses ☐ ☐ No ☐ ☐ Yes
(2) Balance problems or dizziness
☐ ☐ No ☐ ☐ Yes
(3) Ringing in the ears ☐ ☐ No ☐ ☐ Yes
(4) Sensitivity to bright light ☐ ☐ No ☐ ☐ Yes
(5) Irritability ☐ ☐ No ☐ ☐ Yes
(6) Headaches ☐ ☐ No ☐ ☐ Yes
(7) Sleep problems ☐ ☐ No ☐ ☐ Yes

MTBI, it is essential to appreciate that initial screening estimates of the number of service members who sustained an MTBI do not accurately represent either (a) the number of service members who were actually injured (due to false negatives and false positives), or (b) the number of service members who have ongoing problems resulting from the injury. Follow-up assessment to confirm the experience of an MTBI remains challenging because it is based on self-report of the circumstances of an injury event that may have occurred many months earlier, and these retrospective recollections might be unreliable. Moreover, extrapolating from the scientific literature (Belanger, Curtiss, Demery, Lebowitz, & Vanderploeg, 2005; Belanger & Vanderploeg, 2005; Binder, Rohling, & Larrabee, 1997; Frencham, Fox, & Maybery, 2005; Schretlen & Shapiro, 2003), it is likely that most service members who sustained an MTBI during deployment will have recovered fully, or nearly fully, from a cognitive perspective by the time of the post-deployment screening. Therefore the diagnosis of MTBI indicates only the history of injury and does not define the functional outcome or current symptoms. The complexity of estimating diagnostic accuracy, residual problems, and etiology is illustrated in Figure 2.

From both a clinical management and public health perspective, of greatest concern is the number of service members who experience long-term problems

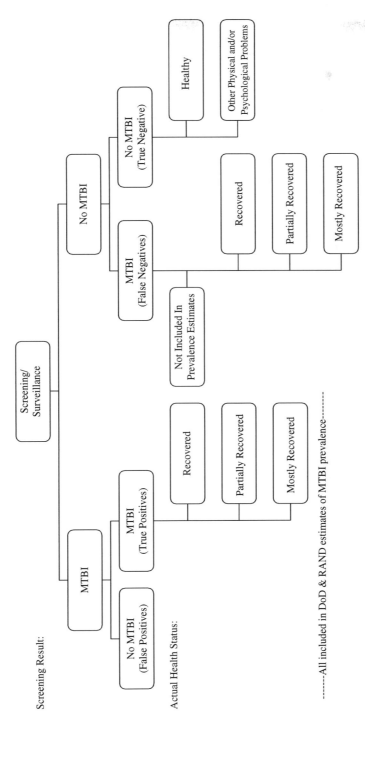

Figure 1 Possible outcomes from the DoD or VA MTBI screening program.

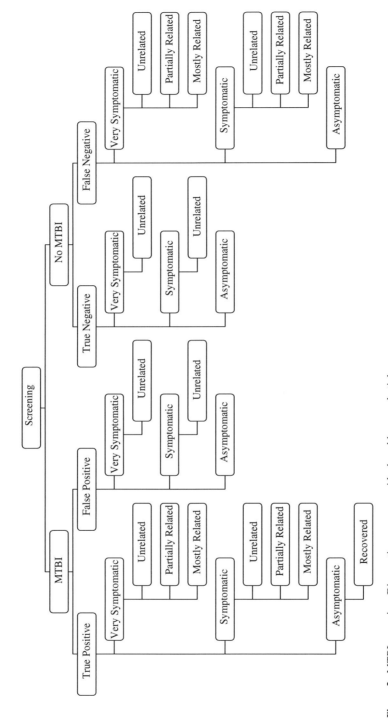

Figure 2 MTBI screening: Diagnostic accuracy, residual problems, and etiology.
Note: "Unrelated" symptoms are caused or maintained by factors such as traumatic stress, depression, chronic pain, insomnia, substance abuse, or life stress.

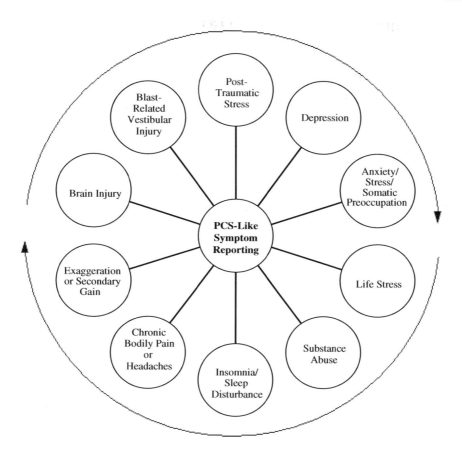

Figure 3 Factors that can influence post-concussion-like symptom reporting post-acutely or long after a mild traumatic brain injury in service members.

resulting from a traumatic brain injury. Most service members who experience a moderate or severe TBI will experience some degree of permanent change in their physical, cognitive, and/or psychological functioning. It is important to note that severity of injury is directly related to prognosis, but this is not absolute. There are patients with severe injury who have very good functional outcome, whereas some who sustain a mild TBI will have poor outcome with persistent symptoms. However, simply reporting symptoms long after an injury does not mean the symptoms are caused by the past injury, because these symptoms are not solely specific to MTBI. It is likely that in many cases the symptoms are due predominantly to other factors such as traumatic stress (e.g., Hoge et al., 2008; Schneiderman, Braver, & Kang, 2008), depression, chronic pain, substance abuse, and community-reintegration issues. Potential for secondary gain (e.g., compensation for permanent effects of injury) could also influence symptom maintenance following MTBI. This is illustrated in Figure 3.

PRIMARY CONCERNS ABOUT THE SCREENING MEASURES

In general, the four-question screening procedure used by the VA (Table 3) and the DoD (Table 4) appears to be reasonable for use in large-scale post-deployment screening. However, our six primary concerns regarding the screening process, some of which are unique to the initial DoD post-deployment screening, are listed below:

(1) Screening for possible TBI was initiated after clinical concern arose from experience in treating returning service members, so not all OEF/OIF service members have been screened. DoD post-deployment TBI screening was only recently mandated in 2008. Therefore hundreds of thousands of service members and veterans, previously deployed, were not systematically screened. VA screening was implemented in 2007 and likely identified some veterans who sustained MTBIs who were not previously screened. However, as of the end of 2008, of the 945,423 separated OEF/OIF veterans, only 42% (400,304) had obtained VA health care since fiscal year 2002 (Kang, 2007).

(2) The post-deployment screening focuses exclusively on the most recent deployment. As a result, injuries sustained in prior deployments will be missed. The Veterans Affairs screening procedure yields a positive result only if the veteran reports current symptoms that might be attributable to the past injury. This approach aligns well with the VA mission to provide care for those experiencing service-related health problems. However, from a surveillance perspective, the true incidence and prevalence of the injury will not be captured by this method (although these data can be retrieved).

(3) Most screening measures focus on single injuries. Not all of them capture multiple injuries. Multiple injuries carry increased risk for long-term problems.

(4) Post-deployment screening, by necessity, is typically implemented in group settings. Service members are highly motivated to move swiftly through the screening process in order to transition home as quickly as possible. Under these circumstances, they might be less forthcoming about reporting deployment-related signs and symptoms of MTBI, more likely resulting in increased false negative than false positive rates.

(5) Because blasts are common in OEF/OIF, it is very likely that some service members who are exposed to one or more blasts but who do *not* experience an MTBI will be misidentified as having sustained an injury (i.e., false positives). The current versions of the screening tools used by the DoD and the VA refer to blast exposure as an "event," without a requirement for "injury." A service member who is in a combat situation involving a blast but who is uninjured might report feeling (a) "dazed," (b) "confused," or (c) both, not because of any neurological effects of the blast itself, but because of an acute stress response and the potentially life-threatening nature of the blast exposure (see Belanger, Uomoto, & Vanderploeg, 2009, for a discussion of this issue). Without verification of the service member's experience by a trained clinician, the screening tool can be expected to falsely classify these service members as having sustained an injury to the brain when, in fact, they did not. We anticipate a significant rate of false positive identification of mild brain injury based on blast "events" leading to reports of feeling dazed, confused, or both in the absence of

actual neurological effects of the blast. This is precisely why screening by survey alone can be misleading and needs to be followed up by detailed clinical assessment. Admittedly, it will not be possible in the foreseeable future to accurately identify all cases. Clinician verification, however, can be used to determine if there was a plausible injury mechanism (e.g., body displacement and hard head strike), immediate injury indicators (e.g., witnessed loss of consciousness or post-traumatic amnesia), and classic acute symptoms in the first 24 hours post injury.

(6) The screening tools used by the DoD and the VA are likely to lead to misidentification of residual symptoms of mild traumatic brain injury in some service members (Belanger et al., 2009). This is because the logic and flow of the questions establishes for the service member an expectation of causation. Expectations of causation can lead to misattribution (Mittenberg, DiGiulio, Perrin, & Bass, 1992) of symptoms to a *past* injury when they are actually caused by *current* problems (e.g., traumatic stress, mild depression, sleep disturbance, chronic bodily pain, or life stress).

The methodology set out in the current screening procedure does not provide a scientifically validated approach to establishing causation. However, the methodology will be interpreted by some clinicians and researchers as reflecting a cause and effect relationship between a past injury and present symptoms. In some cases, this will represent a classic logical fallacy: *post hoc ergo propter hoc* (i.e., "after therefore because of"). This problem with over-identification of residual problems associated with a past MTBI is illustrated with three scenarios, listed below, applied to the DoD post-deployment screening program.

(1) *Double False Positive Scenario*: The service member was involved in an event in which there is a blast. The service member was not injured by the blast, but he or she felt overwhelmed, shocked, and confused in the aftermath of the event. This individual, by definition, will be incorrectly screened as having sustained a mild traumatic brain injury. During the post-deployment period, the service member might endorse three or more symptoms, such as memory problems, irritability, and sleep problems. These symptoms could not be caused by a brain injury because the individual did not sustain a brain injury. However, the screening procedure will (a) falsely identify him or her as having a past brain injury, and (b) falsely identify him or her as having current symptoms from the past injury.

(2) *Misattribution of Symptoms False Positive Scenario*: The service member was involved in an event in which there was a blast. The service member was injured in this event. His or her injuries include a mild traumatic brain injury (i.e., a concussion). The service member fully recovers from this injury in less than 3 weeks. This service member would be correctly screened as having sustained a mild traumatic brain injury. During the post-deployment period, the service member endorses three or more symptoms (e.g., headaches, irritability, and sleep problems), which developed long after the MTBI. These symptoms cannot be caused by the original injury because the service member had recovered from that injury. Thus the screening tool will (a) correctly identify the service member

as sustaining a past mild brain injury, but (b) incorrectly classify the service member as having residual problems from this injury.

(3) *Differential Diagnosis Scenario*: The service member is involved in an event that involves a blast. He or she sustains injuries, including a mild traumatic brain injury. The service member was traumatized by the event because he witnessed the death of a friend and the injuries of other members of his or her team. The service member experienced 90% or more recovery from the mild traumatic brain injury. However, he or she had ongoing problems with traumatic stress and mild depression. During the post-deployment period, the service member endorses three or more symptoms (e.g., irritability, headaches, and sleep problems). In this situation, the screening procedure will (a) correctly identify the original injury, (b) possibly correctly identify some residual symptoms, yet (c) attribute some prominent mental health related symptoms to brain injury alone.

It is important to appreciate that longstanding symptoms and problems in service members or veterans who have sustained one or more MTBIs might be partially or wholly attributable to co-occurring conditions. The most likely co-occurring conditions are post-traumatic stress disorder, depression, chronic pain, chronic sleep problems, and substance abuse disorders. These conditions are associated with symptoms that overlap considerably with typical post-concussion symptoms (Gasquoine, 2000; Gunstad & Suhr, 2004; Hoge et al., 2008; Iverson & McCracken, 1997; Karzmark, Hall, & Englander, 1995; McCauley, Boake, Levin, Contant, & Song, 2001; Schneiderman et al., 2008; Smith-Seemiller, Fow, Kant, & Franzen, 2003; Wilde et al., 2004). The symptoms and problems associated with these conditions can co-occur with the possible lingering effects of MTBIs, or they can mimic the long-term adverse effects of MTBIs. Moreover, it is also possible that long-term symptoms associated with a traumatic brain injury could be misattributed to a mental health condition. Nonetheless, depression, PTSD, chronic pain, and substance abuse are themselves associated with diverse psychological problems and cognitive impairment, and they can result in significant disruption in social and occupational functioning. Therefore it is important to provide accurate differential diagnosis and effective treatment services for service members and veterans with these co-occurring conditions.

ADVANTAGE OF SCREENING: TREATMENT AND REHABILITATION SERVICES

The VA and DoD developed these screening tools, and a clinical process, to identify veterans and service members who were exposed to service-related situations during which they may have suffered an MTBI, and might continue to experience symptoms that could be related to that injury. The screening does not identify the true incidence of MTBI or of residual symptoms and problems associated with MTBI. Rather, it identifies *possible* MTBI. A positive screen simply means that it is possible that the service member experienced an MTBI and, importantly, that the service member has current symptoms and problems. It is well appreciated that symptoms consistent with MTBI can also be related in whole or part to a number of other clinical issues, including post-traumatic stress, depression, vestibular problems, chronic pain, headaches, sleep disturbances, and life stress. Fortunately, initial screening leads to access to specialized and comprehensive assessment, treatment, and rehabilitation services. Through the process of screening and follow-up specialized evaluations, VA has determined that a large percentage of veterans who initially screened positive for the injury (a) didn't actually sustain the injury, or (b) likely recovered from the injury and their current symptoms and problems were most likely caused by something else. Those veterans are provided treatment and rehabilitation services for their ongoing symptoms and problems as a direct result of going through the screening followed by comprehensive evaluations. An additional benefit of the screening process is the increased awareness of TBI throughout the VA system resulting in improved care and access for all veterans with TBI, not only the OEF/OIF population.

CONCLUSIONS

The purpose of this article was to discuss challenges associated with post-deployment screening for MTBI. Multiple screening methods have been used in military, Veterans Affairs, and independent studies, which complicate cross-study comparisons of the resulting epidemiological data. It is essential to appreciate that initial screening estimates of the number of service members who have sustained a possible MTBI do not represent the true incidence or prevalence of (a) the number of service members who were actually injured (due to false negatives and false positives), or (b) the number of service members who have long-term problems resulting from the injury.

We have six primary concerns regarding the screening process, some of which are unique to the initial DoD post-deployment screening. First, because DoD post-deployment MTBI screening was not mandated until May of 2008, hundreds of thousands of service members, previously deployed, were not systematically screened. Second, the post-deployment screening focuses exclusively on the most recent deployment, so injuries sustained in prior deployments will be missed. Third, most screening measures do not carefully document multiple injuries. Fourth, post-deployment health screening, by necessity, typically is done swiftly in group settings. This might contribute to a reduction in the accuracy of the information obtained. Fifth, it is very likely that some service members who are blast-exposed but who do not experience a mild traumatic brain injury will be misidentified as having sustained an MTBI because the blast exposure (a) is referred to as an "event" rather than an "injury," and (b) might cause a service member to feel "dazed" or "confused" psychologically as opposed to neurologically. This is precisely why follow-up clinical evaluation is critically important—many of these false positives will be identified easily during the clinical assessment. Finally, the screening tools are likely to lead to misidentification of residual symptoms of mild traumatic brain injury in some service members whose symptoms are caused by depression, PTSD, life stress, substance abuse, chronic pain, sleep disturbance, or a combination of factors.

We believe that post-deployment screening is important—but no screening methodology will be flawless, and false positives and false negatives are inevitable.

Post-deployment assessment models that include clinician verification of the injury offer advantages over the "survey only" approach, but have not been widely applied (Terrio et al., 2009). Without question, clinician verification, as a secondary screen, can improve screening accuracy. In many cases, false positive results can be easily identified through a follow-up interview (such as when a service member is blast "exposed" from a distance and there is no evidence of injury). True positive results, in many cases, also are easily identified. There are some injury mechanisms and severity indicator descriptions that are associated with a very high probability of MTBI and thus result in injuries that are more readily identifiable. There will, however, continue to be cases that cannot be definitively identified through screening and routine injury surveillance, especially in the absence of contemporaneous medical records, in large part because we do not have a methodology for accurately diagnosing mild brain injuries retrospectively (especially those occurring in theater). Moreover, variability in the training and expertise of those conducting the post-screening assessments will continue to influence the accuracy of injury surveillance in individual cases. The accurate identification of residual symptoms is equally challenging. In the presence of co-morbidity it is extremely difficult to causally link subjective symptoms to a remote MTBI. Traumatic stress, life stress, depression, insomnia, chronic pain, marital and family distress, and substance abuse, singly or in combination, can be the proximate cause for these symptoms. This fact supports the emerging trend in the DoD and VA to simply aggressively *treat what is treatable* regardless of the etiology to try to reduce suffering and improve functioning.

Additional research is necessary to refine the post-deployment sequential screening methodology with the goal of minimizing false negatives during initial screening and minimizing false positives during follow-up evaluations. Training materials and programs could be developed to help clinicians (a) identify common false positive scenarios, (b) reinforce common true positive scenarios, and (c) better appreciate the co-morbidity conundrum. Researchers, government officials, and the media are cautioned that statistics based on screening positive for possible MTBI do not represent the true incidence of the injury or the prevalence of resulting long-term problems. Follow-up clinical evaluations, such as those currently done in the DoD and VA systems, are necessary to more accurately determine the numbers of service members and veterans who have sustained a mild TBI Moreover, these follow-up assessments are critically important for identifying ongoing symptoms and problems (due to brain injury, psychological problems, or both) so service members and veterans can receive timely and effective treatment and rehabilitation services.

AUTHOR NOTES

The authors of this paper, at the time of writing, were all members of the Traumatic Brain Injury Subcommittee of the Defense Health Board. The Defense Health Board is a civilian advisory board to the United States Secretary of Defense. Dr. Kelly is now the Director of the National Intrepid Center of Excellence and has resigned from the TBI subcommittee. The views expressed are those of the authors and do not represent the official position of the Defense Health Board, US Department of Defense, or US Department of Veteran's Affairs.

REFERENCES

Belanger, H. G., Curtiss, G., Demery, J. A., Lebowitz, B. K., & Vanderploeg, R. D. (2005). Factors moderating neuropsychological outcomes following mild traumatic brain injury: A meta-analysis. *Journal of the International Neuropsychological Society, 11*(3), 215–227.

Belanger, H. G., Uomoto, J. M., & Vanderploeg, R. D. (2009). The Veterans Health Administration's (VHA's) Polytrauma System of Care for mild traumatic brain injury: Costs, benefits, and controversies. *Journal of Head Trauma Rehabilitation, 24*(1), 4–13.

Belanger, H. G., & Vanderploeg, R. D. (2005). The neuropsychological impact of sports-related concussion: A meta-analysis. *Journal of the International Neuropsychological Society, 11*(4), 345–357.

Binder, L. M., Rohling, M. L., & Larrabee, J. (1997). A review of mild head trauma. Part I: Meta-analytic review of neuropsychological studies. *Journal of Clinical and Experimental Neuropsychology, 19*(3), 421–431.

Drazen, J. M. (2005). Using every resource to care for our casualties. *New England Journal of Medicine, 352*(20), 2121.

Frencham, K. A., Fox, A. M., & Maybery, M. T. (2005). Neuropsychological studies of mild traumatic brain injury: A meta-analytic review of research since 1995. *Journal of Clinical and Experimental. Neuropsychology, 27*(3), 334–351.

Gasquoine, P. G. (2000). Postconcussional symptoms in chronic back pain. *Applied Neuropsychology, 7*(2), 83–89.

General Accounting Office. (2008, February). *VA Health Care. Mild traumatic brain injury screening and evaluation implemented for OEF/OIF veterans, but challenges remain. GAO-08-276.* Washington, DC: General Accounting Office.

Gunstad, J., & Suhr, J. A. (2004). Cognitive factors in postconcussion syndrome symptom report. *Archives of Clinical Neuropsychology, 19*(3), 391–405.

Hoge, C. W., McGurk, D., Thomas, J. L., Cox, A. L., Engel, C. C., & Castro, C. A. (2008). Mild traumatic brain injury in U.S. soldiers returning from Iraq. *New England Journal of Medicine, 358*(5), 453–463.

Iverson, G. L., & McCracken, L. M. (1997). 'Postconcussive' symptoms in persons with chronic pain. *Brain Injury, 11*(11), 783–790.

Kang, H. (2007). *Analysis of VA health care utilization among US global war on terrorism veterans: Operation Iraqi Freedom, Operation Enduring Freedom.* Veterans Health Administration Office of Public Health and Environmental Hazards.

Karzmark, P., Hall, K., & Englander, J. (1995). Late-onset post-concussion symptoms after mild brain injury: The role of premorbid, injury-related, environmental, and personality factors. *Brain Injury, 9*(1), 21–26.

McCauley, S. R., Boake, C., Levin, H. S., Contant, C. F., & Song, J. X. (2001). Postconcussional disorder following mild to moderate traumatic brain injury: Anxiety, depression, and social support as risk factors and comorbidities. *Journal of Clinical and Experimental Neuropsychology, 23*(6), 792–808.

Mental Health Advisory Team. (2008). *(MHAT-V) Operation Iraqi Freedom 06-08: Iraq. Operation Enduring Freedom 8: Afghanistan, chartered by the Office of the Surgeon Multi-National Force-Iraq, the Office of the Command Surgeon and the Office of the Surgeon General United States Army Medical Command, February 14, 2008.* Available on http://www.armymedicine.army.mil

Mittenberg, W., DiGiulio, D. V., Perrin, S., & Bass, A. E. (1992). Symptoms following mild head injury: Expectation as aetiology. *Journal of Neurology, Neurosurgery and Psychiatry, 55,* 200–204.

Okie, S. (2005). Traumatic brain injury in the war zone. *New England Journal of Medicine, 352*(20), 2043–2047.

Schneiderman, A. I., Braver, E. R., & Kang, H. K. (2008). Understanding sequelae of injury mechanisms and mild traumatic brain injury incurred during the conflicts in Iraq and Afghanistan: Persistent postconcussive symptoms and posttraumatic stress disorder. *American Journal of Epidemiology, 167*(12), 1446–1452.

Schretlen, D. J., & Shapiro, A. M. (2003). A quantitative review of the effects of traumatic brain injury on cognitive functioning. *International Review of Psychiatry, 15*(4), 341–349.

Schwab, K. A., Ivins, B., Cramer, G., Johnson, W., Sluss-Tiller, M., Kiley, K., et al. (2007). Screening for traumatic brain injury in troops returning from deployment in Afghanistan and Iraq: Initial investigation of the usefulness of a short screening tool for traumatic brain injury. *Journal of Head Trauma Rehabilitation, 22*(6), 377–389.

Smith-Seemiller, L., Fow, N. R., Kant, R., & Franzen, M. D. (2003). Presence of post-concussion syndrome symptoms in patients with chronic pain vs mild traumatic brain injury. *Brain Injury, 17*(3), 199–206.

Tanielian, T., & Jaycox, L. H. (Eds.). (2008). Invisible wounds of war: Psychological and cognitive injuries, their consequences, and services to assist recovery. Santa Monica, CA: Rand Corporation.

Terrio, H., Brenner, L. A., Ivins, B., Cho, J. M., Helmick, K., Schwab, K., et al. (2009). Traumatic brain injury screening: Preliminary findings in a U.S. Army Brigade Combat Team. *Journal of Head Trauma Rehabilitation, 24*(1), 14–23.

Wilde, E. A., Bigler, E. D., Gandhi, P. V., Lowry, C. M., Blatter, D. D., Brooks, J., et al. (2004). Alcohol abuse and traumatic brain injury: Quantitative magnetic resonance imaging and neuropsychological outcome. *Journal of Neurotrauma, 21*(2), 137–147.

GIVING CONTEXT TO POST-DEPLOYMENT POST-CONCUSSIVE-LIKE SYMPTOMS: BLAST-RELATED POTENTIAL MILD TRAUMATIC BRAIN INJURY AND COMORBIDITIES

Laura L. S. Howe
VA Palo Alto Health Care System, Palo Alto, CA, USA

In the military and Veterans Administration systems, individuals with potential MTBI are presenting with symptoms in excess of what would be expected based on initial injury characteristics and/or at unexpected time periods based on current research findings. This article investigates factors that might account for the discrepancy between current research expectations and some occurrences in clinical practice. The physics of blast waves, as well as animal and human research, relevant to explosions are reviewed. Additional factors that occur within the military blast exposure milieu are also explored because the context in which an injury occurs can potentially impact symptom severity and course of recovery. Differential diagnoses, iatrogenic illness, diagnosis threat, and symptom embellishment are also considered.

Keywords: Mild traumatic brain injury; Primary blast wave; Post-traumatic stress disorder; Blast injuries; Persistent post-concussive symptoms.

INTRODUCTION

Traumatic brain injury (TBI) is considered to be a signature wound of Operation Enduring Freedom (OEF) and Operation Iraqi Freedom (OIF). TBIs can be differentiated into severity-level classifications as mild, moderate, or severe, based on three acute injury characteristics that are used to determine TBI severity. These injury characteristics include: duration of loss of consciousness (LOC), which is the interruption of awareness of oneself and one's surroundings; Glasgow Coma Scale score (GCS; Teasdale & Jennett, 1974); and duration of post-traumatic amnesia (PTA), which is memory disruption following an injury that results in the inability to store or retrieve new information. All the established severity-level classification systems use characteristics at the time of injury and not characteristics weeks or years later to determine the severity-level classification. It is not the subsequent patient presentation when seeing providers or the public at some later date that determines the initial severity-level classification. This is an important point that is frequently misunderstood.

Address correspondence to: Laura L. S. Howe, VA Palo Alto Health Care System, 3801 Miranda Avenue, Psychology Service (116B), Palo Alto, CA 94304, USA. E-mail: lauralshowe@yahoo.com

© 2009 Psychology Press, an imprint of the Taylor & Francis group, an Informa business

Table 1. VHA/DoD clinical practice guideline for management of concussion/MTBI: TBI classification scheme

Criteria	Severity level		
	Mild	Moderate	Severe
Structural imaging	Normal	Normal or abnormal	Normal or abnormal
Loss of consciousness (LOC)	0–30 min	>30 min and <24 hours	>24 hours
Alteration of consciousness/ mental state	a moment up to 24 hours	>24 hours. Severity based on other criteria	>24 hours. Severity based on other criteria
Post-traumatic amnesia (PTA)	0–1 day	>1 day and <7 days	>7 days
Glasgow Coma Scale (GCS)	13–15	9–12	<9

Alteration of consciousness/mental state must be immediately related to trauma to the head.
VHA/DoD = Veterans Health Administration and Department of Defense.

There is relatively good consensus on the differentiation of moderate and severe injuries, but much less agreement regarding the classification of mild TBI (MTBI) (McCrea, 2008). Within the category of MTBI, most experts differentiate complicated MTBI (i.e., structural injury that is visualized on imaging and/or acute neurological signs on initial examination) from uncomplicated MTBI. In some studies, complicated MTBI has demonstrated a symptom course and recovery similar to moderate injuries (Borgaro, Prigatano, Kwasnica, & Rexer, 2003; Kashluba, Hanks, Casey, & Millis, 2008; Kurca, Sivak, & Kucera, 2006; Williams, Levin, & Eisenberg, 1990). For purposes of this article, MTBI refers to uncomplicated MTBI. The method used by the Veterans Health Administration (VHA) and Department of Defense (DoD) to categorize the three severity levels is presented in Table 1 (Department of Veteran Affairs, 2009). Recent publications have suggested that 11.2% to 19.5% of those deployed may have experienced a MTBI (Hoge et al., 2008; Schwab et al., 2007; Tanielian & Jaycox, 2008).

MILD TRAUMATIC BRAIN INJURY: A BRIEF SUMMARY OF THE LITERATURE

Advances in recent years have significantly furthered our understanding of MTBI (McCrea, 2008). The World Health Organization (WHO) Collaborating Centre Task Force on Mild Traumatic Brain Injury published a detailed review of the literature on MTBI in 2004 (Carroll et al., 2004). The WHO Task Force, which reviewed 120 studies regarding prognosis that met criteria for inclusion in the review, concluded that prognosis after MTBI is highly encouraging (Carroll et al., 2004). Symptoms gradually resolve within days to weeks post injury with little evidence of residual cognitive, behavioral, or academic deficits (Carroll et al., 2004). McCrea et al. (2009), in this special issue of *The Clinical Neuropsychologist*, provide a comprehensive review of the expected course of recovery following MTBI that illustrates: (a) symptomatology is most evident immediately following the injury, (b) delayed onset of symptoms is a very rare occurrence

(McCrea et al., 2003), (c) in the vast majority of cases involving the milder forms of injury there is gradual symptom recovery back to baseline during the first 1 to 2 weeks (Belanger & Vanderploeg, 2005; Lovell et al., 2003; McCrea et al., 2003) and almost all return to baseline functioning within 1 to 3 months (Belanger, Curtiss, Demery, Lebowitz, & Vanderploeg, 2005; Schretlen & Shapiro, 2003), (d) the percentage of subjects endorsing symptoms beyond 1 year post injury is much lower than previous estimates of 15% (Alexander, 1995; McLean, Temkin, Dikmen, & Wyler, 1983) and more likely to be closer to 3% (Alves, Macciocchi, & Barth, 1993; Carroll et al., 2004; Iverson, 2005; McCrea, 2008), (e) MTBI is not associated with long-term persistent neuropsychological impairments (Belanger et al., 2005; Belanger & Vanderploeg, 2005; Dikmen, McLean, & Temkin, 1986; Levin et al., 1987; Schretlen & Shapiro, 2003), (f) symptoms that persist more than several weeks post injury are likely to be related to non-MTBI factors, such as demographic, psychosocial, medical, and/or situational factors (Carroll et al., 2004; Landre, Poppe, Davis, Schmaus, & Hobbs, 2006), and (g) litigation is associated with stable or worsening cognitive functioning over time (Belanger et al., 2005).

Within the Department of Defense (DoD) and the Veterans Health Administration (VHA) systems, individuals with potential TBI which, at most, is at the mild end of the TBI classification continuum are reporting symptoms in excess of expectations and at time periods inconsistent with having experienced a MTBI (Schneiderman, Braver, & Kang, 2008). With this type of discrepancy between scientific research-based expectations and clinical presentations, an explanation is needed. Military investigations have reported 78% to 88% of injuries occurring in Afghanistan and Iraq result from explosive mechanisms, such as improvised explosive devices (IEDs) and landmines (Brookings Institute, 2008; Hoge et al., 2008; Murray et al., 2005; Owens et al., 2008). When considering the bulk of the TBI scientific literature regarding mechanism of injury (e.g., projectile missile, acceleration–deceleration forces, blunt force), primary blast wave emerges as a unique mechanism and injury variable.

EXPLOSIONS: THE DETAILS

Explosions are dynamic, with multiple events occurring in succession and simultaneously. Initially, the blast wave spreads from a point source and consists of a high-pressure shock wave (overpressurization) and a subsequent blast wind that closely follows the shock wave (DePalma, Burris, Champion, & Hodgson, 2005). Then, as the outward spreading energy dissipates, a reversal wind back toward the point source occurs, which ultimately causes underpressurization of the area (DePalma et al., 2005). Many factors, including type of explosive, peak overpressure, duration of the overpressure, impulse (complex wave-forms), location of explosion, proximity to the explosion, environmental hazards, body orientation to the blast, and barriers, impact the damage that may occur due to blast exposure (Clemedson, 1956; DePalma et al., 2005; Elsayed, 1997; White & Richmond, 1959; White, Jones, Damon, & Richmond, 1971).

Mechanisms of injury from blast waves

Explosions result in four potential mechanisms of injury, referred to as primary, secondary, tertiary, and quaternary effects. The primary effects include consequences directly attributable to the blast wave itself. Secondary effects include damage caused by projectiles, such as flying debris and bomb fragments. IEDs utilized in Iraq are often loaded with metallic objects to inflict penetrating injuries as well (DePalma et al., 2005). Tertiary effects include injuries directly attributable to the blast wind that may result in an individual being thrown or moved and a wide range of potential injuries such as fractures, traumatic amputations, or TBI (DePalma et al., 2005; Warden, 2006). Quaternary effects include all other explosion-related effects not accounted for within primary, secondary, and tertiary effects, such as asphyxia, burns, and exposure to toxic inhalants, as well as exacerbation of pre-existing illnesses (DePalma et al., 2005; Taber, Warden, & Hurley, 2006).

Returnees who report symptoms of MTBI indicate being injured by a blast/explosion more so than any other mechanism (Hoge et al., 2008). The secondary, tertiary, and quaternary mechanisms of blast injuries can be characterized as mechanical injuries that are expected to be similar to brain injuries sustained from falls or motor vehicle accidents (Belanger, Kretzmer, Yoash-Gantz, Pickett, & Tupler, 2009a). There is controversy, however, surrounding the effects of the primary blast wave on the brain (Taber et al., 2006). Therefore, we will review the research literature regarding the impact of primary blast wave exposure on cognitive, physical, and emotional functioning.

Primary blast wave injuries: In depth

Primary blast wave injuries are barotraumas. Barotraumas are injuries caused by pressure differences (overpressurization or underpressurization) between the outer surface of the body and internal organs when the primary blast wave impacts the body (Argyros, 1997; DePalma et al., 2005). When the blast wave reaches a living object, three events occur simultaneously: (a) part of the wave is reflected; (b) part of the wave is deflected; and (c) most of the wave is absorbed and propagated through the body as a stress wave, because the human body is a compliant surface (Clemedson & Pettersson, 1956; Leung et al., 2008). These dynamic pressure changes result in a high-frequency stress wave and a low-frequency shear wave at tissue-density interfaces (DePalma et al., 2005; Guy, Glover, & Cripps, 1998). A shear wave resulting from compression of the body wall and structures underneath is hypothesized to be the main source of injury to solid abdominal viscera, mesenteries, and the large bowel (Horrocks & Brett, 2000). In contrast to shear waves, a stress wave has a high amplitude and travels at approximately the speed of sound. This stress wave can potentially injure tissue via spalling (i.e., cavitation created by reflections of a blast wave at the junction of media that consist of different densities or acoustic impedances), implosion (i.e., process by which objects are destroyed by collapsing on themselves), and/or pressure differentials (Leung et al., 2008). The pressure differential creates an external force that causes a sudden acceleration of a surface (e.g., tympanic membrane; Leung et al., 2008; Wightman & Gladish, 2001). However, solid organs with certain characteristics (i.e., small shear modulus and large bulk modulus) will not be significantly compressed and therefore will not experience a large displacement (Clemedson & Pettersson, 1956; Leung et al., 2008).

Air-filled organs and air–fluid interfaces within the body, such as the middle ear, lungs, and GI tract, are the most susceptible to damage from high force blast waves (DePalma et al., 2005; Guy et al., 1998). In an outdoor setting the intensity of the blast wave initially dissipates by a cubed root of the distance from the source (Goh, 2009; Leung et al., 2008). For example, a person 3 meters (10 feet) from the point source experiences nine times more overpressure than a person who is 6 meters (20 feet) from the point source. At further distances, the dissipation transforms to a linear model of decay (Leung et al., 2008). Solid surfaces reflect blast waves (Goh, 2009).

The tympanic membrane is the most susceptible body structure to injury, and can be injured even with minor increases in pressure (i.e., 5 psi or 34.5 kPa). Therefore, it is the most frequently injured structure in the human body via a primary blast wave mechanism (DePalma et al., 2005; Jensen & Bonding, 1993). Because the ear is the most frequently impacted organ at a low pressure differential, it represents an ideal site for detecting minimum threshold effects from the primary blast wave alone and, furthermore, if the tympanic membrane has not been ruptured then the likelihood that the person experienced a significant blast is decreased (Argyros, 1997). Logically then, the likelihood that other air-filled organs have experienced any damage due to the primary effects of an explosion is also significantly decreased. For example, Katz, Ofek, Adler, Abramowitz, and Krausz (1989) investigated 647 bus explosion survivors and found that of the 193 with primary blast injuries, 142 (73.6%) experienced only perforation of the eardrum and 18 presented with isolated pulmonary injuries (9.3%). Likewise, when investigating injuries sustained during a train bombing, Gutierrez et al. (2005) found 99 (40.7%) of 243 victims to have experienced tympanic membrane ruptures and 4 to have experienced pulmonary injuries without ruptured tympanic membranes (1.6%). Related to the brain, Xydakis et al. (2007) found a significant association between tympanic-membrane perforation and LOC in the combat zone (relative risk, 2.76).

Because the tympanic membrane is the most vulnerable structure and may be damaged when other organs are not, it is important to identify symptoms that occur when a tympanic membrane is ruptured. Injury to the ear occurs along a continuum from rupture of the eardrum to dislocation of the ossicles of the middle ear to permanent hearing loss if the oval window or round window are disrupted, with symptoms varying from transient hearing reduction, hearing loss, deafness, tinnitus, vertigo, pain, dizziness, and hemorrhage (DePalma et al., 2005; Hirsch, 1968). It is important to realize that the ear can be easily protected by protective devices (Elsayed, 1997), and individuals who have on protective gear may suffer significant primary blast injury effects without tympanic membrane rupture (Argyros, 1997). Notably, however, even though approximately 37% of Xydakis and colleagues' (2007) sample reported wearing ear protection, the association between tympanic membrane perforation and LOC was still present.

The second body part most susceptible to primary explosion effects is the lung, with pulmonary barotrauma being the most common critical injury of those close to the center point (DePalma et al., 2005). Primary blast wave injury to the brain is hypothesized to include concussion and barotrauma from acute gas embolism (DePalma et al., 2005). With regard to the effects of the primary blast wave, it remains controversial whether brain injury occurs as a primary mechanism involving the blast wave itself as it interacts with the brain or whether a brain injury occurs via a secondary process, such as blast-induced dysfunction in the circulatory system or pulmonary systems (Leung et al., 2008). For example, it is hypothesized that primary blast wave effects (i.e., changes in pressure) can lead to cavitation in blood vessels, which can result in air or gas emboli causing a cerebral infarct (Mayorga, 1997; Okie, 2005). Brain injury secondary to a cerebral infarct, whether due to air emboli or another cause, would not be classified as MTBI. It is unknown if a primary blast wave can result in a secondary process that results in brain injury in humans but does not rise to the level of a noticeable infarct.

Animal studies on blast injury

The vast majority of the research conducted regarding blast injury has been conducted on animals. Animal studies suggest that primary blast waves alone, without secondary, tertiary, and quaternary effects, can in some circumstances cause damage to brain tissue and result in cognitive deficits (Cernak et al., 1996; Kaur et al., 1995). Contrary to the belief that the skull protects the brain from primary blast wave impact, Clemedson and Pettersson (1956) found that the shock wave amplitude and waveform did not significantly decrease when passing through rabbit skulls (in rats, see also Chavko, Koller, Prusaczyk, & McCarron, 2007).

The importance of the direction of impact was demonstrated in animal studies that showed different blast energy dissipation mechanics, depending on orientation of the head to the blast exposure (see, for example, Chavko et al., 2007). Five repeated blast waves in succession have been shown in animal models using sheep and swine to reduce the injury threshold from peak overpressures, compared to one blast exposure (Richmond, Yelverton, & Fletcher, 1981, as cited in Leung et al., 2008). Yang, Wang, Tang, and Ying (1996) found similar results when using weak blast exposures. Significant public attention has centered around the possibility that multiple blast exposures without associated alteration in consciousness may produce brain dysfunction (Glasser, 2007, as cited in French & Parkinson, 2008); however, "in the absence of supporting data such speculation may serve to simply raise unnecessary anxiety in deployed service members" (French & Parkinson, 2008, p. 1006).

Bauman et al. (2009) presented a swine model of explosive blast injury to the brain. Three situations were modeled: the blast tube which equated with a free-field blast situation, the Humvee surrogate, and the four-sided building with an entrance and no roof (Bauman et al., 2009). Each design took measures to minimize significant movement of the swine during blast exposure (Bauman et al., 2009). The researchers found structure variables (e.g., size, percent enclosed) significantly impacted the amplitude, frequency, and time to decay of the blast waves, and more importantly that the pressures were conducted into the brain as measured by fiberoptic pressure transducers that were implanted within the brain and vasculature. Two weeks after blast exposure the swine demonstrated reduced coordination of the metacarpals of the forelimbs, but additional studies are required to clarify if the disruption in functioning is due to brain injury, peripheral neuromuscular injury, or a combination of both. The researchers also found white matter fiber degeneration and astrocytosis in swine exposed to primary blast waves (Bauman et al., 2009). Similarly, Cernak, Wang, Jiang, Bian, and Savic (2001) found the formation of cytoplasmic vacuoles and myelin alterations in the hippocampus of primary blast-exposed rodents, even when the blast was focused on the thorax and the head was protected. The extent of cognitive impairment and biochemical changes was correlated with blast injury severity.

Extrapolations from animal research to humans are limited by numerous factors, including concerns regarding the blast wave generators themselves (Bauman et al., 2009) and also anatomical differences such as skull size, shape, and geometry between animals and humans (Sipos, Mulder, Koolstra, & van Eijden, 2008). Animal models, however, should not be dismissed and the cumulative findings suggest primary blast wave does have an impact on the brain in some situations. By extension, if primary blast wave by itself can in some cases result in moderate to severe brain injury, then it is theoretically possible that primary blast wave can also result in MTBI in some situations.

Human blast injury studies investigating cognition

Blast exposure may result in no injury, monotrauma (e.g., isolated ruptured tympanic membrane), or polytrauma. Polytrauma injuries are defined as injuries to more than one body area or organ systems that result in physical, cognitive, and/or psychosocial impairments (Department of Veterans Affairs, 2005). When comparing blast versus nonblast induced injuries, Sayer et al. (2008a) found that mechanism of injury did not predict outcomes as measured by Functional Independence Measure (FIM) scores; however, patients injured via a blast exposure had more soft tissue, eye, oral and maxillofacial, otologic, and penetrating brain injuries, auditory impairments, and symptoms of post-traumatic stress disorder (PTSD). Similarly, Warden (2006) found that patients injured via blast were more likely to have acute stress disorder, lower limb amputations, seizures, and skull fracture.

Several studies have been published investigating post-deployment symptoms and injuries (e.g., Hoge, Auchterlonie, & Milliken, 2006; Hoge et al., 2008; Sayer et al., 2008a). However, there is a strong need for studies investigating the effect of blast wave injury on human brain functioning and expected trajectories of recovery when brain dysfunction occurs. At this time, there appears to only be one full-length peer-reviewed article investigating blast injuries and cognitive functioning in humans that is based on group comparisons and not case studies. Belanger et al. (2009a) compared individuals with TBI due to blast versus TBI due to non-blast-related mechanisms on select neuropsychological measures and found that severity of injury, not mechanism of injury, was predictive of performance on verbal learning and memory measures. One of the strengths of the Belanger et al. (2009a) study was that they screened the sample for insufficient effort. Other studies investigating the blast mechanism of injury with regards to brain functioning have not consistently reported screening the participants for effort (i.e., performance validity), which can introduce a confound into the data and make the data difficult to interpret.

Warden et al. (2009) report a case study of suspected primary blast wave-associated TBI. The patient was exposed to multiple blast waves within a few hours. It is known that no secondary or tertiary blast effects co-occurred during her exposure to the primary blast waves because although she experienced altered awareness, she remained conscious throughout the event (Warden et al., 2009). At the time of blast exposure she experienced concussion-like symptoms (i.e., headache, balance problems, dizziness, and vomiting). MR imaging 3 months later was consistent with a resolving hematoma (Warden et al., 2009), but not definitive. The symptoms may have been due to brain concussion or the primary blast wave exposure, but they may have been due to other factors, such as dehydration or emotional trauma. Additionally, because the positive neuroimaging findings were identified months later they cannot be definitively attributed to the blast exposure. The location of the finding on imaging was the middle of the cerebellum. It is possible the findings could reflect a hypertensive bleed from either barotraumas, which caused an increase in blood pressure to the brain, or acute stress-related hypertension.

It is important that practitioners do not overgeneralize from the Warden case report to assume that every blast exposure results in a TBI or that this case report definitely demonstrated TBI due to primary blast wave exposure. Due to the complex nature of blast exposures, it would be highly improbable that all exposures result in a TBI. More data are needed to characterize the consequences of primary blast wave on the brain in humans. In nonblast MTBI research, contextual factors sometimes play a role in symptom development and maintenance. Therefore, the contextual milieu of blast injuries will be reviewed.

CONTEXT OF INJURY AND THE POST-DEPLOYMENT ENVIRONMENT

The situational context in which blast exposures occur and the post-deployment environment are important variables in post-concussion syndrome-like symptom creation, maintenance, and recovery. Some of these variables may explain why individuals with blast-related potential MTBI appear to be reporting symptoms and trajectories of recovery not consistent with what is expected. For example, Vasterling et al. (2006) compared 654 soldiers on select cognitive tests before and after deployment to a matched sample of 307 soldiers who were not deployed and found that being deployed was associated with an increased negative affect state and decreased neuropsychological test scores on sustained attention, verbal learning, and visuospatial memory tasks with an improvement in reaction time scores. Some of the contextual variables associated with deployment are reviewed below.

Co-occurring complexities

Post-concussive symptoms generally fall into three categories. Somatic symptoms include headache, dizziness, fatigue, noise/light sensitivity, and sleep disturbances. Cognitive symptoms include confusion, attention problems, reduced processing speed, memory difficulties, and executive dysfunction. Emotional and behavioral symptoms include depression, anxiety, irritability, apathy, and mood labiality. Numerous studies have demonstrated that post-concussion syndrome (PCS) symptoms are not specific to MTBI, in that patient groups without MTBI histories and even the general population endorse PCS symptoms (see Boake et al., 2005; Iverson & Lange, 2003; Landre et al., 2006; Meares et al., 2006; Meares et al., 2008). For example, individuals in psychotherapy who do not have a history of head injury report elevated levels of PCS symptoms (Fox, Lees-Haley, Earnest, & Dolezal-Wood, 1995). Additionally, Suhr and Gunstad (2002b) reported that depression accounted for elevated levels of PCS symptoms including cognitive symptoms more so than a history of head injury. Lees-Haley, Fox, and Courtney (2001) found symptoms associated with a MTBI diagnosis, such as feeling dazed, confusion, and subjective memory complaints, were endorsed in similar levels in patients exposed to traumatic events without TBI. Similarly, Iverson and McCracken (1997) found 39% of an outpatient pain sample met criteria for PCS even though none had a history of head injury. Frénisy et al. (2006) found that polytrauma patients who had not experienced a TBI endorsed high rates of neurobehavioral symptoms, including attention and memory complaints, concept organization difficulties and mood symptoms, such as irritability, mood swings, suspiciousness, decreased motivation, and guilt, again illustrating that physical injuries may produce symptoms that are associated with PCS as well.

Because many conditions and diagnoses can produce symptoms that are also associated with PCS, it is important to know what conditions may potentially account for the reported PCS-like symptoms months to years post injury at a time when the symptoms are less likely to be related to the remote potential MTBI. Differential diagnosis of PCS-like symptoms in the blast exposure population includes but is not limited to brain injury, chronic pain secondary to physical injury (e.g., back pain, headaches), physical injury even without chronic pain (e.g., ear drum rupture, traumatic amputation), sleep disturbances, anxiety spectrum disorders, including, but not limited to PTSD, depression, substance abuse disorders, somatoform disorders (e.g., conversion disorders, somatization disorders, hypochondriasis), factitious disorders, medication side effects, misattribution bias, diagnosis threat, symptom embellishment for secondary gain (i.e., malingering), and premorbid factors (e.g., learning disabilities). All these differentials may present with symptoms that overlap with PCS (e.g., Gasquoine, 2000; Gunstad & Suhr, 2004; Hoge et al., 2008; Iverson & McCracken, 1997; Karzmark, Hall, & Englander, 1995; McCauley, Boake, Levin, Contant, & Song, 2001; Schneiderman et al., 2008; Smith-Seemiller, Fow, Kant, & Franzen, 2003; Wilde et al., 2004). For example, concussion, PTSD, and chronic pain share the symptoms of fatigue, sleep disturbance, mood disturbance, psychosocial distress, and cognitive complaints (e.g., concentration and short-term memory), which can lead to role changes and decrements in everyday functioning. It is important to realize the differential diagnoses are not all mutually exclusive. For example, a patient may have chronic pain due to physical injuries (e.g., knee pain or back injury), PTSD, a history of remote MTBI, and also embellish symptoms for secondary gain (e.g., to increase service connection). Numerous potential comorbid conditions with overlapping symptoms add complexity to the diagnostic puzzle. This also creates numerous potential patient presentations. Due to the complexities of combat blast exposure, practitioners should be aware of the differential diagnoses, their associated symptoms, base rates, and the trajectory of recovery from each potential comorbid condition. This will aid the practitioner when diagnosing the patient and creating treatment plans.

Transient and chronic pain are important diagnostic considerations when assessing late-occurring or persistent PCS-like symptom presentations. Mechanisms of blast exposure can result in injuries that lead to transient or chronic pain (e.g., flying debris, falling, pressure changes). Transient and chronic pain can impact physical, social, cognitive, and emotional domains of functioning with resultant negative consequences for peer and family relationships. Pain can disrupt sleep patterns and negatively impact sexual functioning. Additionally, medications used for pain control may have side effects that create PCS-like symptoms.

Post-traumatic stress disorder (PTSD) and the anxiety spectrum disorders also need to be considered in the combat-exposed population. A higher prevalence of PTSD has been documented in combat veterans compared to the general population (Kessler, Sonnega, Bromet, Hughes, & Nelson, 1995; Kulka, 1990). PTSD symptoms in active duty military have been found in approximately 5% of soldiers prior to deployment (Hoge et al., 2004), whereas estimates of PTSD after return from OIF have been estimated to range from 13% to 17% (Hoge et al., 2004; Hoge, Terhakopian, Castro, Messer, & Engel, 2007). Physical injury while in combat is a risk factor for developing PTSD (Hoge et al., 2004, 2007; Koren, Norman, Cohen, Berman, & Klein, 2005). Studies that compared injured versus non-injured soldiers from Vietnam found two to three times higher rates of PTSD in soldiers who were injured (Kulka, 1990; Pitman, Altman, & Macklin, 1989). Patients with combat-related PTSD often present with comorbidities (Brady, Killeen, Brewerton, & Lucerini, 2000; Hryvniak & Rosse, 1989). Combat-related PTSD has been associated with more severe functional impairments in some studies (Prigerson, Maciejewski, & Rosenheck, 2001). PTSD, unlike MTBI, has been demonstrated to be associated with long-term negative health consequences, such as cardiovascular disease (Bullman, Kang, & Thomas, 1991; Dirkzwager, van der Velden, Grievink, & Yzermans, 2007; Kang, Bullman, & Taylor, 2006). Many recent studies have demonstrated the high prevalence of PTSD and other psychiatric illness resulting from the Afghanistan and Iraq wars (e.g., Erbes, Westermeyer, Engdahl, & Johnsen, 2007; Hoge et al., 2006, 2008; Jakupcak et al., 2007; Kolkow, Spira, Morse, & Grieger, 2007; Milliken, Auchterlonie, & Hoge, 2007). Hoge et al. (2008) found that 44% of soldiers with MTBI and associated LOC also met criteria for PTSD. Hoge et al. (2008) found that, when adjusting for PTSD and depression, MTBI was no longer significantly associated with PCS symptoms (except headache) or physical health outcomes. Therefore PTSD is an important consideration when assessing and working with patients who present with physical injuries and/or potential TBI during combat.

Substance abuse disorders, depressive disorders, conversion disorders, hypochondriasis, and factitious disorders can all produce symptoms that are among the non-specific symptoms of PCS. Sleep disturbances that co-occur or are caused by many of these diagnoses can produce PCS-like symptoms (e.g., irritability and fatigue), as well. Medication side effects can also produce PCS-like symptoms. Even symptoms that some believe are unique or indicative of MTBI, such as visual changes, vertigo or other balance problems, and auditory deficits and tinnitus, may actually be associated with some of the physical impacts of blasts, rather than MTBI (e.g., tympanic membrane rupture). Similarly, Iverson (2006) reported that substantial minorities of civilians with depression report "classic" post-concussion-like symptoms, such as dizziness (31%), nausea (41%), and noise sensitivity (50%).

It is important to realize that multiple diagnoses and symptoms can be entangled. For example, medication side effects may result in sleep disturbances, which negatively impact mood, which in turn can intensify subjective distress related to chronic pain symptoms and result in increased doses of pain medication that may further worsen sleep patterns. It is crucial to treat these patients with a mechanism of injury approach, which does not solely treat the presenting symptoms but instead utilizes interdisciplinary team care to address patients' physical, psychological, rehabilitative, and prosthetic needs while being mindful of the context and base rates of comorbidities (Scott, Belanger, Vanderploeg, Massengale, & Scholten, 2006). The mechanism of injury approach is similar to a biospsychosocial approach. When treating symptoms in isolation, there is a risk of decreasing one symptom (e.g., pain) while increasing others (e.g., sleep disturbances, mood disturbance, cognitive complaints). Misattribution of symptoms is discussed next.

Iatrogenic illness, diagnosis threat, and misattribution bias

Several studies have found an increase in symptom endorsement over time, either between participants (e.g., Belanger et al., 2009a) or within participants (e.g., Milliken et al., 2007). Various explanations have been advanced including (a) recovery from TBI may be associated with increased recovery of distressing memories, (b) physiological changes that persist (e.g., vestibular changes, hearing loss, tinnitus) may result in increased anxiety responses over time, and (c) awareness of symptoms may increase with time (Belanger et al., 2009a). While these are possibilities, it is also possible that the DoD and VHA systems along with the public milieu may be functioning in a way to create, maintain, and/or accentuate the symptoms in some select cases. As noted earlier, it is unlikely that persistent or late-occurring symptoms are related to a potential remote MTBI for the overwhelming majority of cases. However, symptoms that are shared with other conditions, such as substance abuse, sleep disorders, and mood disorders, can persist if not properly treated. Additionally, symptoms associated with MTBI can occur in normal healthy adults (Iverson & Lange, 2003). These facts, combined with the reality that misinformation about MTBI (e.g., base rate, recovery trajectory, and future implications) is in the public domain, create a situation where expectations may result in individuals misattributing their symptoms to an improper source (e.g., remote potential MTBI) when they actually stem from other comorbid conditions or everyday life fluctuates. Studies have investigated this phenomenon, which is called misattribution bias (e.g., Mittenberg, DiGiulio, Perrin, & Bass, 1992).

Some patients with a history of MTBI have been found to under-report pre-injury levels of PCS symptoms (Mittenberg et al., 1992). Also, when study participants without a history of TBI were asked to imagine the symptoms of a MTBI they reported symptoms typically endorsed by patients after a MTBI (Mittenberg et al., 1992). With ambiguous stimuli, such as internal states, individuals interpret the event based largely on their expectation of that experience (Gunstad & Suhr, 2001). Taken together the relevant literature suggests that if there is an expectation of initial and continued symptoms that some individuals will in fact experience these symptoms (Mittenberg et al., 1992). Gunstad and Suhr suggested that Mittenberg's "expectation as etiology" hypothesis may be too specific and perhaps a "good old days" hypothesis would be more appropriate, meaning that after a negative event people may attribute all symptoms to that negative event.

The concept of "diagnosis threat" is similar to the "expectation as etiology" theory. Suhr and Gunstad (2002a, 2005) found that when participants were randomly assigned to a group informed they were being assessed due to a history of MTBI, versus a group given neutral instructions that did not call attention to the remote MTBI, the former group performed more poorly on neuropsychological test measures. This suggests a psychological mechanism, termed "diagnosis threat", that can negatively impact performance on some neuropsychological test measures (Suhr & Gunstad, 2002a, 2005). This is especially problematic when the symptoms of the genuine diagnosis are commonly occurring symptoms among the general public, in that normal experience may function to reinforce the mistaken belief that the person is indeed "sick." Misinformation in the public domain that does not differentiate the severity levels of TBI and suggests MTBI has long-term deficits similar to a severe TBI has the potential to be harmful to those who experience a blast exposure.

Mittenberg, Tremont, Zeilinski, Fichera, and Rayls (1996) investigated brain injury outcomes as a function of two informational responses to injury. These authors found that an intervention consisting of extensive written instructions and a meeting with a therapist for information and general advice to gradually return to premorbid activities before discharge ($n = 29$) versus routine discharge information consisting of advice to rest ($n = 29$) resulted in reduced symptoms and disability at 6 months post-injury via interview. Other studies have also found that providing patients with information regarding the normal course and trajectory of recovery after MTBI can decrease symptom prevalence in children (Ponsford et al., 2001) and adults (Ponsford et al., 2002). These and similar studies suggest that provision of accurate information regarding expected symptoms, the trajectory of recovery along with suggested coping strategies within 1 week of sustaining a concussion results in fewer symptoms and reduced anxiety subsequently (Mittenberg et al., 1996; Paniak, Toller-Lobe, Durand, & Nagy, 1998; Paniak, Toller-Lobe, Reynolds, Melnyk, & Nagy, 2000; Wade, Crawford, Wenden, King, & Moss, 1997; Wade, King, Wenden, Crawford, & Caldwell, 1998).

It is not known if informational approaches would work as well at a later time point (Belanger, Uomoto, & Vanderploeg, 2009b). There are several reasons simple informational interventions may not be as helpful with persistent or later-occurring PCS-like symptoms in the blast exposure population. First, it is possible that misattribution over an extended period of time may lead to a psychological investment in the symptoms on multiple levels. Social roles, financial compensation, perceived self-efficacy, and personal life expectations may all be altered by prolonged periods of misattributed PCS-like symptoms. Second, in some cases the PCS-like symptoms may be due to comorbid condition(s). Simply informing the patients they should not have symptoms due to a remote potential MTBI will not alleviate symptoms stemming from a different source. This underscores the importance of appropriate differential assessment and diagnosis based on a mechanism of injury approach (Scott et al., 2006). In either situation, if symptoms stem from a different etiology or iatrogenic symptoms were created, symptom resolution will require a mental paradigm shift in the individual. It is important for clinicians to get these patients "treatment ready," which means aiding them with the mental paradigm shift and helping them to consider that their current symptoms may be related to psychological or physical factors not involving the brain. In some instances this process may require more than one discussion, and individuals and their families may go through a range of emotions during and after the discussions. The reallocation of the longstanding misattribution of symptoms to a different cause may require recreation of personal identity on some level.

External incentives: Secondary gain can lead to symptom embellishment

External incentives are known to shape behavior. There are external incentives that can occur when claiming an injury or embellishing the severity of an injury while on active duty. While in theatre, an injury can potentially excuse a solider from duty for a certain period of time or result in a change of duties. In extreme cases an injury may result in the solider being discharged from the service on medical grounds. Within the VHA and DoD, benefits vary depending on the nature and severity of the injury sustained.

Within the VHA system, recognition of an injury can result in a veteran obtaining a service-related disability rating (0% to 100%). The percent of service connection impacts disability payments monthly, access to health care, co-payments for services, access to vocational training, and educational expense reimbursement. New programs are developed to cater to the needs of the soldiers and veterans to make sure they are properly compensated for injuries obtained in the line of service. One example is the Servicemembers' Group Life Insurance Traumatic Injury Protection Program (TSGLI), which can result in a large one-time sum of money (up to 100 K) being dispersed to those who are injured (https://www.hrc.army.mil/site/crsc/tsgli/index.html).

Numerous researchers have reported that diagnoses that rely solely on self-report and subjective evidence can be feigned and misrepresented, and that symptom embellishment is a concern within a compensation context (Greiffenstein & Baker, 2008; Mittenberg, Patton, Canyock, & Condit, 2002; Peterson, 1998). Some have argued that the VHA disability program can have unintended consequence of promoting illness due to financial incentives and the structure of the system (Mossman, 1996).

Veterans claiming disability status due to PTSD is one area that has raised concerns about secondary gain incentives in the VHA disability system (Sayer, Spoont, Nelson, Clothier, & Murdoch, 2008b). Sayer et al. (2008b) hypothesized this may have been due to the fact a PTSD diagnosis depends heavily on self-report, rather than objective markers. The program may create incentives for veterans to magnify their symptom presentation to maximize their service connection level (Frueh, Hamner, Cahill, Gold, & Hamlin, 2000). Burket and Whitley (1998) suggested that some veterans use the VHA mental health system to establish a basis for their PTSD claims and then withdraw from services once their claim is finalized. Several studies have shown that as a group veterans who are seeking disability status for PTSD report more severe PTSD symptoms and show more frequent symptom exaggeration on MMPI-2 validity indices compared to veterans with PTSD who are not seeking disability status (Frueh, Gold, & de Arellano, 1997; Frueh et al., 2000; Frueh, Smith, & Barker, 1996; Gold & Frueh, 1998). Studies investigating service utilization and disability-seeking status have shown mixed findings, with some finding a decrease in service use after an increase in PTSD service connection rating to 100% (Office of Inspector General, 2005). In contrast, after controlling for compensation-seeking status, Sayer et al. (2008b) found an increase in mental health service usage among participants who were no longer compensation seeking, suggesting that services were not being used merely to justify a PTSD claim (Sayer et al., 2008b). Notably, however, when administering symptom validity measures to Vietnam Veterans with chronic combat-related PTSD who presented for PTSD residential treatment, Freeman, Powell, and Kimbrell (2008) found a 53% clear symptom exaggeration rate on the SIRS, with SIRS scores significantly correlated with self-reported PTSD symptom severity on the clinician-administered PTSD scale (CAPS). Additional studies are needed to clarify these findings.

Instances of exaggeration have been reported within the military context by the media. The Associated Press released a news story on April 11, 2009, stating that although the DoD reported only 21 surviving POWs from the first Gulf War in 1991, the VHA was paying disability benefits to 286 service members who reported being taken prisoner. Similarly, although there are only approximately 560 officially recognized POWs from Vietnam (661 returned alive and approximately 100 have died since then), the VHA reported paying benefits to 966 Vietnam POWs. Reportedly, approximately 2000 veterans who were pretending to be POWs have been discovered, with some having received cumulative benefits over the years in excess of 400,000 dollars (Associated Press, April 11, 2009 by Allen Breed).

Because TBI is considered a signature wound of the current conflicts and, as with PTSD, MTBI is a diagnosis often made based on subjective report, it is important for clinicians and policy makers to be aware of the potential for symptom embellishment and malingering of MTBI. Researchers have reported that external incentives, such as monetary gain from litigation, correlate with persistent or worsening PCS symptoms over time (Belanger et al., 2005). Similarly, in a meta-analysis, Binder and Rohling (1996) demonstrated that financial incentives had more of an impact on neuropsychological test performance than MTBI. Likewise, Green, Lees-Haley, and Allen (2002) reported that compromised effort had more of an impact on memory test scores than neurological disease. Returning to a military context, when investigating soldiers returning from service in Operation Iraqi Freedom or Operation Enduring Freedom, it was found that 17% (4 of 23) of patients evaluated at a Polytrauma Network Site (Level 2) failed symptom validity testing, consistent with embellishing of symptoms (Whitney, Shepard, Williams, Davis, & Adams, 2009).

When clinicians were made aware of potential threats to assessment validity, detection of PTSD simulation improved (Hickling, Blanchard, Mundy, & Galovski, 2002). It is important that clinicians screen for symptom validity and remain aware of the potential pull for symptom embellishment due to multiple external incentives associated with establishment of injury. It stands to reason that education regarding this possibility should be provided to practitioners within the DoD and VHA system of care for all levels of practitioners, not just neuropsychologists and rehabilitation specialists. It is also important to note that encouraging clinicians to remain cognizant of potential symptom embellishment and malingering in no way infers that individuals who sustained injuries while on active duty should be denied benefits. With finite resources available, it is important that individuals are compensated at the level of injury obtained and that compensation is related to actual occurrences of injury.

CONTEXT OVERVIEW: SUMMARY

Exposure to an explosion can create a complex situation. Situational variables (e.g., tympanic membrane rupture, intense fear) can result in symptoms that are also associated with a MTBI. Those injured in blast explosion scenarios often have co-occurring physical injuries and numerous comorbid potential diagnoses. Misinformation within the public domain and system variables can potentially lead to misattribution of symptoms. It is crucial for providers to remember that TBI severity is determined by injury characteristics at the time of the injury and not patient presentation months or years later. Since many persons with potential MTBI do not have contemporaneous medical documentation and do not present with unequivocal signs of neurologic injury (e.g., brain-imaging findings, hemiparesis, etc.), confirmation of an initial TBI may not be possible. The implication is not that such persons do not deserve treatment for their symptoms, but that it remains unknown whether these symptoms are due, in whole or in part, to TBI. Months and years after the injury, the scientific literature suggests that persistent or late-occurring symptoms are related to non-brain-injury factors. In addition, the DoD and VHA systems contain external incentives, which for some individuals can lead to embellishment of injuries and maintenance of a sick role.

Clinicians need to be mindful that patients may misattribute symptoms to an MTBI, even years after an event. Clinicians should attend to these issues when assessing and treating individuals with PCS-like symptoms. With education, skill building, and reassurance, clinicians can help foster the mental paradigm shift required to prevent and alleviate the misattribution of symptoms. It is also important for clinicians and researchers to remember that primary blast wave is a unique phenomenon that challenges what we already know and believe about MTBI. Until additional research is completed, clinicians are advised to remain open-minded regarding whether blast injury creates differences in mechanisms, trajectory, and symptom severity, compared to other types of MTBI.

BRIEF RECOMMENDATIONS FOR ASSESSMENT AND TREATMENT

Clinicians need to be aware that their actions can help alleviate or perpetuate the symptoms experienced by a patient via iatrogenic effects (i.e., inadvertent adverse mental and/or physical effects that occur in a patient due to a healthcare professional's intervention). Therefore, DoD and VHA employees who interact with the soldiers and veterans, and who have diagnostic authority (e.g., conduct the clinical reminders or MTBI screenings), or therapists who work with the patients in rehabilitation or vocational contexts, who could be viewed by the patient as having diagnostic authority, should be educated regarding the current MTBI findings and the complex post-deployment environment. Such education may occur through hospital-based continuing education modules similar to the required HIPAA security and privacy trainings. Consistent with Mittenberg et al.'s work (1996), psychoeducation regarding the expected recovery from MTBI should be given at the time an individual screens positive on a TBI screen or clinical reminder. Although this intervention will not alleviate symptoms stemming from other causes, an informational handout for patients, such as the ones created by the Defense and Veterans Brain Injury Center (DVBIC), may help alleviate any misattribution or diagnosis threat that can occur in the interim between a positive screening and obtaining a more thorough evaluation. A mechanism of injury approach, which is similar to a biopsychosocial approach, that takes a holistic view of the patient and situation should be utilized. All of the co-occurring psychological, physical, and diagnostic complexities including the system's external incentives need to be taken into consideration when interacting with and treating the patients.

Additional studies are needed that investigate the cognitive and emotional aspects of primary blast injury closer in time to the exposure, to determine if the expected trajectory of recovery is consistent with other mechanisms of injury. Studies investigating the comorbid complexities and what treatments work best are also needed. Psychosocial and educational interventions utilized with patients who present with persistent PCS symptoms should be monitored and the positive and negative outcomes need to be disseminated.

AUTHOR NOTE

The views expressed in this manuscript are the author's and do not reflect the views or official policies of the US Government or the Veterans Health Administration.

ACKNOWLEDGMENT

The author would like to thank Johnny Davis, Louis French, Grant Iverson, and Rosemarie Moser for their thoughtful review and comments on a draft of this manuscript. The author would also like to thank the blind reviewers for their helpful comments and Jerry Sweet for his valuable editorial assistance.

REFERENCES

Alexander, M. P. (1995). Mild traumatic brain injury: Pathophysiology, natural history, and clinical management. *Neurology, 45*(7), 1253–1260.

Alves, W., Macciocchi, S. N., & Barth, J. T. (1993). Post-concussive symptoms after uncomplicated head injury. *Journal of Head Trauma Rehabilitation, 8*, 48–59.

Argyros, G. J. (1997). Management of primary blast injury. *Toxicology, 121*, 105–115.

Bauman, R. A., Ling, G. S., Tong, L., Januszkiewicz, A., Agoston, D., et al. (2009). An introductory characterization of combat-casualty-care relevant swine model of closed head injury resulting from exposure to explosive blast. *Journal of Neurotrauma, 26*(6), 841–860.

Belanger, H. G., Curtiss, G., Demery, J. A., Lebowitz, B. K., & Vanderploeg, R. D. (2005). Factors moderating neuropsychological outcomes following mild traumatic brain injury: A meta-analysis. *Journal of the International Neuropsychological Society, 11*(3), 215–227.

Belanger, H. G., Kretzmer, T., Yoash-Gantz, R., Pickett, T., & Tupler, L. A. (2009a). Cognitive sequelae of blast-related versus other mechanisms of brain trauma. *Journal of the International Neuropsychological Society, 15*(1), 1–8.

Belanger, H. G., Uomoto, J. M., & Vanderploeg, R. D. (2009b). The Veterans Health Administration System of Care for Mild Traumatic Brain Injury: Costs, benefits, and controversies. *Journal of Head Trauma Rehabilitation, 24*(1), 4–13.

Belanger, H. G., & Vanderploeg, R. D. (2005). The neuropsychological impact of sports-related concussion: A meta-analysis. *Journal of the International Neuropsychological Society, 11*(4), 345–357.

Binder, L. M., & Rohling, M. L. (1996). Money matters: A meta-analytic review of the effects of financial incentives on recovery after closed-head injury. *The American Journal of Psychiatry, 153*(1), 7–10.

Boake, C., McCauley, S. R., Levin, H. S., Pedroza, C., Contant, C. F., et al. (2005). Diagnostic criteria for postconcussional syndrome after mild to moderate traumatic brain injury. *The Journal of Neuropsychiatry and Clinical Neurosciences, 17*, 350–356.

Borgaro, S. R., Prigatano, G. P., Kwasnica, C., & Rexer, J. L. (2003). Cognitive and affective sequelae in complicated and uncomplicated mild traumatic brain injury. *Brain Injury, 17*(3), 189–198.

Brady, K. T., Killeen, T. K., Brewerton, T., & Lucerini, S. (2000). Comorbidity of psychiatric disorders and post-traumatic stress disorder. *Journal of Clinical Psychiatry, 61*(Suppl 7), 22–32.

Breed, A. (2009, April 11). *POW claimants exceed recorded POWs*. Associated Press.

Brookings Institute. (2008). Iraq Index. Retrieved March 24, 2009, from http://www.brookings.edu/saban/iraq-index.aspx

Bullman, T. A., Kang, H. K., & Thomas, T. L. (1991). Post-traumatic stress disorder among Vietnam veterans on the Agent Orange Registry. A case-control analysis. *Annals of Epidemiology, 1*, 505–512.

Burkett, B. G., & Whitley, G. (1998). *Stolen valor: How the Vietnam generation was robbed of its heroes and history*. Dallas, TX: Verity.

Carroll, L. J., Cassidy, J. D., Peloso, P. M., Borg, J., von Holst, H., et al. (2004). Prognosis for mild traumatic brain injury: Results of the WHO Collaborating Centre Task Force on Mild Traumatic Brain Injury. *Journal of Rehabilitaion Medicine, 43*(Suppl), 84–105.

Cernak, I., Savic, J., Malicevic, Z., Zunic, G., Radosevic, P., et al. (1996). Involvement of the central nervous system in the general response to pulmonary blast injury. *The Journal of Trauma, 40*, S100–S104.

Cernak, J., Wang, Z., Jiang, J., Bian, X., & Savic, J. (2001). Ultrastructural and functional characteristics of blast injury-induced neurotrauma. *The Journal of Trauma, 50*(4), 695–706.

Chavko, M., Koller, W. A., Prusaczyk, W. K., & McCarron, R. M. (2007). Measurement of blast wave by miniature fiber optic pressure transducer in the rat brain. *Journal of Neuroscience Methods, 159*, 277–281.

Clemedson, C. J. (1956). Blast injury. *Physiological Review, 36*(3), 336–354.

Clemedson, C. J., & Pettersson, H. (1956). Propagation of a high explosive air shock wave through different parts of an animal body. *The American Journal of Physiology, 184*, 119–126.

DePalma, R. G., Burris, D. G., Champion, H. R., & Hodgson, M. J. (2005). Blast injuries. *The New England Journal of Medicine, 352*, 1335–342.

Department of Veterans Affairs. (2005). *Veterans Health Administration VHA Directive 2005–024: Polytrauma Rehabilitation Centers.* Washington, DC: Department of Veteran Affairs.

Department of Veteran Affairs. (2009). *VA/DoD clinical practice guideline for management of concussion/mild traumatic brain injury.* Washington, DC: Department of Veteran Affairs.

Dikmen, S., McLean, A., & Temkin, N. (1986). Neuropsychological and psychosocial consequences of minor head injury. *Journal of Neurology, Neurosurgery & Psychiatry, 49*(11), 1227–1232.

Dirkzwager, A. J., van der Velden, P. G., Grievink, L., & Yzermans, C. J. (2007). Disaster related post-traumatic stress disorder and physical health. *Psychosomatic Medicine, 69*, 435–440.

Elsayed, N. M. (1997). Toxicology of blast overpressure. *Toxicology, 121*, 1–15.

Erbes, C., Westermeyer, J., Engdahl, B., & Johnsen, E. (2007). Post-traumatic stress disorder and service utilization in a sample of service members from Iraq and Afghanistan. *Miliary Medicine, 172*(4), 359–363.

Fox, D., Lees-Haley, P., Earnest, K., & Dolezal-Wood, S. (1995). Post-concussive symptpoms: Baserates and etiology in psychiatric patients. *The Clinical Neuropsychologist, 9*, 89–92.

Freeman, T., Powell, M., & Kimbrell, T. (2008). Measuring symtpom exaggeration in Veterans with chronic post-traumatic stress disorder. *Psychiatric Research, 158*, 374–380.

French, L. M., & Parkinson, G. W. (2008). Assessing and treating veterans with traumatic brain injury. *Journal of Clinical Psychology: In Session, 6418*, 1004–1013.

Frénisy, M. C., Bénony, H., Chahraoui, K., Minot, D., d'Athis, P., et al. (2006). Brain injured patients versus multiple trauma patients: Some neurobehavioral and psychopathological aspects. *The Journal of Trauma, 60*(5), 1018–1026.

Frueh, B. C., Gold, P. B., & de Arellano, M. A. (1997). Symptom overreporting in combat veterans evaluated for PTSD: Differentiation on the basis of compensation seeking status. *Journal of Personality Assessment, 68*, 369–384.

Frueh, B. C., Hamner, M. B., Cahill, S. P., Gold, P. B., & Hamlin, K. L. (2000). Apparent symptom overreporting in combat veterans evaluated for PTSD. *Clinical Psychology Review, 20*, 853–885.

Frueh, B. C., Smith, D. W., & Barker, S. E. (1996). Compensation seeking status and psychometric assessment of combat veterans seeking treatment for PTSD. *Journal of Traumatic Stress, 9*, 427–439.

Gasquoine, P. G. (2000). Postconcussional symptoms in chronic back pain. *Applied Neuropsychology, 7*(2), 83–89.

Goh, S. H. (2009). Bomb blast mass casualty incidents: Initial triage and management of injuries. *Singapore Medical Journal, 50*(1), 101–105.

Gold, P. B., & Frueh, B. C. (1999). Compensation-seeking and extreme exaggeration of psychopathology among combat veterans evaluated for post-traumatic stress disorder. *The Journal of Nervous and Mental Disease, 187*, 680–684.

Green, P., Lees-Haley, P. R., & Allen, L. M. (2002). The Word Memory Test and the validity of neuropsychological test scores. *Journal of Forensic Neuropsychology, 2*, 97–124.

Greiffenstein, M. F., & Baker, W. J. (2008). Validity testing in dually diagnosed post-traumatic stress disorder and mild closed head injury. *The Clinical Neuropsychologist, 22*, 565–582.

Gunstad, J., & Suhr, J. A. (2001). "Expectation as etiology" versus "the good old days": Postconcussion syndrome symptom reporting in athletes, headache suffers, and depressed indviduals. *Journal of the International Neuropsychological Society, 7*, 323–333.

Gunstad, J., & Suhr, J. A. (2004). Cognitive factors in postconcussion syndrome symptom report. *Archives of Clinical Neuropsychology, 19*(3), 391–405.

Gutierrez de Ceballos, J. P., Fuentes, F. T., Diaz, D. P., Sanchez, M. S., Llorente, C. M., & Guerrero Sanz, J. E. (2005). Casualties treated at the closet hospital in the Madrid, March 11, terrorist bombings. *Critical Care Medicine, 33*, S107–S112.

Guy, R. J., Glover, M. A., & Cripps, N. P. (1998). The pathophysiology of primary blast injury and its implications for treatment. Part I: The thorax. *Journal of the Royal Naval Medical Service, 84*, 79–86.

Hickling, E. J., Blanchard, E. B., Mundy, E., & Galovski, T. E. (2002). Detection of malingered MVA related post-traumatic stress disorder: An investigation of the ability to detect professional actors by experienced clinicians, psychological tests, and psychophysiological assessment. *Journal of Forensic Psychology Practice, 2*, 33.

Hirsch, F. G. (1968). Effects of overpressure on the ear: A review. *Annals of the New York Academy of Sciences, 152*, 146–162.

Hoge, C. W., Auchterlonie, J. L., & Milliken, C. S. (2006). Mental health problems, use of mental health services, and attrition from military service after returning from deployment to Iraq or Afghanistan. *Journal of the American Medical Association, 295*(9), 1023–1032.

Hoge, C. W., Castro, C. A., Messer, S. C., McGurk, D., Cotting, D. I., et al. (2004). Combat duty in Iraq and Afghanistan, mental health problems, and barriers to care. *The New England Journal of Medicine, 351*, 13–22.

Hoge, C. W., McGurk, D., Thomas, J. L., Cox, A. L., Engel, C. C., et al. (2008). Mild traumatic brain injury in U.S. soldiers returning from Iraq. *The New England Journal of Medicine, 358*(5), 453–463.

Hoge, C. W., Terhakopian, A., Castro, C. A., Messer, S. C., & Engel, C. C. (2007). Association of post-traumatic stress disorder with somatic symptoms, health care visits, and absenteeism among Iraq war veterans. *The American Journal of Psychiatry, 164*, 150–153.

Horrocks, C., & Brett, S. (2000). Blast injury. *Current Anaesthesia and Critical Care, 11*, 113–119.

Hryvniak, M. R., & Rosse, R. B. (1989). Concurrent psychiatric illness in inpatients with post-traumatic stress disorder. *Military Medicine, 154*(8), 399–401.

Iverson, G. L. (2005). Outcome from mild traumatic brain injury. *Current Opinion in Psychiatry, 18*(3), 301–317.

Iverson, G. L. (2006). Misdiagnosis of the persistent postconcussion syndrome in patients with depression. *Archives of Clinical Neuropsychology, 21*(4), 303–310.

Iverson, G. L., & Lange, R. T. (2003). Examination of "postconcussion-like" symptoms in a healthy sample. *Applied Neuropsychology, 10*(3), 137–144.

Iverson, G. L., & McCracken, L. M. (1997). 'Postconcussive' symptoms in persons with chronic pain. *Brain Injury, 11*(11), 783–790.

Jakupcak, M., Conybeare, D., Phelps, L., Hunt, S., Holmes, H. A., et al. (2007). Anger, hostility, and aggression among Iraq and Afghanistan War veterans reporting PTSD and subthreshold PTSD. *Journal of Trauma Stress, 20*(6), 945–954.

Jensen, J. H., & Bonding, P. (1993). Experimental pressure induced rupture of the tympanic membrane in man. *Acta Oto-Laryngologica, 113*(1), 62–67.

Kang, H. K., Bullman, T. A., & Taylor, J. W. (2006). Risk of selected cardiovascular diseases and post-traumatic stress disorder among former World War II prisoners of war. *Annals of Epidemiology, 16*, 381–386.

Karzmark, P., Hall, K., & Englander, J. (1995). Late-onset post-concussion symptoms after mild brain injury: The role of premorbid, injury-related, environmental, and personality factors. *Brain Injury*, *9*(1), 21–26.

Kashluba, S, Hanks, R. A., Casey, J. E., & Millis, S. R. (2008). Neuropsychologic and functional outcome after complicated mild traumatic brain injury. *Archives of Physical Medicine and Rehabilitation*, *89*(5), 904–911.

Katz, E., Ofek, B., Adler, J., Abramowitz, H. B., & Krausz, M. M. (1989). Primary blast injury after a bomb explosion in a civilian bus. *Annals of Surgery*, *209*, 484–488.

Kaur, C., Singh, J., Lim, M. K., Ng, B. L., Yap, E. P., et al. (1995). The response of neurons and microglia to blast injury in the rat brain. *Neuropathology and Applied Neurobiology*, *21*, 787–794.

Kessler, R. C., Sonnega, A., Bromet, E., Hughes, M., & Nelson, C. B. (1995). Post-traumatic stress disorder in the National Comorbidity Survey. *Archives of General Psychiatry*, *52*(12), 1048–1060.

Kolkow, T. T., Spira, J. L., Morse, J. S., & Grieger, T. A. (2007). Post-traumatic stress disorder and depression in health care providers returning from deployment to Iraq and Afghanistan. *Military Medicine*, *172*(5), 451–455.

Koren, D., Norman, D., Cohen, A., Berman, J., & Klein, E. M. (2005). Increased PTSD risk with combat-related injury: A matched comparison study of injured and uninjured soldiers experiencing the same combat events. *The American Journal of Psychiatry*, *162*(2), 276–282.

Kulka, R. A. (1990). *Trauma and the Vietnam war generation: Report of findings from the National Vietnam veterans readjustment study*. New York: Brunner/Mazel.

Kurca, E., Sivak, S., & Kucera, P. (2006). Impaired cognitive functions in mild traumatic brain injury patients with normal and pathologic magnetic resonance imaging. *Neuroradiology*, *48*(9), 661–669.

Landre, N., Poppe, C. J., Davis, N., Schmaus, B., & Hobbs, S. E. (2006). Cognitive functioning and postconcussive symptoms in trauma patients with and without mild TBI. *Archives of Clinical Neuropsychology*, *21*(4), 255–273.

Lees-Haley, P. R., Fox, D. D., & Courtney, J. C. (2001). A comparison of complaints by mild brain injury claimants and other claimants describing subjective experiences immediately following their injury. *Archives of Clinical Neuropsychology*, *16*, 689–695.

Leung, L. Y., VandeVord, P. J., Dal Cengio, A. L., Bir, C., Yang, K. H., et al. (2008). Blast related neurotrauma: A review of cellular injury. *Molecular and Cellular Biomechanics*, *5*(3), 155–168.

Levin, H. S., Mattis, S., Ruff, R. M., Eisenberg, H. M., Marshall, L. F., et al. (1987). Neurobehavioral outcome following minor head injury: A three-center study. *Journal of Neurosurgery*, *66*(2), 234–243.

Lovell, M. R., Collins, M. W., Iverson, G. L., Field, M., Maroon, J. C., et al. (2003). Recovery from mild concussion in high school athletes. *Journal of Neurosurgery*, *98*(2), 296–301.

Mayorga, M. A. (1997). The pathology of primary blast overpressure injury. *Toxicology*, *121*, 17–28.

McCauley, S. R., Boake, C., Levin, H. S., Contant, C. F., & Song, J. X. (2001). Postconcussional disorder following mild to moderate traumatic brain injury: Anxiety, depression, and social support as risk factors and comorbidities. *Journal of Clinical and Experimental Neuropsychology*, *23*(6), 792–808.

McCrea, M. (2008). *Mild traumatic brain injury and post-concussion syndrome: The new evidence base for diagnosis and treatment*. New York: Oxford University Press.

McCrea, M., Guskiewicz, K. M., Marshall, S. W., Barr, W. B., Randolph, C., et al. (2003). Acute effects and recovery time following concussion in collegiate football players. *Journal of the American Medical Association*, *290*, 2556–2563.

McCrea, M., Iverson, G., McAllister, T., Hammeke, T. A., Powell, M., et al. (2009). An intergrated review of recovery after mild traumatic brain injury (MTBI): Implications for clinical management. *The Clinical Neuropsychologist, 23*(8), 1368–1390.

McLean Jr, A., Temkin, N. R., Dikmen, S., & Wyler, A. R. (1983). The behavioral sequelae of head injury. *Journal of Clinical Neuropsychology, 5*(4), 361–376.

Meares, S., Shores, E. A., Batchelor, J., Baguley, I., Chapman, J., et al. (2006). The relationship of psychological and cognitive factors and opioids in the development of the postconcussion syndrome in general trauma patients with mild traumatic brain injury. *Journal of the International Neuropsychoogical Society, 12*(6), 792–801.

Meares, S., Shores, E. A., Taylor, A. J., Batchelor, J., Bryant, R. A., et al. (2008). Mild traumatic brain injury does not predict acute postconcussion syndrome. *Journal of Neurology, Neurosurgery & Psychiatry, 79*(3), 300–306.

Milliken, C. S., Auchterlonie, J. L., & Hoge, C. W. (2007). Longitudinal assessment of mental health problems among active and reserve component soldiers returning from the Iraq war. *Journal of the Amercan Medical Association, 298*(18), 2141–2148.

Mittenberg, W., DiGiulio, D. V., Perrin, S., & Bass, A. E. (1992). Symptoms following mild head injury: Expectation as aetiology. *Journal of Neurology, Neurosurgery & Psychiatry, 55*, 200–204.

Mittenberg, W., Patton, C., Canyock, E. M., & Condit, D C. (2002). Base rates of malingering and symptom exaggeration. *Journal of Clinical and Experimental Neuropsychology, 24*(8), 1094–1102.

Mittenberg, W., Tremont, G., Zeilinski, R. E., Fichera, S., & Rayls, K. R. (1996). Cognitive-behavioural prevention of postconcussion syndrome. *Archives of Neurology, 11*, 139–145.

Mossman, D. (1996). Veterans affairs disability compensation: A case study in counter-therapeutic jurisprudence. *Bulletin of the American Academy of Psychiatry and the Law, 24*(1), 27–44.

Murray, C. K., Reynolds, J. C., Schroeder, J. M., Harrison, M. B., Evans, O. M., et al. (2005). Spectrum of care provided at an echelon II medical unit during Operation Iraqi Freedom. *Military Medicine, 170*, 516–520.

Office of Inspector General. (2005). *Review of state variances in VA disability compensation payments* (Report #05-00765-137). Washington, DC: Department of Veterans Affairs.

Okie, S. (2005). Traumatic brain injury in the war zone. *The New England Journal of Medicine, 352(20)*, 2043–2047.

Owens, B. D., Kragh, J. F., Wenke, J. C., Macaitis, J., Wade, C. E., et al. (2008). Combat wounds in Operation Iraqi Freedom and Operation Enduring Freedom. *Journal of Trauma, 64*, 295–299.

Paniak, C., Toller-Lobe, G., Durand, A., & Nagy, J. (1998). A randomized trial of two treatments for mild traumatic brain injury. *Brain Injury, 12*, 1011–1023.

Paniak, C., Toller-Lobe, G., Reynolds, S., Melnyk, A., & Nagy, J. (2000). A randomized trial of two treatments for mild traumatic brain injury: 1 year follow-up. *Brain Injury, 14*, 219–226.

Peterson, D. I. (1998). A study of 249 patients with litigated claims of injury. *The Neurologist, 4*, 131–137.

Pitman, R. K., Altman, B., & Macklin, M. L. (1989). Prevalence of post-traumatic stress disorder in wounded Vietnam veterans. *American Journal of Psychiatry, 146*(5), 667–669.

Ponsford, J., Willmott, C., Rothwell, A., Cameron, P., Ayton, G., et al. (2001). Impact of early intervention on outcome after mild traumatic brain injury in children. *Pediatrics, 108*(6), 1297–1303.

Ponsford, J., Willmott, C., Rothwell, A., Cameron, P., Kelly, A. M., et al. (2002). Impact of early intervention on outcome following mild head injury in adults. *Journal of Neurology, Neurosurgery, & Psychiatry, 73*(3), 330–332.

Prigerson, H. G., Maciejewski, P. K., & Rosenheck, R. A. (2001). Combat trauma: Trauma with highest risk of delayed onset and unresolved post-traumatic stress disorder symptoms, unemployment, and abuse among men. *The Journal of Nervous and Mental Diseases, 189(2)*, 99–108.

Sayer, N. A., Chiros, C. E., Sigford, B., Scott, S., Clothier, B., et al. (2008a). Characteristics and rehabilitation outcomes among patients with blast and other injuries sustained during the Global War on Terror. *Archives of Physical Medicine and Rehabilitation, 89*, 163–170.

Sayer, N. A., Spoont, M., Nelson, D. B., Clothier, B., & Murdoch, M. (2008b). Changes in psychiatric status and service use associated with continued compensation seeking after claim determinations for post-traumtic stress disorder. *Journal of Traumatic Stress, 21*, 40–48.

Schneiderman, A. I., Braver, E. R., & Kang, H. K. (2008). Understanding sequelae of injury mechanisms and mild traumatic brain injury incurred during the conflicts in Iraq and Afghanistan: Persistent postconcussive symptoms and post-traumatic stress disorder. *American Journal of Epidemiology, 167*(12), 1446–1452.

Schretlen, D. J., & Shapiro, A. M. (2003). A quantitative review of the effects of traumatic brain injury on cognitive functioning. *International Review of Psychiatry, 15*(4), 341–349.

Schwab, K. A., Ivins, B., Cramer, G., Johnson, W., Sluss-Tiller, M., et al. (2007). Screening for traumatic brain injury in troops returning from deployment in Afghanistan and Iraq: Initial investigation of the usefulness of a short screening tool for traumatic brain injury. *Journal of Head Trauma Rehabilitation, 22*(6), 377–389.

Scott, S. G., Belanger, H. G., Vanderploeg, R. D., Massengale, J., & Scholten, J. (2006). Mechanism-of-injury approach to evaluating patients with blast-related polytrauma. *Journal of the American Osteopathic Association, 106*(5), 265–270.

Sipos, R., Mulder, L., Koolstra, J., & van Eijden, T. (2008). Development of the micro architecture and mineralization of the basilar part of the pig occipital bone. *Connect Tissue Research, 49*(1), 22–29.

Smith-Seemiller, L., Fow, N. R., Kant, R., & Franzen, M. D. (2003). Presence of post-concussion syndrome symptoms in patients with chronic pain vs mild traumatic brain injury. *Brain Injury, 17*(3), 199–206.

Suhr, J. A., & Gunstad, J. (2002a). "Diagnosis Threat": The effect of negative expectations on cognitive performance in head injury. *Journal of Clinical and Experimental Neuropsychology, 24* (4), 448–457.

Suhr, J. A., & Gunstad, J. (2002b). Postconcussive symptom report: The relative influence of head injury and depression. *Journal of Clinical and Experimental Neuropsychology, 24*(8), 981–993.

Suhr, J. A., & Gunstad, J. (2005). Further exploration of the effect of "diagnosis threat" on cognitive performance in individuals with mild head injury. *Journal of the International Neuropsychological Society, 11*(1), 23–29.

Taber, K. H., Warden, D. L., & Hurley, R. A. (2006). Blast-related brain injury: What is known? *Journal of Neuropsychiatry and Clinical Neuroscience, 18*, 141–145.

Tanielian, T., & Jaycox, L. H. (Eds.). (2008). *Invisible wounds of war: Psychological and cognitive injuries, their consequences, and services to assist recovery.* Santa Monica, CA: Rand Corporation.

Teasdale, G., & Jennett, B. (1974). Assessment of coma and impaired consciousness; A practical scale. *Lancet, 2*, 81–84.

Vasterling, J. J., Proctor, S. P., Amoroso, P., Kane, R., Heeren, T., et al. (2006). Neuropsychological outcomes of army personnel following deployment to the Iraq war. *Journal of the American Medical Association, 296*(5), 519–529.

Wade, D. T., Crawford, S., Wenden, F. J., King, N. S., & Moss, N. E. (1997). Does routine follow-up after head injury help? A randomized controlled trial. *Journal of Neurology, Neurosurgery & Psychiatry, 62*, 478–484.

Wade, D. T., King, N. S., Wenden, F. J., Crawford, S., & Caldwell, F. E. (1998). Routine follow-up after head injury. A second randomized controlled trial. *Journal of Neurology, Neurosurgery & Psychiatry, 65*, 177–183.

Warden, D. (2006). Military TBI during the Iraq and Afghanistan wars. *Journal of Head Trauma Rehabilitation, 21*(5), 398–402.

Warden, D. L., French, L. M., Shupenko, L., Fargus, J., Riedy, G., et al. (2009). Case report of a solider with primary blast injury. *Neuroimage, 47*(Suppl. 2), T152–T153.

Wightman, J., & Gladish, S. (2001). Explosions and blast injuries. *Annals of Emergency Medicine, 37*, 644–678.

White, C. S., Jones, R. K., Damon, E. R., & Richmond, D. R. (1971). *The biodynamics of airblast* (Technical Report, DNA 2738-T). Washington, DC: Department of Defense.

White, C. S., & Richmond, D. R. (1959). *Blast biology* (Technical Progress Report, TID-5764). Washington, DC: Atomic Energy Commision.

Whitney, K. A., Shepard, P. H., Williams, A. L., Davis, J. J., Adams, K. M. (2009) The Medical Symptom Validity Test in the evaluation of Operation Iraqi Freedom/Operation Enduring Freedom soldiers: A preliminary study. *Archives of Clinical Neuropsychology, 24*(2), 145–152.

Wilde, E. A., Bigler, E. D., Gandhi, P. V., Lowry, C. M., Blatter, D. D., et al. (2004). Alcohol abuse and traumatic brain injury: Quantitative magnetic resonance imaging and neuropsychological outcome. *Journal of Neurotrauma, 21*(2), 137–147.

Williams, D. H., Levin, H. S., & Eisenberg, H. M. (1990). Mild head injury classification. *Neurosurgery, 27*(3), 422–428.

Xydakis, M. S., Bebarta, V. S., Harrison, C. D., Conner, J. C., Grant, G. A., et al. (2007). Tympanic-membrane perforation as a marker of concussive brain injury in Iraq. *The New England Journal of Medicine, 357*(8), 830–831.

Yang, Z., Wang, Z., Tang, C., & Ying, Y. (1996). Biological effects of weak blast waves and safety limits for internal organ injury in the human body. *The Journal of Trauma, 40*(3 Suppl), S81–S84.

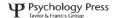

PSYCHOPHARMACOLOGICAL ISSUES IN THE TREATMENT OF TBI AND PTSD

Thomas W. McAllister
Dartmouth Medical School, Lebanon, NH, USA

Recognition of the frequency of the co-occurrence of traumatic brain injury (TBI) and post-traumatic stress disorder (PTSD) is a relatively recent development in both fields. As a result there has been little work on effective treatment strategies for those with both conditions. In fact studies of PTSD treatment often exclude those with a history of TBI, and studies of the treatment of TBI sequelae have often excluded participants with psychiatric disorders such as PTSD. Thus although evidence-based approaches for the treatment of PTSD and for the sequelae TBI are emerging, little is known about the use of psychotropic medications to treat individuals with co-morbid TBI/PTSD. The growing cohort of military personnel with high rates of exposure to TBI and concurrent PTSD calls attention to the need for improved treatment strategies, and for clarification of whether medications currently used to treat PTSD or the sequelae of TBI are effective in the co-morbid condition. In the absence of informative treatment studies, clinicians are faced with uncertainty about whether to use conventional approaches, alter these approaches in some way, or to shy away from these interventions for fear of exacerbating symptoms of the other condition. This situation is further complicated by the fact that many clinicians tend to be more familiar with medication approaches in one disorder or the other. This paper reviews the use of medications for the treatment of PTSD, the neuropsychiatric sequelae of TBI, and the co-morbid condition. General principles are suggested and particular attention is directed to situations where the use of medication for one condition might exacerbate symptoms of the other disorder. Directions for future research are suggested.

Keywords: TBI; PTSD; Pharmacological treatment.

INTRODUCTION

Traumatic brain injury (TBI) and post-traumatic stress disorder (PTSD) are two of the characteristic sequelae of the current conflicts in Iraq and Afghanistan. The psychological trauma associated with combat, coupled with the high rate of exposure to blast injuries has resulted in a cohort of military personnel with symptoms suggestive of both PTSD and persistent sequelae of TBI. This co-morbid condition has been described to a limited extent in civilians (Bryant, Moulds, Guthrie, & Nixon, 2003; Bryant & Harvey, 1999a, 1999b; Harvey, Brewin, Jones, & Kopelman, 2003), but little is known about its occurrence and treatment in

---

Address correspondence to: Thomas W. McAllister, M.D., Section of Neuropsychiatry, Dartmouth-Hitchcock Medical Center, 1 Medical Center Drive, Lebanon, New Hampshire 03756, USA. E-mail: Thomas.w.mcallister@dartmouth.edu

military populations. This paper offers a review of pharmacological interventions for symptoms commonly associated with TBI and PTSD, and outlines an approach to the co-morbid condition.

EPIDEMIOLOGICAL ISSUES

Epidemiology of TBI in combat veterans

Even during peacetime the military has high rates of TBI (Ommaya, Ommaya, Dannenberg, & Salazar, 1996). Estimates of TBI in the current conflicts are significantly higher than in previous wars (Warden, 2006). The Joint Theater Trauma Registry reported that 22% of the wounded soldiers passing through the Landstuhl Regional Medical Center had injuries to the head, face, or neck (Okie, 2005). The recent Rand report (Tanielian & Jaycox, 2008) suggested a 19% rate of probable TBI in a telephone survey of almost 2000 previously deployed service members, although the authors and others (Hoge, Goldberg, & Castro, 2009) point out that the screening methodology may overestimate the true number. Nevertheless, as Warden has pointed out, the rate of brain injury appears increased relative to the 12–14% seen in the Vietnam War (Okie, 2005), perhaps related to improved survival rates associated with the use of body armor, increased awareness of TBI, and the mode of warfare (blast attacks) (Warden, 2006). The emergence of improvised explosive devices (IEDs) as a primary mode of attack has called attention to the effects of "blast injury" (see, e.g., Cernak, Wang, Jiang, Bian, & Savic, 2001; Mayorga, 1997; Warden, 2006). It is not known whether the effects of blast on the brain are related to the mechanical effects of the associated over-pressurized wave with distortion of vascular tissue, neural tissue, or both, the inertial effects of being buffeted by the alternating high and low pressure events, some other mechanism, or a combination of these factors. It is clear that other injury mechanisms often come into play, including impact forces (coming into contact with an object), inertial forces (rapid acceleration/deceleration of the brain), and penetrating injuries from shrapnel or debris.

Outcome after TBI varies according to the severity of the injury as well as a variety of other factors including pre-injury medical and psychiatric factors, psychosocial stressors and support systems, pain, genotype, and other factors (De Silva et al., 2009; Green et al., 2008; Jordan, 2007; Steyerberg et al., 2008). A full discussion of this topic is beyond the scope of this article (for reviews see Perel, Edwards, Wentz, & Roberts, 2006; Willemse-van Son, Ribbers, Verhagen, & Stam, 2007), but it is worth noting that in both civilian and military contexts the majority of brain injuries are classified as "mild" (Kraus et al., 2005; Warden, 2006). The great majority of individuals with a mild injury report complaints in three broad areas after mild TBI: cognition (memory, attention, slowed thinking), somatic problems (headache, disequilibrium, fatigue), and emotional troubles (irritability, dysphoria, anxiety) (Levin et al., 1987). Fortunately the majority of individuals report improvement of symptoms over several days to weeks after injury, and most are free of complaint and measurable deficits 3–6 months after injury (Carroll, et al., 2004; McAllister, 2005; McAllister & Arciniegas, 2002). Nevertheless some individuals have persistent symptoms that they attribute to their injury. The literature often suggests that 15% of individuals will have persistent or chronic problems based on a study by Rutherford et al. (Rutherford, Merrett, & McDonald, 1979). However, as Greiffenstein (2009) has pointed out, this study may overestimate the number of individuals with persistent symptoms in that several of those with persistent symptoms were felt to be malingering when initially seen 6 weeks after the injury. The etiology of persistent symptoms is a subject of some debate, with proposed etiologies including subtle diffuse axonal injury, the development of psychiatric disorders such as depression or PTSD, and litigation/ compensation concerns (for discussion see Bigler, 2008; McAllister, 2005). Evidence in support of these various theories is often variable but suggests that litigation/ compensation influences risk of persistent symptoms (see e.g., Belanger, Curtiss, Demery, Lobowitz, & Vanderploeg, 2005; Binder & Rohling, 1996), and the presence of psychiatric conditions (Mooney & Speed, 2001; Mooney, Speed, & Sheppard, 2005) are particularly important factors. Recent work suggests that this is also true in military populations, and that the presence of depression and PTSD may account for much of the distress in individuals who also suffered a mild TBI (Hoge et al., 2009; Schneiderman, Braver, & Kang, 2008).

Epidemiology of PTSD in combat veterans

Among veterans of the current conflicts in Iraq and Afghanistan, PTSD prevalence has been estimated to be 17% with no apparent female:male difference (Hoge et al., 2004) although others have reported somewhat lower rates (Schneiderman et al., 2008). These figures differ from the civilian population, where the prevalence of PTSD is approximately 8% with a 2:1 female:male ratio (Kessler, Sonnega, Bromet, Hughes, & Nelson, 1995). Given the well-known dose– response relationship between traumatic exposure and PTSD onset, and the threat to life associated with the current combat scenario, it is not surprising that the prevalence of PTSD is high.

Epidemiology of co-morbid TBI and PTSD

There is some controversy in the civilian literature about the prevalence of co-morbid TBI and PTSD (see Harvey et al., 2003). TBI is associated with partial or complete amnesia for the event, whereas a core symptom of PTSD is recurrent memory and re-experiencing of the event. Thus some have questioned the ability to have both conditions, particularly after a mild TBI (MTBI) (Sbordone & Liter, 1995). On the other hand clinicians frequently encounter individuals who have intrusive memories of events immediately before or after the accident, or have patchy amnesia with some islands of preserved memory. A related issue is whether full re-experiencing phenomena are required for the diagnosis of PTSD, or at least its functional equivalent. For example Warden et al. (1997) found that none of 47 military patients with TBI met *full* criteria for PTSD, because none had re-experiencing symptoms of the event. However 13% of the patients did experience the avoidance and arousal symptom clusters of PTSD, suggesting that individuals can develop a form of PTSD without the re-experiencing symptoms. Bryant and Harvey (1998; Harvey & Bryant, 1998a, 1998b) have shown that rates of acute stress disorder 1 month after a motor vehicle accident are comparable in those with and those without a TBI. Furthermore, acute stress disorder is a good predictor of those who go on to develop PTSD 6 months after injury. Of interest in these studies is that the TBI group with PTSD was significantly more symptomatic than the TBI group without PTSD. Bombardier et al. (2006) reported that of 124 civilians studied 6 months after injury, 11% had PTSD symptoms but only 5.6% met full criteria. This suggests that different reported prevalence rates may reflect different PTSD assessment methods. Sumpter and McMillan (2006) found that using a self-report questionnaire to diagnose PTSD after TBI resulted in a case rate of 59%, whereas using a clinician-administered structured interview resulted in a case rate of only 3%. As noted earlier, the recent reports of Schneiderman et al. (2008) and Hoge et al. (2008) suggest that the co-morbid condition is common in the cohort of military service members involved in Operations Enduring Freedom and Iraqi Freedom (OEF/OIF).

It is important to point out that much of the above discussion considers the frequency of co-morbid TBI and PTSD from the *same* event, and focuses primarily on the civilian population. Less is known about the co-morbid condition in military populations and in those exposed to psychologically traumatic events at time points different from when they experienced a TBI. Anecdotal reports from clinics working with OEF/OIF military personnel and veterans suggest the latter scenario is quite common.

There is also a complex interaction between TBI and psychiatric illness in general, not simply PTSD. It has been established in the civilian populations that TBI, including MTBI, increases the risk of developing psychiatric illness (Ashman et al., 2004; Deb, Lyons, & Koutzoukis, 1998; Fann et al., 2004; Hibbard, Uysal, Kepler, Bogdany, & Silver, 1998; Massagli et al., 2004; van Reekum, Cohen, & Wong, 2000). Furthermore, in both civilian and military populations, the development of psychiatric illness is associated with increased rates of persistent post-concussive symptoms (McAllister & Arciniegas, 2002; Tanielian & Jaycox, 2008). Hoge et al. (2008) surveyed 2525 army personnel 3–4 months after deployment in OIF. Based on self-report, soldiers were categorized as not injured, having sustained a TBI with loss of consciousness (4.9%), a TBI with altered consciousness (10.3%), or other injuries (17.2%). The individuals reporting TBI had significantly increased rates of PTSD, and those with a history of loss of consciousness had significantly higher rates of depression. TBI, especially with loss of consciousness, was associated with numerous physical health problems; however when adjusted for the presence or absence of PTSD and depression, only headache and heart pounding were associated with a history of TBI with loss of consciousness.

Schneiderman et al. (2008) in a questionnaire survey of 2235 OEF/OIF military personnel assessed at least 5 months after return from deployment found TBI rates of 12% and PTSD rates of 11%. PTSD was increased in individuals with a history of TBI, and post-concussive symptoms in the TBI group were increased in those who also had PTSD. The results of both this study (Schneiderman et al., 2008) and the Hoge et al. study (2008) must be interpreted cautiously in that both relied on a questionnaire methodology to determine TBI "caseness," and the validity of this screening methodology has been questioned (Hoge et al., 2009).

Nevertheless it seems reasonable to posit that military personnel serving in the current conflicts face increased exposure to TBI, which in turn increases their risk for developing a variety of psychiatric disorders. These disorders then amplify the disability associated with the TBI. In the context of war, then, it is not surprising that stress-related disorders and depression are highly prevalent. Unfortunately, much debate has centered on ways of determining if a constellation of symptoms is due to PTSD or MTBI, with a tendency to question the validity of the role of mild brain injury. However, whether persistent symptoms are attributed to a previous TBI or to a current psychiatric disorder does not change the fact that the individual suffered a TBI. The more germane question, especially from a treatment standpoint, is whether the current symptoms are better attributed to the remote TBI with persistent symptoms, co-morbid conditions such as PTSD and/or depression, or a combination of these factors.

The literature reviewed above suggests that TBI, PTSD and the co-morbid condition occur frequently in military personnel involved in the current conflicts. Although a full discussion of the neuropathophysiology of TBI and PTSD is beyond the scope of this paper (see, e.g., Bigler, 2007; Bremner, 2007; Friedman & Davidson, 2007; Neumeister et al., 2005), it is worth noting that each disorder has a characteristic profile of brain regions that are vulnerable to biomechanical trauma or psychological trauma (Stein & McAllister, 2009) and that several of these brain regions including the hippocampus, the amygdala, as well as orbito-frontal and prefrontal cortices are related to the genesis of neuropsychiatric symptoms in *both* conditions. This suggests that important neurobiological as well as psychological mechanisms contribute to the co-morbid condition. With this as background, several issues in the pharmacological approach to co-morbid TBI/PTSD are addressed.

DOES TBI ALTER THE PHARMACOLOGICAL APPROACH TO PSYCHIATRIC DISORDERS?

It is important to acknowledge several issues relevant to the use of medications in this clinical context. As noted it is only recently acknowledged that co-morbid TBI and PTSD is an important clinical syndrome and thus there is no evidence base addressing medication approaches to treatment. In the absence of a clear evidence base, one typically falls back on so-called expert opinion or consensus. Due to the newness of the field, there are few such recognized experts and little has been written on the topic. An alternative approach is to consider treatments used in similar or analogous clinical situations. This approach is complicated by an asymmetric evidence base on effective treatments in PTSD and in TBI. There is a more robust evidence base for an array of treatments for PTSD than there is for treatment of the neuropsychiatric sequelae of TBI, although the recent IOM reports (Institute of Medicine, 2008, 2009) on both conditions were rather skeptical of the evidence supporting common practices in both conditions.

In any case existing evidence may not be applicable to co-morbid TBI/PTSD for several reasons. Many PTSD treatment studies have carefully excluded individuals with a history of TBI (and other co-morbid conditions such as depression, and substance abuse) and the few systematic treatment studies of neuropsychiatric sequelae of TBI have generally excluded individuals with PTSD and other psychiatric disorders. This highlights the importance of distinguishing medication efficacy from effectiveness. It may be possible to demonstrate a statistical effect of a medication in a carefully selected population. This is not the same as showing effectiveness in the population for which the medication is most commonly prescribed. Additionally, many earlier military studies of PTSD were of Vietnam era veterans, implying a certain chronicity of symptoms not yet true of the OEF/OIF cohort. Earlier studies also have a preponderance of male participants, whereas studies of civilian trauma often have a larger percentage of women participants. It is not clear that a particular intervention found efficacious in a civilian population will have the same benefit in military populations (Institute of Medicine, 2008).

Perhaps the most fundamental question is whether a history of TBI alters the response to standard pharmacological agents and thus whether treatment approaches require modification. There are some theoretical reasons to think that response to pharmacological agents might differ after a TBI. TBI is associated with dysregulation of several neurotransmitter systems integral to the homeostasis of mood, emotional control and cognition (e.g., the catecholaminergic, serotonergic, and cholinergic systems) raising the possibility that medications that work through modulation of these neurotransmitters might behave differently after an injury. In so far as a brain injury results in actual loss of neurons in brain regions modulating emotional control and cognition, there might be less substrate on which pharmacologic agents can work and this might alter the side effect profile.

Interestingly a review of the literature (Warden, 2006) found an inadequate evidence base on the pharmacotherapy of the neuropsychiatric sequelae of TBI. Pharmacologic treatments of affective disorders/anxiety/psychosis, cognition, and aggression were reviewed. Studies were scored on the basis of design, implementation, and sample size as being Class I (highest), Class II, or Class III evidence (weakest). Based on the profile of evidence, a determination was made as to whether there was sufficient support to establish that treatment as a standard of care (strong evidence), a guideline (moderate evidence), or an option (lowest level of evidence). For the most part the evidence was Class III consisting of case reports and small case series, or clinical trials with methodological limitations or small sample sizes, greatly limiting the strength of the conclusions that could be drawn. With respect to the treatment of mood disorders, psychosis, and anxiety, evidence in support of the efficacy of standard psychotropic regimens (e.g., antidepressants) did not rise above the option level. For cognition, the evidence supported the use of donepezil and methylphenidate for treatment of attention and speed of information processing at a guideline level, donepezil for the treatment of memory deficits at a guideline level, and bromocriptine for the treatment of executive deficits. For aggression, evidence for the use of beta blockers (propranolol, pindolol) was considered at a guideline level. There was no significant evidence that side effects were more evident in individuals with TBI, although many clinicians adopt a lower dosing strategy and slower titration (McAllister, 2008).

PHARMACOLOGICAL APPROACH TO AN INDIVIDUAL WITH TBI AND PSYCHOLOGICAL HEALTH PROBLEMS

As noted, the evidence base for pharmacological interventions in an individual with TBI and psychological health problems, particularly PTSD, is scarce. Nevertheless this is a common clinical problem, and there are some general principles that are reasonable to consider while acknowledging that these suggestions should not become enshrined as doctrine. These principles may change over time as appropriate studies are completed to address some of these critical issues. The following discussion represents one framework for such an approach based on the author's clinical experience and integrated summary of limited available literature.

Need for a comprehensive approach

In addition to PTSD, TBI is associated with a variety of other neuropsychiatric sequelae (McAllister, 2008). A thorough understanding of the pre-injury history, the profile of the injury, and the context in which the injury occurred is critical to a nuanced appraisal of the current difficulties and how best to determine the cause of the presenting symptoms (McAllister, 2007, 2008; Stein & McAllister, 2009). It is important to be aware that the sequelae of the injury can alter the presentation of psychiatric and behavioral disorders, and thus standard assessment instruments and diagnostic criteria may not completely apply (see McAllister, 2007). Emerging neurodiagnostic techniques such as newer neuroimaging modalities can be helpful but should not be overly emphasized (Belanger, Vanderploeg, R., Curtiss, G., & Warden, 2007). An appreciation for the normal trajectory of recovery after injury, particularly mild TBI, is critical to putting the current symptoms in perspective (Hoge et al., 2009; McCrea et al., 2009 this issue).

Although this paper focuses on pharmacological interventions, it should be emphasized that the effectiveness of medication is greatly enhanced in the context of addressing the full array of an individual's psychosocial needs. It is worth noting that there is a strong evidence base supporting the use of cognitive interventions for individuals with TBI (Cicerone et al., 2000; Cicerone, Levin, Malec, Stuss, & Whyte, 2006) and that the recent Institute of Medicine report on PTSD found stronger support for the use of cognitive behavioral interventions in the treatment of PTSD than it did for medication interventions (Institute of Medicine, 2008).

Of interest is an absence of studies addressing whether the combination of medication and cognitive therapies is more effective than either treatment alone. Combined medication and cognitive therapy approaches have been explored in other psychiatric disorders such as depression, where it appears that both approaches are fairly similar in efficacy but may differ somewhat in terms of which patients benefit from which intervention, and there is some evidence that combination therapy is more effective than either monotherapy for some patients (Feldman, 2007; Hollon et al., 2005; Pampallona, Bollini, Tibaldi, Kupelnick, & Munizza, 2004). In the context of TBI and PTSD, the absence of data on the efficacy of combination approaches is an important gap in our knowledge base, particularly since it is common for individuals to receive such combination approaches clinically. For example we do not know whether cognitive remediation approaches in combination with a catecholaminergic agent such as methylphenidate, or procholinergic agents (cholinesterase inhibitors) lead to greater cognitive gains in individuals with TBI. Nor has it been established that cognitive behavioral therapies for PTSD (exposure based techniques or cognitive processing techniques) are more effective in combination with medications (e.g., SSRIs).

Importance of diagnostic clarity

As with any clinical condition, a proper evaluation is the foundation of a sound treatment plan. TBI occurs at high rates in military and also other populations at high risk for PTSD including victims of domestic violence (Galea et al., 2008) and incarcerated populations (Fann et al., 2004). The overlap between the symptoms frequently endorsed by individuals with a history of TBI and those with a history of PTSD require careful assessment of both conditions. For example, both groups may note problems in cognition (memory, attention), somatic concerns (headache), and affective dysregulation (impulsivity, irritability, anxiety), particularly in the time period shortly after the traumatic event (whether psychological, biomechanical, or both). Thus, accurate causal attribution of specific symptoms to a particular etiology may be difficult if not impossible. It is best in such situations for the clinician to keep an open mind about attribution, while at the same time establishing a clear etiological hypothesis in order to inform the therapeutic decision making. As a general rule, treatment trials should be initiated with one agent at a time, with a clear diagnostic formulation (e.g., "I am treating TBI related cognitive deficits," or "I am treating PTSD related sleep disturbance").

Duration of treatment trials

It is not possible to define an adequate trial that fits all clinical situations. Pharmacological agents differ with respect to pharmacokinetic properties and onset of action. The concurrent use of other medications or the presence of other medical disorders may alter the adequacy of a therapeutic trial and influence the frequency and intensity of medication-associated side effects. Nevertheless, trials of most psychotropics should be at least 2 weeks in duration (if tolerated) at a dose generally considered therapeutic. Trials lasting 4 to 8 weeks are much more informative. Both TBI and PTSD are associated with a heightened reactivity to environmental changes. Thus, the longer the treatment trial, the more confidence one has in assessing efficacy. There is also a strong sense among clinicians that the TBI population has a heightened sensitivity to medication side effects, necessitating lower starting doses, and longer titration intervals. This also necessitates longer treatment trials.

USE OF TREATMENT ALGORITHMS FOR IDIOPATHIC PSYCHIATRIC DISORDERS AS MODELS

In the absence of a robust evidence base informing us about the treatment of behavioral disorders after TBI, most clinicians use treatment algorithms developed for idiopathic psychiatric disorders. This approach is supported by the limited available evidence (Warden et al., 2006) as well as expert opinion (e.g., Alderfer, Arciniegas, & Silver, 2005). When using this approach with PTSD, however, there are some concerns. Although understanding of the pathophysiology of PTSD has progressed over the last two decades, and focused on the neural substrates of fear conditioning/emotional processing, the stress response, and the modulation of these systems by prefrontal cortex, pharmacotherapeutic approaches have focused more on interventions used to treat depression, anxiety, and mood instability (Friedman & Davidson, 2007). Thus, the majority of the literature addresses the efficacy of antidepressants, anxiolytics, antipsychotics, and anticonvulsants. The interpretation of this evidence varies greatly depending on the system used to weight the methodological rigor of the studies considered. The reader is referred to two recent extensive reviews of this topic for additional details (Friedman & Davidson, 2007; Institute of Medicine, 2008).

POTENTIAL EFFECTS OF STANDARD TREATMENTS FOR TBI OR PTSD

Consonant with the overlap in symptoms between these two conditions, many classes of medications (for example SSRIs) are used to treat various symptoms of both conditions (see discussion below). However, this approach can have some pitfalls and it is important to consider potential effects of a given agent or class of agent on the domains of cognition, arousal, sleep, and neurological function, as these are domains on which standard psychotropic regimens can have adverse effects after a TBI.

Cognition

Both TBI and PTSD are commonly associated with cognitive complaints and deficits (McAllister, 2008; Vasterling et al., 2002) although these are typically more of a concern in the TBI population. Many of the medications commonly used in both conditions such as antipsychotics, anticonvulsants, and some anxiolytics can be associated with cognitive slowing and problems with memory and attention. Adrenergic agents can either enhance or impair cognition depending on their receptor agonist profile and their dose (see below for further discussion). Thus, particular care should be given to monitoring cognitive function when prescribing these agents.

As noted, cognitive behavioral therapies are a mainstay of PTSD treatment (Institute of Medicine, 2008). The impact that psychotropic medications may have on cognitive behavioral therapies shown to be effective in PTSD is unclear. Theoretically, medications known to impact attention and memory processes could alter the efficacy of psychotherapies that depend on intact cognitive processes in order to be effective.

Arousal

Individuals with TBI may complain of excessive fatigue, or demonstrate reduced arousal or apathy. Conversely, those with PTSD typically have excessive arousal as a core component of the disorder, particularly in response to certain environmental contexts. Agents such as central nervous stimulants that enhance catecholaminergic tone (e.g., methylphenidate) are commonly used to treat arousal and cognitive deficits in individuals with TBI, but in theory could exacerbate core symptoms of PTSD.

Sleep

Disordered sleep is common in both individuals with TBI and those with PTSD. Following mild TBI, complaints of excessive fatigue and problems with sleep are very common (Kraus et al., 2005; Vaishnavi, Makley, & Rao, in press). The mechanism underlying this is not entirely clear but may be related to persistent neurotransmitter dysregulation as well as an overall sense that the individual is working harder mentally and physically to maintain performance after an injury. Sleep disruptions characterized by fragmented sleep and nightmares are very common in individuals with PTSD (Raskind et al., 2007). Many of the psychotropics have complex effects on sleep, thus it is helpful for clinicians to familiarize themselves with these effects, discuss potential sleep changes with the patient, and monitor changes in sleep as the medication trial progresses.

Neurological function

Individuals with a history of TBI have higher rates of seizures and may have problems with disequilibrium or balance, vision, and hearing (Cosetti & Lalwani, in press; Kapoor & Ciuffreda, in press), as well as other neurological concerns. Individuals with PTSD have less marked neurological abnormalities as a general rule but have been reported to have higher rates of subtle neurological abnormalities (Pitman et al., 2006). Many of the psychotropics can have adverse effects on sensory processing, gait, and balance, and are associated with increased rates of seizures. Thus, again, it is helpful for the clinician to bear these issues in mind when choosing a medication and to monitor for emergence or worsening of these symptoms during treatment.

Alterations in dosing

Related to the above concerns most expert opinion suggests that conventional dosing strategies be altered in individuals with a history of TBI and ongoing sequelae (McAllister, 2008). Starting doses should be reduced and titration intervals prolonged. Clinicians should be alert to therapeutic responses at lower than expected doses and should not feel compelled to push through to higher "therapeutic" doses unless warranted by an incomplete response. Although a full discussion of all psychotropic agents that might be useful in co-morbid TBI/PTSD is beyond the scope of this paper, the use of the major classes of common psychotropic agents is reviewed below (see Table 1 for a summary).

Table 1 Psychotropic categories: Uses in TBI, PTSD, and co-morbid TBI/PTSD

Medication class	Common uses in TBI	Common uses in PTSD	Potential issues in co-morbid TBI/PTSD
Antidepressants (SSRIs, tricyclics, heterocyclics, monoamine oxidase inhibitors)	Treatment of depression Sometimes used to treat aggression SSRIs used to treat anxiety	SSRIs used to treat PTSD Sxs (2 agents approved) Treatment of depression SSRIs used to treat other anxiety sxs	Little evidence base Anticholinergic effects may worsen cognitive complaints/deficits Some agents may lower seizure threshold
Antipsychotics (conventionals such as haloperidol; atypicals such as risperidone, olanzapine)	Often used to treat aggression (evidence base limited) Psychotic syndromes after TBI	Augment antidepressants Treatment of aggression/agitation	Little evidence base Extrapyramidal syndromes May worsen cognitive complaints/deficits at higher doses Metabolic syndrome
Anxiolytics (benzodiazepines, SSRIs, buspirone)	Treatment of anxiety or agitation	SSRIs used to treat PTSD sxs and other anxiety sxs	Little evidence base Some concerns that benzodiazepines: – result in "disinhibition" in TBI – may worsen arousal and cognitive complaints/deficits after TBI – may worsen neurological deficits (gait, balance) – potential for abuse
Anticonvulsants (phenytoin, carbamazepine, valproic acid, lamotrigine, others)	Seizure prophylaxis Seizure management Mood stabilization Aggression/agitation (evidence of efficacy lacking)	Seizure management Mood Stabilization Treatment of core PTSD sxs (evidence of efficacy weak)	Little evidence base Potential for dermatologic, hepatic, and bone marrow toxicity Worsen cognitive complaints/deficits

Catecholaminergic/ adrenergic agents (CNS stimulants, alpha adrenergic agents such as guanfacine or clonidine, beta-blocking agents such as propranolol)	*CNS stimulants (e.g., methylphenidate) often used to treat arousal or memory/attention problems after TBI* *Guanfacine and clonidine used to treat cognitive complaints/deficits*	*Beta blockers have been used in effort to prevent PTSD and to treat hyperarousal* *Trial of guanfacine showed no effect*	*Little evidence base* *Stimulants could exacerbate hyperarousal associated with PTSD* *Beta blockers may worsen cognitive complaints/deficits after TBI* *Potential for abuse with stimulants*
Cholinergic agents (acetylcholinesterase inhibitors such as donepezil)	*Treatment of cognitive complaints/deficits after TBI*	*Not commonly used in PTSD*	*Little evidence base* *Unclear whether cholinergic agents would impact on emotional processing in PTSD* *Unclear whether cholinergic agents would impact on efficacy of cognitive therapies in either condition*

The major categories of psychotropic agents commonly used in individuals with sequelae of TBI and in individuals with PTSD. Potential issues in the use of these agents in those with both conditions are summarized in the far right column.

ISSUES IN THE USE OF THE MAJOR CLASSES OF PSYCHOTROPIC AGENTS

Antidepressants

Rationale and use in TBI. The Neurobehavioral Guidelines Workgroup (Warden et al., 2006) reviewed the use of antidepressants in TBI through 2004. Although there were numerous case reports and small case series covering a variety of classes of antidepressants, methodological issues limited the recommendations to an optional level only (their weakest category of evidence). This conclusion applied to a variety of classes of antidepressants including SSRIs, tricyclics, and MAOIs, as well as more novel agents. More recently, Ashman et al. (in press) reported a 10-week, double-blind, placebo-controlled study of 52 individuals with remote, predominantly moderate-to-severe TBI. Participants received sertraline 25–200 mg daily or placebo. A total of 59% percent of persons receiving sertraline responded (defined by at least a 50% drop in Hamilton Rating Scale) while only 32% of those treated with placebo responded. Although these rates did not statistically significantly differ, this may be related to sample size. Despite the limited evidence base, expert opinion of most TBI clinicians consider SSRIs to be the first line choice for TBI patients with depression (Alderfer et al., 2005).

Rationale and use in PTSD. Antidepressants are often considered the first-line approach to the pharmacologic management of PTSD. However, the only two agents approved by the U.S. Food and Drug Administration (FDA) for the treatment of PTSD are the selective serotonin reuptake inhibitors paroxetine and sertraline. Treatment guidelines established by several groups including the American Psychiatric Association (APA, 2006) the Management of Post-traumatic Stress Working Group of VA and the Department of Defense (VA/DoD)(Veterans Health Administration/Department of Defense, 2004), the British National Institute for Clinical Excellence (NICE) (National Institute for Health and Clinical Excellence, 2005), the International Society for Traumatic Stress Studies (ISTSS) (Foa, Keane, & Friedman, 2000), and the Australian Centre for Posttraumatic Mental Health of the Australian National Health and Medical Research Council (Australian Centre for Posttraumatic Mental Health, 2007), have largely supported the use of antidepressants, in particular SSRIs, albeit with varying degrees of confidence. However, this relative consensus has been called into question by the recent Institute of Medicine Report (Institute of Medicine, 2008). This committee found 14 SSRI studies that met its rigorous inclusion criteria and half were judged to provide only modest information due to various methodological limitations. Of the seven studies judged to be most informative, four were positive (Brady et al., 2000; Davidson, Rothbaum, Kolk, Sikes, & Farfel, 2001; Martenyi, Brown, Zhang, Prakash, & Koke, 2002; Tucker et al., 2001), and three were negative (Friedman, Marmar, Baker, Sikes, & Farfel, 2007; van der Kolk et al., 2007; Zohar et al., 2002). Perhaps of more concern is that the two studies in veterans (Friedman et al., 2007; Zohar et al., 2002) were negative. As a result, the IOM committee concluded that the evidence was inadequate to determine the efficacy of SSRIs in the treatment of PTSD (although there was a dissenting opinion) and highlighted several methodological concerns in the studies to date. The first concern is the consistently high dropout rates in the treatment arms (typically in the range of 30%). The second is the frequent use of a last observation carried forward approach to data analysis, which in the presence of high dropout rates can inflate apparent treatment effects. The third concern noted in the report is that most of the studies have been sponsored by the pharmaceutical industry.

Rationale and use in comorbid TBI/PTSD. There is no literature on the use of antidepressants in individuals with co-morbid TBI/PTSD. Clinical experience suggests that standard approaches can be effective. However it may be helpful to start with lower doses and slow upward titration intervals. In addition, it is worth considering potential impact on cognition and seizure threshold when choosing an antidepressant regimen. In so far as cognitive complaints or deficits are evident, it may be best to avoid medications with a heavy anticholinergic burden due to the concern that such individuals may be more sensitive to cognitive impairing anticholinergic effects. Thus, SSRIs might be preferred initially to tricyclic antidepressants. However, many of the SSRIs also have anticholinergic effects (e.g., paroxetine), thus medications such as sertraline or citalopram might be better tolerated. The recent IOM report on TBI (Institute of Medicine, 2008) concluded that TBI was associated with an increase in seizure risk, particularly within the first year of injury. Although the evidence was strongest for penetrating, severe, and moderate injuries, concern was also raised for those with mild TBI. Thus, medications such as buproprion, maprotiline, and amoxapine, which may be associated with increased seizure frequency in vulnerable populations, should not be first-line medications, and if used should be titrated slowly and given in divided doses (Coffey, 2007).

Anticonvulsants

Rationale and use in TBI. Anticonvulsants are typically used in three contexts after TBI: to prevent or treat seizures, to treat aggression, and for mood stabilization. It is fairly common to encounter individuals taking anticonvulsants who do not know why these agents have been prescribed. Many of these agents can have toxic effects on liver and bone marrow, as well as cognitive dulling effects, and therefore should be used judiciously (Agrawal, Timothy, Pandit, & Manju, 2006; Haltiner, Temkin, Winn, & Dikmen, 1996) and the rationale for their use should be clarified. For example anticonvulsants are effective in treating chronic seizures associated with TBI (Agrawal et al., 2006; Teasell, Bayona, Lippert, Villamere, & Hellings, 2007). These agents are also effective in the prophylaxis against post-traumatic epilepsy but only within the first week after the injury. Use beyond that time frame does not appear to reduce seizure risk and thus is not warranted (Agrawal et al., 2006; Teasell et al., 2007).

The Neurobehavioral Guidelines group (Warden et al., 2006) failed to find compelling evidence that these agents were particularly efficacious in either the treatment of aggression or in the treatment of mood disorders after TBI. However, this finding is more accurately characterized as an "absence of evidence" rather than "evidence of absence." There is a wide array of case reports and small case series supporting the use of anticonvulsants in both of these contexts but the strength of the evidence is weak. In addition there is evidence that anticonvulsants can reduce aggression associated with mood disorders (depression, mania) (Grunze, 2008; Weisler, Cutler, Ballenger, Post, & Ketter, 2006), dementia (Konovalov, Muralee, & Tampi, 2008; Passmore, Gardner, Polak, & Rabheru, 2008) and other neuropsychiatric conditions (e.g., Rogawski & Loscher, 2004).

Rationale and use in PTSD. Interest in the use of anticonvulsants to treat PTSD comes from several fronts. One hypothesis of the etiology of PTSD is that re-experiencing symptoms are caused by a kindling mechanism analogous to models of seizure genesis. Many of the anticonvulsants are effective in blocking these processes, and thus might be effective in PTSD. In addition, many of the newer anticonvulsants act on the glutamate and GABA systems. Glutamine is the major excitatory, and GABA the major inhibitory, neurotransmitter of the brain. Both of these neurotransmitter systems appear to play a role in the etiology of PTSD. Thus, medications that modulate either system might impact PTSD symptoms. However, both of these neurotransmitter systems have a complex array of receptors that vary in distribution across the brain, making simple predictions of effect difficult.

There are two broad families of glutamine receptors; ionotropic and metabotropic. Stimulation of the former results in a change in configuration of certain membrane pores resulting in the flow of various ions into the neuron. This results in activation of certain cell signaling processes. Most attention in PTSD has focused on the ionotropic receptors of which there are three classes: NMDA, kainite, and AMPA. These receptors play a role in critical cognitive functions such as learning, memory, extinction, and fear conditioning. One theory of PTSD is that excessive activation of the stress response results in overactivation of the glutamatergic system with heightened fear conditioning (Friedman & Davidson, 2007; Southwick et al., 2007). Under normal circumstances this system is modulated by the GABA system. Evidence of reduced GABA function in individuals with PTSD has given rise to interest in medications that enhance GABAergic function. Of additional note is that stimulation of certain serotonergic receptors (e.g., 5-HT-1A) in the amygdala enhances this GABA role in damping down the fear circuit, providing a rationale for the use of pro-serotonergic agents (Friedman & Davidson, 2007).

Evidence for the efficacy of anticonvulsants in PTSD consists mainly of case reports, small series, and open label trials. The IOM report did review three randomized clinical trials (Davidson, Brady, Mellman, Stein, & Pollack, 2007; Hertzberg et al., 1999; Tucker et al., 2007). Neither the use of Tiagabine (Davidson et al., 2007) nor Topiramate (Tucker et al., 2007) were better than placebo. A small study ($n=15$) of lamotrigine (Hertzberg et al., 1999) did show effect of drug compared to placebo. The authors of the IOM report concluded that there was inadequate evidence to determine the efficacy of anticonvulsants.

Rationale and use in co-morbid TBI/PTSD. There is no research on the use of anticonvulsants in the treatment of co-morbid TBI/PTSD. In theory this class of medication might be useful both from the perspective of treating mood disorders (a "mood stabilizer" role) and of treating impulsive anger, irritability, and aggression. However, at this time it is not known whether anticonvulsants will be helpful. When using these agents, clinicians should be aware of their potential to exacerbate cognitive deficits, particularly in individuals with TBI. Additionally, some of the newer anticonvulsants can be associated with adverse changes in mood and behavior (Cramer, DeRue, Devinsky, Edrich, & Trimble, 2003; Mula, Monaco, & Trimble, 2004; Mula, Trimble, Yuen, Liu, & Sander, 2003).

Antipsychotics

Rationale and use in TBI. Following a TBI, antipsychotics are most commonly used to treat aggression, or other forms of impulse discontrol, and psychosis. With respect to aggression, the Neurobehavioral Guidelines group (Warden et al., 2006) did not include any articles on the use of antipsychotics in the 52 papers it reviewed in the treatment of aggression. Anecdotal evidence suggests that despite this absence of evidence and systematic investigation, atypical antipsychotics are frequently the first agents chosen by clinicians treating aggression and agitation after TBI. Although there is evidence of efficacy in the treatment of aggression associated with other neuropsychiatric populations such as autistic spectrum conditions (McDougle, Stigler, Erickson, & Posey, 2008), use in TBI is not strongly supported in the literature to date.

Use of both conventional and atypical antipsychotics for the treatment of psychosis after TBI was discussed by the Neurobehavioral Guidelines group (Warden et al., 2006) although the evidence consisted of two case reports only. However, expert opinion (Arciniegas, Harris, & Brousseau, 2003; McAllister & Ferrell, 2002) suggests that careful use of these agents to treat clearcut psychotic syndromes can be useful, although initial dosing and titration intervals are typically adjusted as described earlier.

Thus, despite broad use of these agents to treat a variety of neuropsychiatric sequelae of TBI, it should be noted that there is very little empirical support for this practice and these agents are not without significant hazards including extrapyramidal symptoms, development of an involuntary movement disorder, metabolic complications, and cardiac complications (Ray, Chung, Murray, Hall, & Stein, 2009). Thus, these medications should not be first-line agents and the clinician should periodically assess the need for their ongoing use.

Rationale and use in PTSD. There has been some interest in the use of atypical antipsychotics in the treatment of PTSD. The rationale follows from their utility as adjunctive agents in the treatment of other psychiatric disorders such as depression, as well as the observation that some of these medications can be useful in the management of sleep and impulse control problems. Many studies have used these agents either in individuals who have not responded to more conventional approaches, or as adjunctive interventions in partial responders. Again, the small case series and open label trials have given some indication of benefit but the more rigorous randomized trials, of which there are few, have been less promising. Of the latter, five of the studies used risperidone (Bartzokis, Lu, Turner, Mintz, & Saunders, 2005; Hamner et al., 2003; Monnelly, Ciraulo, Knapp, & Keane, 2003; Padala et al., 2006; Reich, Winternitz, Hennen, Watts, & Stanculescu, 2004) and two used olanzapine (Butterfield et al., 2001; Stein, Kline, & Matloff, 2002).

The largest of the studies had a total of 33 participants in the treatment arm (Bartzokis et al., 2005) and most of the studies had high dropout rates. Five of these studies did show statistically significant drug effects, although the effects sizes were quite small and the study limitations limited the strength of the evidence. The IOM report (Institute of Medicine, 2008) concluded that there was inadequate evidence to determine whether there is an effect, but did note that three studies suggested an adjunctive effect of risperidone. The APA, VA/DoD, NICE, ISTSS, and Australian guidelines (American Psychiatric Association, 2006; Australian Centre for Posttraumatic Mental Health, 2007; Foa, Dancu, Zayfert, Mueser, & Descamps, 1997; National Institute for Health and Clinical Excellence, 2005; Veterans Health Administration/Department of Defense, 2004) were similarly skeptical in their appraisal of the evidence for this class of medications.

Rationale and use in co-morbid TBI/PTSD. There is no literature on the use of antipsychotics in co-morbid TBI/PTSD. In theory low doses of these agents might be useful in the treatment of psychotic symptoms complicating this condition. However, there is no empirical support for this as yet. In both PTSD and TBI the evaluation of psychotic symptoms and the attribution of the cause of those symptoms can be quite complex. For example, in TBI psychotic symptoms can be seen in the period of post-traumatic amnesia, as a complication of post-traumatic epilepsy, associated with a mood disorder (depression or mania), or as a schizophrenia-like disorder. It is critical to carefully assess the underlying cause, as the approach to treatment varies significantly. Anticonvulsants might be more appropriate if the psychotic symptoms are part of an epileptic syndrome (e.g., ictal or peri-ictal psychosis), whereas antidepressants might be a better choice if the psychosis is more likely associated with a severe depressive syndrome.

Individuals with PTSD may experience a variety of dissociative phenomena that can resemble psychotic symptoms although the time course is usually briefer than that associated with typical psychotic symptoms. In addition, some extreme forms of avoidant behavior and the reasons stated for engaging in this behavior can lead the clinician to consider whether these overvalued ideas have crossed the line into delusional thinking. The time course and consistency of the behaviors, and the degree to which the person is influenced by the beliefs can be helpful clues, but at times one is left to consider an empirical trial of antipsychotics in an effort to relieve distress. This should only be done to test the notion that the target behaviors are driven by an underlying psychosis, and clear milestones of improvement should be identified in advance. If the medication does not result in improvement it should be discontinued and the etiology of the symptoms reconsidered.

Anxiolytics

Rationale and use in TBI. Individuals with a history of TBI have increased rates of anxiety disorders (Fann et al., 2004; Hibbard et al., 1998). Medication approaches to anxiety typically consist of three options: benzodiazepines, buspirone, and SSRIs. The Neurobehavioral Guidelines group

(Warden et al., 2006) found only a single case report that was considered Level III evidence (option) for the use of Venlafaxine (a mixed serotonin and norepinephrine reuptake inhibitor) in the treatment of anxiety symptoms. Expert opinion generally expresses concern about the use of benzodiazepines in individuals with TBI, based on fears that many such individuals have compromised cognition, arousal, and coordination, and use of benzodiazepines might further impair function in these domains (Arciniegas & Silver, 2006; Lee, Lyketsos, & Rao, 2003). Another concern is the high rate of substance abuse in the TBI population, and use of medications with abuse and dependence potential might put recovering individuals at risk for relapse. SSRIs have thus become the front-line agents not only for depression but for the treatment of generalized anxiety and other anxiety disorders. Although this may make sense, there is little empirical research to inform practice.

Rationale and use in PTSD. The conceptualization of PTSD as a form of anxiety disorder has led to interest in the use of anxiolytics. Evidence in support of the use of the SSRIs has been described above. With respect to anxiety, it is of interest that excessive stress has been associated with dysregulation of serotonergic receptors including downregulation of the anxiolytic 5-HT-1A family, and upregulation of the anxiety provoking 5-HT-2A family (Friedman & Davidson, 2007) providing a theoretical rationale for the use of SSRIs in this population. Unfortunately, benzodiazepines as a class have not proven to be particularly useful in preventing PTSD in acutely traumatized individuals (Gelpin, Bonne, Peri, Brandes, & Shalev, 1996; Mellman, Bustamante, David, & Fins, 2002; Pitman & Delahanty, 2005), nor in the management of fully developed PTSD (Friedman & Davidson, 2007; Institute of Medicine, 2008).

Rationale and use in co-morbid TBI/PTSD. There are no trials of anxiolytics in co-morbid TBI/PTSD. The concerns with respect to benzodiazepines in individuals with TBI also apply to this population, but there is no confirming evidence at this time, and one is hard pressed to suggest that TBI is more than a relative contraindication to the use of benzodiazepines. Thus, as with so many of these medications, it is best to proceed with caution, bearing in mind the theoretical concerns and being alert to the possibility that benzodiazepines might be associated with some degradation of motor and cognitive function. Buspirone is a reasonable alternative, recalling that the onset of action for this agent is several weeks. Thus, it is helpful to reduce the expectations for a rapid cure when discussing a trial of this medication.

Other agents

A variety of other agents have been used in the management of PTSD or TBI symptoms, but for the most part the evidence is quite limited with respect to their efficacy, particularly in military populations, and most especially in individuals with co-morbid TBI and PTSD. However, several are mentioned here as clinicians may encounter individuals being treated with these agents, or asked to consider prescribing them for particular patients.

D-Cycloserine. This is an agent being investigated primarily in PTSD. D-Cycloserine was originally developed as an antibiotic for the treatment of tuberculosis. It has NMDA partial agonist properties and interest in its use comes from a presumed effect on learning and fear extinction through its modulation of NMDA receptors. Preclinical work (Yamamoto et al., 2008), as well as some human studies in various anxiety disorders (Davis, Ressler, Rothbaum, & Richardson, 2006; Norberg, Krystal, & Tolin, 2008) have suggested a role for this compound as an adjunct to cognitive behavioral therapy. Use in a small study ($n = 11$) of individuals with PTSD (Heresco-Levy et al., 2002) failed to show a significant effect on PTSD measures although there was modest improvement in the numbing and avoidance symptom clusters and cognitive measures. Larger clinical trials are currently under way.

Adrenergic agents. These may play a role in the treatment of both individuals with TBI and those with PTSD. Their role in co-morbid TBI/PTSD is quite unclear at this time. The rationale for the use of these agents is complex and differs across the two conditions.

Rationale and use in TBI. Following TBI there is dysregulation of central adrenergic tone, particularly in the prefrontal cortex (PFC) and related working memory (WM) circuitry associated with the hallmark cognitive complaints (memory and attention) (McAllister, Flashman, Sparling, & Saykin, 2004). Alpha-1 and beta receptor agonists can worsen cognitive symptoms, whereas alpha-2 agonists may (in a dose-sensitive fashion) improve cognition. The literature suggests that catecholaminergic systems, particularly adrenergic systems, are critical to executive functioning, fear conditioning, and emotional processing. These effects are complex, and vary according to brain region, receptor type, and dose and agonist/antagonist profile of agent. In general, alpha-2 adrenergic agonists facilitate executive function, and may improve PTSD symptoms, whereas other agonists and norepinephrine at higher doses may impair cognitive function and exacerbate PTSD (Arnsten & Li, 2005; Arnsten, 2007).

Rationale and use of adrenergic agents in PTSD. A full explication of the complex role of the adrenergic system in PTSD is beyond the scope of this paper but the reader is referred to several recent discussions of this topic (Arnsten, 2007; Strawn & Geracioti, 2008; van Stegeren, 2008). Both acute and chronic stress increase firing of noradrenergic neurons. This may increase the efficiency of emotional memory and fear conditioning in the amygdala and related emotional memory processing circuitry, predominantly through stimulation of beta and alpha-1 adrenergic receptors. Under normal circumstances these responses are dampened by PFC input through interaction with Alpha-2 adrenergic receptors. However, response of PFC alpha-2 adrenergic receptors to norepinephrine follows an inverted "U" dose–response profile. In the presence of excessive norepinephrine release, as in acute and chronic stress, this critical dampening effect of the PFC on amygdala activation is taken off line and may contribute to the absence of extinction and pathological remembering that are a hallmark of PTSD (Arnsten, 2007). Presynaptic activation of alpha-2 receptors in the amygdala also acts to reduce release of catecholamines, opening the possibility for dampening fear conditioning and consolidation of emotional memory. These observations have led to attempts to manipulate memory consolidation and extinction through medications that act on the adrenergic system. The overall strategy has been to block alpha-1 and beta-adrenergic receptors to reduce fear conditioning and emotional memory consolidation, or to increase alpha-2 activity to increase PFC inhibition of emotional memory processing. For example, Pitman et al. (2002) used the beta blocker propranolol to reduce consolidation of traumatic memories in individuals with recent trauma. A variety of investigators have used the alpha-1 antagonist prazosin to reduce the nightmares associated with PTSD (Raskind et al., 1996, 2007; Taylor et al., 2008, 2006). Taylor et al. (2006) used daytime prazosin in a small number of individuals with civilian PTSD and found a reduction in a general distress measure as well as reduced PTSD symptoms. In a recent study, Taylor et al. (2008) found that prazosin improved several measures of sleep architecture and reduced both nightmares and non-nightmare distressed awakenings in 13 individuals with civilian PTSD.

Alpha-2 agonists (clonidine, guanfacine) have been used with the thought that they reduce output of noradrenergic neurons arising in the locus coeruleus, and through amygdala connections dampen stress-related activation associated with fear conditioning. A second rationale is that small doses of alpha-2 agonists enhance activation in prefrontal cortex with subsequent enhanced modulation of emotional memory processing and fear conditioning in the amygdala (Arnsten, 2007). However, attempts to treat PTSD with these medications have not been particularly fruitful. Neylan et al. (2006) failed to find a significant difference between guanfacine and placebo in a population with military PTSD.

Rationale and use in co-morbid TBI/PTSD. The above discussion presents a treatment dilemma for the clinician treating co-morbid TBI/PTSD: interventions that improve one condition may worsen the other. For example, some agents that dampen adrenergic tone and improve PTSD symptoms (e.g., beta adrenergic blockade) exacerbate TBI related cognitive complaints (WM) (Chamberlain, Muller, Blackwell, Robbins, & Sahakian, 2006), and interventions that increase norepinephrine (NE) release and improve cognitive function (e.g., catecholamine agonists such as methylphenidate) may exacerbate PTSD symptoms.

CRF antagonists

One of the initiating events in the stress response is the release of corticotrophin releasing factor (CRF) from the median eminence of the hypothalamus. This in turn stimulates the release of adrenal corticotrophin releasing hormone (ACTH) and the subsequent downstream increase in release of glucocorticoids from the adrenal glands. In addition to this hormonal function, CRF functions as a neurotransmitter with CRF-containing neurons and CRF receptors present in neocortex, hippocampus, amygdala, and other regions (Risbrough & Stein, 2006). CRF appears to modulate a variety of other neurotransmitters including serotonin and the catecholamines (Risbrough & Stein, 2006). In light of these key roles, agents that block CRF might well be useful in the prevention and or treatment of PTSD. To date, however, no trials of CRF altering agents have been reported.

Need for additional research

It is apparent from the above review that several key questions would benefit from targeted research. The overarching question is whether not the history of a TBI, particularly a mild TBI alters an individual's response to conventional therapies. Thus as clinical trials of agents or nonpharmacological interventions move forward, it will be important to characterize the study populations in terms of TBI history. Rather than eliminating these individuals from studies, it would be helpful either to stratify the sample in terms of presence or absence of a history of TBI, or to make a comorbid population the focus of the study. In designing these trials, the severity of the injury, as well as the presence or absence of cognitive complaints/deficits should be carefully characterized, as not all TBIs of similar apparent severity are in fact the same. Conversely, we know something about the treatment of cognitive complaints and deficits after TBI, but we know little about how to treat the cognitive complaints and deficits associated with PTSD (Vasterling et al., 2006). Studies of the effects on PTSD symptoms of catecholaminergic and cholinergic augmentation strategies for cognitive complaints/deficits are needed. As noted, there are certain brain regions that are vulnerable to both TBI and the effects of chronic stress. Further research on the mechanisms of how these regions and the relevant circuitry connecting them are effected by both psychological and biomechanical mechanisms would be helpful and might lead to innovative interventions to prevent the development of psychiatric sequelae such as PTSD in those who suffer a TBI. Another important gap in the treatment literature is whether evidence-based non-pharmacological therapies (such as cognitive remediation for cognitive complaints/deficits after TBI or cognitive behavioral therapies for PTSD) in combination with pharmacological intervention are more effective than either intervention alone.

SUMMARY

The study of PTSD and TBI is relatively young, and the topic of co-morbid TBI/PTSD has only recently been recognized as an important clinical concern. The emergence of a large cohort of military personnel with high rates of PTSD and high rates of exposure to TBI has drawn attention to the fact that little is known about the most effective treatment approaches to this complex clinical condition. Clinicians who are expert in the treatment of PTSD typically have little experience with the neuropsychiatric sequelae of TBI, and those with experience in TBI often have little experience in the evaluation and management of PTSD. Although there is an emerging evidence base for best-practice approaches to PTSD on the one hand, and TBI sequelae on the other, the evidence base informing treatment of the co-morbid condition is non-existent. Thus, at this time clinicians opting for medication approaches to treatment must rely on approaches and algorithms developed for the treatment of PTSD symptoms, the sequelae of TBI, or idiopathic psychiatric disorders. Although this is a reasonable starting place, it is important to consider the areas in which these approaches may fall short and may increase the risk of adverse outcomes. Several guiding principles may inform this approach. Although this paper focuses on pharmacological issues, a comprehensive approach taking into account the full spectrum of psychosocial issues impacting the patient will be most effective. Many patients will be resistant to taking medications for a variety of reasons and will require psychotherapeutic approaches. Although it seems logical that some individuals would benefit from a combination of pharmacologic and psychotherapeutic interventions there are no data on this approach to date.

Proper attribution of symptoms to either the chronic sequelae of TBI, or to PTSD, or the combination of these disorders is desirable but not always possible with any degree of certainty. Nevertheless diagnostic clarity is important to strive for and should inform the pharmacologic approach, even if in a hypothesis-driven empiric fashion. Treatment trials should be of sufficient duration to ascertain whether the agent is of sufficient therapeutic value to warrant continuation of the drug.

Although the absence of an adequate evidence base to properly guide treatment often results in an approach predicated on medications used in the absence of the other condition (e.g., treating PTSD as one would if the person did not have a TBI), there is insufficient evidence to determine whether these interventions will be as effective in this context. Furthermore there is at least theoretical concern that one could worsen the clinical situation with some medication approaches. Particular attention should be paid to the effect of medications on the domains of cognition, arousal, sleep, and neurological function, where arguably desirable effects for one condition may exacerbate symptoms of the co-morbid condition. Overall a thoughtful, cautious, patient approach that is undertaken while addressing the array of issues of importance to the individual, and places the potential gains from a given medication in a realistic context, is likely to be most effective.

ACKNOWLEDGMENTS

Work supported by: NIH grants R01 HD048176, 1RO1NS055020, and CDMRP grant PT075446.

REFERENCES

Agrawal, A., Timothy, J., Pandit, L., & Manju, M. (2006). Post-traumatic epilepsy: An overview. *Clinical Neurology and Neurosurgery, 108*(5), 433–439.

Alderfer, B. S., Arciniegas, D. B., & Silver, J. M. (2005). Treatment of depression following traumatic brain injury. *Journal of Head Trauma Rehabilitation, 20*(6), 544–562.

American Psychiatric Association (2006). *American psychiatric association practice guidelines for the treatment of psychiatric disorders.* Arlington, VA: American Psychiatric Publishing.

Arciniegas, D. B., Harris, S. N., & Brousseau, K. M. (2003). Psychosis following traumatic brain injury. *International Review of Psychiatry, 15*(4), 328–340.

Arciniegas, D. B., & Silver, J. M. (2006). Pharmacotherapy of posttraumatic cognitive impairments [review]. *Behavioural Neurology, 17*(1), 25–42.

Arnsten, A., & Li, B-M. (2005). Neurobiology of executive functions: Catecholamine influences on prefrontal cortical functions. *Biological Psychiatry, 57*(11), 1377–1384.

Arnsten, A. F. T. (2007). Catecholamine and second messenger influences on prefrontal cortical networks of "representational knowledge": A rational bridge between genetics and the symptoms of mental illness. *Cerebral Cortex, 17*(Suppl 1), 6–15.

Ashman, T., Cantor, J., Gordon, W., Spielman, L., Flanagan, S., Ginsberg, A., et al. (2009). A randomized controlled trial of sertraline for the treatment of depression in individuals with traumatic brain injury. *General Hospital Psychiatry, 90*(5), 733–740.

Ashman, T. A., Spielman, L. A., Hibbard, M. R., Silver, J. M., Chandna, T., & Gordon, W. A. (2004). Psychiatric challenges in the first 6 years after traumatic brain injury: Cross-sequential analyses of axis i disorders. *Archives of Physical Medicine and Rehabilitation, 85*(Suppl 2), S36–42.

Australian Centre for Posttraumatic Mental Health (2007). *Austrailian guidelines for the treatment of adults with acute stress disorder and posttraumatic stress disorder.* Melbourne, Victoria: ACPMH.

Bartzokis, G., Lu, P. H., Turner, J., Mintz, J., & Saunders, C. S. (2005). Adjunctive risperidone in the treatment of chronic combat-related posttraumatic stress disorder. *Biological Psychiatry, 57*(5), 474–479.

Belanger, H., Curtiss, G., Demery, J., Lobowitz, B., & Vanderploeg, R. (2005). Factors moderating neuropsychological outcomes following mild traumatic brain injury: A meta-analysis. *Journal of the International Neuropsychological Society, 11,* 215–227.

Belanger, H., Vanderploeg, R., Curtiss, G., & Warden, D. (2007). Recent neuroimaging techniques in mild traumatic brain injury. *Journal of Neuropsychiatry and Clinical Neurosciences, 19*(1), 5–20.

Bigler, E. (2008). Neuropsychology and clinical neuroscience of persistent post-concussive syndrome. *Journal of the International Neuropsychological Society, 14,* 1–22.

Bigler, E. D. (2007). Anterior and middle cranial fossa in traumatic brain injury: Relevant neuroanatomy and neuropathology in the study of neuropsychological outcome [review; 119 refs]. *Neuropsychology, 21*(5), 515–531.

Binder, L. M., & Rohling, M. L. (1996). Money matters: A meta-analytic review of the effects of financial incentives on recovery after closed-head injury [see comments]. *American Journal of Psychiatry, 153*(1), 7–10.

Bombardier, C., Fann, J., Temkin, N., Esselman, P., Pelzer, E., Keough, M., et al. (2006). Posttraumatic stress disorder symptoms during the first six months after traumatic brain injury. *Journal of Neuropsychiatry and Clinical Neurosciences, 18*(4), 501–508.

Brady, K., Pearlstein, T., Asnis, G. M., Baker, D., Rothbaum, B., Sikes, C. R., et al. (2000). Efficacy and safety of sertraline treatment of posttraumatic stress disorder: A randomized controlled trial. *JAMA, 283*(14), 1837–1844.

Bremner, J. D. (2007). Functional neuroimaging in post-traumatic stress disorder. *Expert Review of Neurotherapeutics, 7*(4), 393–405.

Bryant, R., Moulds, M., Guthrie, R., & Nixon, R. (2003). Treating acute stress disorder following mild traumatic brain injury. *American Journal of Psychiatry, 160*(3), 585–587.

Bryant, R. A., & Harvey, A. G. (1998). Relationship between acute stress disorder and posttraumatic stress disorder following mild traumatic brain injury. *American Journal of Psychiatry, 155*(5), 625–629.

Bryant, R. A., & Harvey, A. G. (1999a). Postconcussive symptoms and posttraumatic stress disorder after mild traumatic brain injury. *Journal of Nervous and Mental Disease, 187*(5), 302–305.

Bryant, R. A., & Harvey, A. G. (1999b). The influence of traumatic brain injury on acute stress disorder and post-traumatic stress disorder following motor vehicle accidents. *Brain Injury, 13*(1), 15–22.

Butterfield, M. I., Becker, M. E., Connor, K. M., Sutherland, S., Churchill, L. E., & Davidson, J. R. (2001). Olanzapine in the treatment of post-traumatic stress disorder: A pilot study. *International Clinical Psychopharmacology, 16*(4), 197–203.

Carroll, L. J., Cassidy, J. D., Peloso, P. M., Borg, J., von Holst, H., Holm, L., et al. (2004). Prognosis for mild traumatic brain injury: Results of the WHO collaborating centre task force on mild traumatic brain injury. *Journal of Rehabilitation Medicine, 43*(Suppl), 84–105.

Cernak, I., Wang, Z., Jiang, J., Bian, X., & Savic, J. (2001). Ultrastructural and functional characteristics of blast injury-induced neurotrauma. *Journal of Trauma, 50*(4), 695–706.

Chamberlain, S. R., Muller, U., Blackwell, A. D., Robbins, T. W., & Sahakian, B. J. (2006). Noradrenergic modulation of working memory and emotional memory in humans. *Psychopharmacology, 188*(4), 397–407.

Cicerone, K., Dahlberg, C., Kalmar, K., Langenbahn, D. M., Malec, J., Bergquist, T. F., et al. (2000). Evidence-based cognitive rehabilitation: Recommendations for clinical practice. *Archives of Physical Medicine and Rehabilitation, 81*, 1596–1615.

Cicerone, K., Levin, H., Malec, J., Stuss, D., & Whyte, J. (2006). Cognitive rehabilitation interventions for executive function: Moving from bench to bedside in patients with traumatic brain injury. *Journal of Cognitive Neuroscience, 18*(7), 1212–1222.

Coffey, C. (2007). Disturbances of mood, emotion, and affect. In C. E. Coffey & J. M. Silver (Eds.), *Guide to neuropsychiatric therapeurics*. Philadelphia: Lippincott Williams & Wilkins.

Cosetti, M., & Lalwani, A. (in press). Dizziness, imbalance and vestibular dysfunction after traumatic brain injury. In J. Silver, T. McAllister, & S. Yudofsky (Eds.), *Textbook of traumatic brain injury* (2nd ed.). Washington, DC: Amercan Psychiatric Publishing.

Cramer, J., DeRue, K., Devinsky, O., Edrich, P., & Trimble, M. (2003). A systematic review of the behavioral effects of levetiracetam in adults with epilepsy, cognitive disorders, or an anxiety disorder during clinical trials. *Epilepsy Behav, 4*, 124–132.

Davidson, J. R., Brady, K., Mellman, T. A., Stein, M. B., & Pollack, M. H. (2007). The efficacy and tolerability of tiagabine in adult patients with post-traumatic stress disorder. *Journal of Clinical Psychopharmacology, 27*(1), 85–88.

Davidson, J. R., Rothbaum, B. O., Kolk, B. A. v. d., Sikes, C. R., & Farfel, G. M. (2001). Multicenter, double-blind comparison of sertraline and placebo in the treatment of posttraumatic stress disorder. *Archives of General Psychiatry, 58*(5), 485–492.

Davis, M., Ressler, K., Rothbaum, B. O., & Richardson, R. (2006). Effects of d-cycloserine on extinction: Translation from preclinical to clinical work. *Biological Psychiatry, 60*, 369–375.

De Silva, M., Roberts, I., Perel, P., Edwards, P., Kenward, M., Fernandes, J., et al. (2009). Patient outcome after traumatic brain injury in high-, middle- and low-income countries: Analysis of data on 8927 patients in 46 countries. *International Journal of Epidemiology, 38*(2), 452–458.

Deb, S., Lyons, I., & Koutzoukis, C. (1998). Neuropsychiatric sequelae one year after a minor head injury. *Journal of Neurology, Neurosurgery and Psychiatry, 65*(6), 899–902.

Fann, J. R., Burington, B., Leonetti, A., Jaffe, K., Katon, W. J., & Thompson, R. S. (2004). Psychiatric illness following traumatic brain injury in an adult health maintenance organization population [see comment]. *Archives of General Psychiatry, 61*(1), 53–61.

Feldman, G. (2007). Cognitive and behavioral therapies for depression: Overview, new directions, and practical recommendations for dissemination. *Psychiatric Clinics of North America, 30*(1), 39–50.

Foa, E., Dancu, C., Zayfert, C., Mueser, K., & Descamps, M. (1997). *Therapist guide: Brief cognitive behavior therapy for post-traumatic stress disorders in survivors of childhood sexual abuse*. White River Junction, VT: National Center for Post-Traumatic Stress Disorder, Veterans Affairs Medical and Regional Office Center.

Foa, E., Keane, T., & Friedman, M. (2000). *Effective treatments for PTSD: Practice guidelines from the international society for traumatic stress studies*. New York: Guilford Press.

Friedman, M. J., & Davidson, J. R. T. (2007). Pharmacotherapy for PTSD. In M. J. Friedman, T. M. Keane, & P. A. Resick (Eds.), *Handbook of PTSD* (pp. 376–405). New York: Guilford Press.

Friedman, M. J., Marmar, C., Baker, D., Sikes, C., & Farfel, G. (2007). Randomized, double-blind comparison of sertraline and placebo for post-traumatic stress disorder in a department of veterans affairs setting. *Journal of Clinical Psychiatry, 68*, 711–720.

Galea, S., Ahern, J., Tracy, M., Hubbard, A., Cerda, M., Goldmann, E., et al. (2008). Longitudinal determinants of posttraumatic stress in a population-based cohort study. *Epidemiology, 19*, 47–54.

Gelpin, E., Bonne, O., Peri, T., Brandes, D., & Shalev, A. Y. (1996). Treatment of recent trauma survivors with benzodiazepines: A prospective study. *Journal of Clinical Psychiatry, 57*(9), 390–394.

Green, R., Colella, B., Hebert, D., Bayley, M., Kang, H., Till, C., et al. (2008). Prediction of return to productivity after severe traumatic brain injury: Investigations of optimal neuropsychological tests and timing of assessment. *Archives of Physical Medicine and Rehabilitation, 89*(12 Suppl), S51–60.

Greiffenstein, M. (2009). Clinical myths of forensic neuropsychology. *The Clinical Neuropsychologist, 23*, 286–296.

Grunze, H. (2008). The effectiveness of anticonvulsants in psychiatric disorders. *Dialogues in Clinical Neuroscience, 10*(1), 77–89.

Haltiner, A., Temkin, N., Winn, H., & Dikmen, S. (1996). The impact of posttraumatic seizures one year neuropsychological and psychological outcome after head injury. *Journal of the International Neuropsychological Society, 2*, 494–504.

Hamner, M. B., Faldowski, R. A., Ulmer, H. G., Frueh, B. C., Huber, M. G., & Arana, G. W. (2003). Adjunctive risperidone treatment in post-traumatic stress disorder: A preliminary controlled trial of effects on comorbid psychotic symptoms. *International Clinical Psychopharmacology, 18*(1), 1–8.

Harvey, A., Brewin, C., Jones, C., & Kopelman, M. (2003). Coexistence of posttraumatic stress disorder and traumatic brain injury: Towards a resolution of the paradox. *Journal of the International Neuropsychological Society, 9*(4), 663–676.

Harvey, A. G., & Bryant, R. A. (1998a). Acute stress disorder after mild traumatic brain injury. *Journal of Nervous and Mental Disease, 186*(6), 333–337.

Harvey, A. G., & Bryant, R. A. (1998b). Predictors of acute stress following mild traumatic brain injury. *Brain Injury, 12*(2), 147–154.

Heresco-Levy, U., Kremer, I., Javitt, D. C., Goichman, R., Reshef, A., Blanaru, M., et al. (2002). Pilot-controlled trial of d-cycloserine for the treatment of post-traumatic stress disorder. *International Journal of Neuropsychopharmacology, 5*(4), 301–307.

Hertzberg, M. A., Butterfield, M. I., Feldman, M. E., Beckham, J. C., Sutherland, S. M., Connor, K. M., et al. (1999). A preliminary study of lamotrigine for the treatment of posttraumatic stress disorder. *Biological Psychiatry, 45*(9), 1226–1229.

Hibbard, M. R., Uysal, S., Kepler, K., Bogdany, J., & Silver, J. (1998). Axis i psychopathology in individuals with traumatic brain injury. *Journal of Head Trauma Rehabilitation, 13*(4), 24–39.

Hoge, C., Castro, C., Messer, S., McGurk, D., Cotting, D., & Koffman, R. (2004). Combat duty in Iraq and Afghanistan, mental health problems, and barriers to care. *New England Journal of Medicine, 351,* 13–22.

Hoge, C., Goldberg, H., & Castro, C. (2009). Care of war veterans with mild traumatic brain injury – flawed perspectives. *New England Journal of Medicine, 360*(16), 1588–1591.

Hoge, C., McGurk, D., Thomas, J., Cox, A., Engel, C., & Castro, C. (2008). Mild traumatic brain injury in U.S. Soldiers returning from Iraq. *New England Journal of Medicine, 358*(5), 453–463.

Hollon, S., Jarrett, R., Nierenberg, A., Thase, M., Trivedi, M., & Rush, A. (2005). Psychotherapy and medication in the treatment of adult and geriatric depression: Which monotherapy or combined treatment? *Journal of Clinical Psychiatry, 66*(4), 455–468.

Institute of Medicine (2008). *Treatment of posttraumatic stress disorder: An assessment of the evidence.* Washington, DC: The National Academies Press.

Institute of Medicine (2009). *Gulf war and health, volume 7: Long-term consequences of traumatic brain injury.* Washington, DC: The National Academies Press.

Jordan, B. D. (2007). Genetic influences on outcome following traumatic brain injury. *Neurochemical Research, 32,* 905–915.

Kapoor, N., & Ciuffreda, K. (in press). Vision problems. In J. Silver, T. McAllister, & S. Yudofsky (Eds.), *Textbook of traumatic brain injury* (2nd ed.). Washington, DC: Amercan Psychiatric Publishing.

Kessler, R. C., Sonnega, A., Bromet, E., Hughes, M., & Nelson, C. B. (1995). Posttraumatic stress disorder in the national comorbidity survey. *Archives of General Psychiatry, 52,* 1048–1060.

Konovalov, S., Muralee, S., & Tampi, R. (2008). Anticonvulsants for the treatment of behavioral and psychological symptoms of dementia: A literature review. *International Psychogeriatrics, 20*(2), 293–308.

Kraus, J., Schaffer, K., Ayers, K., Stenehjem, J., Shen, H., & Afifi, A. A. (2005). Physical complaints, medical service use, and social and employment changes following mild traumatic brain injury: A 6-month longitudinal study. *Journal of Head Trauma Rehabilitation, 20*(3), 239–256.

Lee, H. B., Lyketsos, C. G., & Rao, V. (2003). Pharmacological management of the psychiatric aspects of traumatic brain injury. *International Review of Psychiatry, 15*(4), 359–370.

Levin, H. S., Mattis, S., Ruff, R. M., Eisenberg, H. M., Marshall, L. F., Tabaddor, K., et al. (1987). Neurobehavioral outcome following minor head injury: A three-center study. *Journal of Neurosurgery, 66*(2), 234–243.

Martenyi, F., Brown, E. B., Zhang, H., Prakash, A., & Koke, S. C. (2002). Fluoxetine versus placebo in posttraumatic stress disorder. *Journal of Clinical Psychiatry, 63*(3), 199–206.

Massagli, T., Fann, J., Burington, B., Jaffe, K., Katon, W., & Thompson, R. (2004). Psychiatric illness after mild traumatic brain injury in children. *Archives of Physical Medicine and Rehabilitation, 85,* 1428–1434.

Mayorga, M. A. (1997). The pathology of primary blast overpressure injury. *Toxicology, 121*(1), 17–28.

McAllister, T. (2005). Mild brain injury and postconcussive symptoms. In J. Silver, S. Yudofsky, & T. McAllister (Eds.), *Textbook of traumatic brain injury* (2nd ed., pp. 279–308). Arlington, VA: American Psychiatric Press, Inc.

McAllister, T. (2007). Neuropsychiatric aspects of TBI. In N. Zasler, D. Katz, & R. Zafonte (Eds.), *Brain injury medicine: Principles and practice* (pp. 835–864). New York: Demos Medical Publishing, Inc.

McAllister, T. (2008). Neurobehavioral sequelae of traumatic brain injury: Evaluation and treatment. *World Psychiatry, 7,* 3–10.

McAllister, T., & Ferrell, R. (2002). Evaluation and treatment of psychosis after traumatic brian injury. *NeuroRehabilitation, 17*, 357–368.

McAllister, T. W., & Arciniegas, D. (2002). Evaluation and treatment of postconcussive symptoms. *NeuroRehabilitation, 17*(4), 265–283.

McAllister, T. W., Flashman, L. A., Sparling, M. B., & Saykin, A. J. (2004). Working memory deficits after traumatic brain injury: Catecholaminergic mechanisms and prospects for treatment – a review. *Brain Injury, 18*(4), 331–350.

McCrea, M., Iverson, G., McAllister, T., Hammeke, T., Powell, M., Barr, W., et al. (2009). An integrated review of recovery after mild traumatic brain injury (MTBI): Implications for clinical management. *The Clinical Neuropsychologist, 23*(8), 1368–1390.

McDougle, C. J., Stigler, K. A., Erickson, C. A., & Posey, D. J. (2008). Atypical antipsychotics in children and adolescents with autistic and other pervasive developmental disorders. *Journal of Clinical Psychiatry, 69*(Suppl 4), 15–20.

Mellman, T. A., Bustamante, V., David, D., & Fins, A. I. (2002). Hypnotic medication in the aftermath of trauma. *Journal of Clinical Psychiatry, 63*(12), 1183–1184.

Monnelly, E. P., Ciraulo, D. A., Knapp, C., & Keane, T. (2003). Low-dose risperidone as adjunctive therapy for irritable aggression in posttraumatic stress disorder. *Journal of Clinical Psychopharmacology, 23*(2), 193–196.

Mooney, G., & Speed, J. (2001). The association between mild traumatic brain injury and psychiatric conditions. *Brain Injury, 15*, 865–877.

Mooney, G., Speed, J., & Sheppard, S. (2005). Factors related to recovery after mild traumatic brain injury. *Brain Injury, 19*(12), 975–987.

Mula, M., Monaco, F., & Trimble, M. (2004). Use of psychotropic drugs in patients with epilepsy: Interactions and seizure risk. *Expert Review of Neurotherapeutics, 4*(6), 953–964.

Mula, M., Trimble, M., Yuen, A., Liu, R., & Sander, J. (2003). Psychiatric adverse events during levetiracetam therapy. *Neurology, 61*, 704–706.

National Institute for Health and Clinical Excellence (2005). *Post-traumatic stress disorder (PTSD): The management of ptsd in adults and children in primary and secondary care.* London: National Institute for Clinical Excellence.

Neumeister, A., Wood, S., Bonne, O., Nugent, A. C., Luckenbaugh, D. A., Young, T., et al. (2005). Reduced hippocampal volume in unmedicated, remitted patients with major depression versus control subjects. *Biological Psychiatry, 57*(8), 935–937.

Neylan, T. C., Lenoci, M., Franklin, K. W., Metzler, T. J., Henn-Haase, C., Hierholzer, R. W., et al. (2006). No improvement of posttraumatic stress disorder symptoms with guanfacine treatment. *American Journal of Psychiatry, 163*, 2186–2188.

Norberg, M., Krystal, J., & Tolin, D. (2008). A meta-analysis of d-cycloserine and the facilitation of fear extinction and exposure therapy. *Biological Psychiatry, 63*, 1118–1126.

Okie, S. (2005). Traumatic brain injury in the war zone [see comment]. *New England Journal of Medicine, 352*(20), 2043–2047.

Ommaya, A., Ommaya, A., Dannenberg, A., & Salazar, A. (1996). Causation, incidence, and costs of traumatic brain injury in the U.S. Military medical system. *Journal of Trauma, 40*(2), 211–217.

Padala, P. R., Madison, J., Monnahan, M., Marcil, W., Price, P., Ramaswamy, S., et al. (2006). Risperidone monotherapy for post-traumatic stress disorder related to sexual assault and domestic abuse in women. *International Clinical Psychopharmacology, 21*(5), 275–280.

Pampallona, S., Bollini, P., Tibaldi, G., Kupelnick, B., & Munizza, C. (2004). Combined pharmacotherapy and psychological treatment for depression: A systematic review. *Archives of General Psychiatry, 61*, 714–719.

Passmore, M., Gardner, D., Polak, Y., & Rabheru, K. (2008). Alternatives to atypical antipsychotics for the management of dementia-related agitation. *Drugs and Aging, 25*(5), 381–398.

Perel, P., Edwards, P., Wentz, R., & Roberts, I. (2006). Systematic review of prognostic models in traumatic brain injury. *BMC Medical Informatics & Decision Making, 6,* 38.

Pitman, R., Sanders, K., Zusman, R., Healy, A., Cheema, F., Lasko, N., et al. (2002). Pilot study of secondary prevention of posttraumatic stress disorder with propranolol. *Biological Psychiatry, 51*(2), 189–192.

Pitman, R. K., & Delahanty, D. L. (2005). Conceptually driven pharmacologic approaches to acute trauma. *CNS Spectrums, 10*(2), 99–106.

Pitman, R. K., Gilbertson, M. W., Gurvits, T. V., May, F. S., Lasko, N. B., Metzger, L. J., et al. (2006). Clarifying the origin of biological abnormalities in PTSD through the study of identical twins discordant for combat exposure. *Annals of the New York Academy of Sciences, 1071,* 242–254.

Raskind, M., Peskind, E., Hoff, D., Hart, K., Holmes, H., Warren, D., et al. (2007). A parallel group placebo controlled study of prazosin for trauma nightmares and sleep disturbance in combat veterans with post-traumatic stress disorder [see comment]. *Biological Psychiatry, 61*(8), 928–934.

Raskind, M. A., Peskind, E. R., Kanter, E. D., Petrie, E. C., Radont, A., Thompson, C., et al. (1996). Prazosin reduces nightmares and other PTSD symptoms in combat veterans: A placebo-controlled study. *American Journal of Psychiatry, 153*(11), 1503.

Ray, W., Chung, C., Murray, K., Hall, K., & Stein, C. (2009). Atypical antipsychotic drugs and the risk of sudden cardiac death. *New England Journal of Medicine, 360,* 225–235.

Reich, D. B., Winternitz, S., Hennen, J., Watts, T., & Stanculescu, C. (2004). A preliminary study of risperidone in the treatment of posttraumatic stress disorder related to childhood abuse in women. *Journal of Clinical Psychiatry, 65*(12), 1601–1606.

Risbrough, V., & Stein, M. (2006). Role of corticotropin releasing factor in anxiety disorders: A translational research perspective. *Hormones and Behavior, 50*(4), 550–561.

Rogawski, M. A., & Loscher, W. (2004). The neurobiology of antiepileptic drugs for the treatment of nonepileptic conditions. *Nature Medicine, 10*(7), 685–692.

Rutherford, W., Merrett, J., & McDonald, J. (1979). Symptoms at one year following concussion from minor head injuries. *Injury Prevention, 10*(3), 225–230.

Sbordone, R. J., & Liter, J. C. (1995). Mild traumatic brain injury does not produce posttraumatic stress disorder. *Brain Injury, 9*(4), 405–412.

Schneiderman, A., Braver, E., & Kang, H. (2008). Understanding sequelae of injury mechanisms and mild traumatic brain injury incurred during the conflicts in Iraq and Afghanistan: Persistent postconcussive symptoms and posttraumatic stress disorder. *American Journal of Epidemiology, 167,* 1446–1452.

Southwick, S., Davis, L., Aikins, D., Rasmusson, A., Barron, J., & Morgan, C. I. (2007). Neurobiological alterations associated with PTSD. In M. J. Friedman, T. M. Keane, & P. A. Resick (Eds.), *Handbook of PTSD*. New York: Guilford Publications.

Stein, M., & McAllister, T. (2009). A beating of minds: Exploring the convergence of posttraumatic stress disorder and mild traumatic brain injury. *American Journal of Psychiatry, 166,* 768–776.

Stein, M. B., Kline, N. A., & Matloff, J. L. (2002). Adjunctive olanzapine for SSRI-resistant combat-related PTSD: A double-blind, placebo-controlled study. *American Journal of Psychiatry, 159*(10), 1777–1779.

Steyerberg, E., Mushkudiani, N., Perel, P., Butcher, I., Lu, J., McHugh, G., et al. (2008). Predicting outcome after traumatic brain injury: Development and international validation of prognostic scores based on admission characteristics. *PLoS Med*, *5*(8), e168.

Strawn, J., & Geracioti, T. J. (2008). Noradrenergic dysfunction and the psychopharmacology of posttraumatic stress disorder. *Depression and Anxiety*, *25*(3), 260–271.

Sumpter, R., & McMillan, T. (2006). Errors in self-report of post-traumatic stress disorder after severe traumatic brain injury. *Brain Injury*, *20*(1), 93–99.

Tanielian, T., & Jaycox, L. H. (Eds.). (2008). *Invisible wounds of war: Psychological and cognitive injuries, their consequences, and services to assist recovery*. Washington, DC: RAND Corporation.

Taylor, F., Martin, P., Thompson, C., Williams, J., Mellman, T., Gross, C., et al. (2008). Prazosin effects on objective sleep measures and clinical symptoms in civilian trauma posttraumatic stress disorder: A placebo-controlled study. *Biological Psychiatry*, *63*(6), 629–632.

Taylor, F. B., Lowe, K., Thompson, C., McFall, M. M., Peskind, E. R., Kanter, E. D., et al. (2006). Daytime prazosin reduces psychological distress to trauma specific cues in civilian trauma posttraumatic stress disorder. *Biological Psychiatry*, *59*(7), 577–581.

Teasell, R., Bayona, N., Lippert, C., Villamere, J., & Hellings, C. (2007). Post-traumatic seizure disorder following acquired brain injury. *Brain Injury*, *21*(2), 201–214.

Tucker, P., Trautman, R. P., Wyatt, D. B., Thompson, J., Wu, S. C., Capece, J. A., et al. (2007). Efficacy and safety of topiramate monotherapy in civilian posttraumatic stress disorder: A randomized, double-blind, placebo-controlled study. *Journal of Clinical Psychiatry*, *68*(2), 201–206.

Tucker, P., Zaninelli, R., Yehuda, R., Ruggiero, L., Dillingham, K., & Pitts, C. D. (2001). Paroxetine in the treatment of chronic posttraumatic stress disorder: Results of a placebo controlled, flexible dosage trial. *Journal of Clinical Psychiatry*, *62*(11), 860–868.

Vaishnavi, S., Makley, M., & Rao, V. (in press). Sleep disturbances and fatigue. In J. Silver, T. McAllister, & S. Yudofsky (Eds.), *Textbook of traumatic brain injury* (2nd ed.). Washington, DC: Amercan Psychiatric Publishing.

van der Kolk, B. A., Spinazzola, J., Blaustein, M. E., Hopper, J. W., Hopper, E. K., Korn, D. L., et al. (2007). A randomized clinical trial of eye movement desensitization and reprocessing (EMDR), fluoxetine, and pill placebo in the treatment of posttraumatic stress disorder: Treatment effects and long-term maintenance. *Journal of Clinical Psychiatry*, *68*(1), 37–46.

van Reekum, R., Cohen, T., & Wong, J. (2000). Can traumatic brain injury cause psychiatric disorders? *Journal of Neuropsychiatry and Clinical Neuroscience*, *12*, 316–327.

van Stegeren, A. H. (2008). The role of the noradrenergic system in emotional memory. *Acta Psychologica*, *127*(3), 532–541.

Vasterling, J., Proctor, S., Amoroso, P., Kane, R., Heeren, T., & White, R. (2006). Neuropsychological outcomes of army personnel following deployment to the Iraq war. *JAMA*, *296*(5), 519–529.

Vasterling, J. J., Duke, L. M., Brailey, K., Constans, J. I., Allain, A. N.Jr., & Sutker, P. B. (2002). Attention, learning, and memory performances and intellectual resources in vietnam veterans: PTSD and no disorder comparisons. *Neuropsychology*, *16*(1), 5–14.

Veterans Health Administration/Department of Defense (2004). *VA/DOD clinical practice guideline for the management of post-traumatic stress*. Washington, DC: Department of Veterans Affairs.

Warden, D. (2006). Military TBI during the Iraq and Afghanistan wars. *Journal of Head Trauma Rehabilitation*, *21*(5), 398–402.

Warden, D. C., Labbate, L. A., Salazar, A. M., Nelson, R., Sheley, E., Staudenmeier, R., et al. (1997). Posttraumatic stress disorder in patients with traumatic brain injury and amnestic for the event. *Journal of Neuropsychiatry and Clinical Neurosciences, 9*, 18–22.

Warden, D. L., Gordon, B., McAllister, T. W., Silver, J. M., Barth, J. T., et al. (2006). Guidelines for the pharmacologic treatment of neurobehavioral sequelae of traumatic brain injury. *Journal of Neurotrauma, 23*(10), 1468–1501.

Weisler, R., Cutler, A., Ballenger, J., Post, R., & Ketter, T. (2006). The use of antiepileptic drugs in bipolar disorders: A review based on evidence from controlled trials. *CNS Spectrums, 11*(10), 788–799.

Willemse-van Son, A., Ribbers, G., Verhagen, A., & Stam, H. (2007). Prognostic factors of long-term functioning and productivity after traumatic brain injury: A systematic review of prospective cohort studies. *Clinical Rehabilitation, 21*(11), 1024–1037.

Yamamoto, S., Morinobu, S., Fuchikami, M., Kurata, A., Kozuru, T., & Yamawaki, S. (2008). Effects of single prolonged stress and d-cycloserine on contextual fear extinction and hippocampal NMDA receptor expression in a rat model of PTSD. *Neuropsychopharmacology, 33*(9), 2108–2116.

Zohar, J., Amital, D. C., Miodownik, M. K., Bleich, A., Lane, R. M., & Austin, C. (2002). Double-blind placebo-controlled pilot study of sertraline in military veterans with posttraumatic stress disorder. *Journal of Clinical Psychopharmacology, 22*(2), 190–195.

AN INTEGRATED REVIEW OF RECOVERY AFTER MILD TRAUMATIC BRAIN INJURY (MTBI): IMPLICATIONS FOR CLINICAL MANAGEMENT

Michael McCrea[1,2], Grant L. Iverson[3,4], Thomas W. McAllister[5], Thomas A. Hammeke[2], Matthew R. Powell[1], William B. Barr[6], and James P. Kelly[7,8]

[1]Neuroscience Center, Waukesha Memorial Hospital, WI, [2]Department of Neurology, Medical College of Wisconsin, WI, USA, [3]Department of Psychiatry, University of British Columbia, Vancouver, BC, [4]British Columbia Mental Health & Addiction Services, Vancouver, BC, Canada, [5]Section of Neuropsychiatry, Dartmouth Medical School, Lebanon, NH, [6]Departments of Neurology and Psychiatry, New York University School of Medicine, NY, [7]Departments of Neurosurgery and Physical Medicine and Rehabilitation, University of Colorado Denver School of Medicine, CO, USA, and [8]National Intrepid Center of Excellence, Defense Centers of Excellence for Psychological Health and TBI, U.S. Department of Defense, Bethesda, MD, USA

> *The diagnosis and treatment of mild traumatic brain injury (MTBI) have historically been hampered by an incomplete base of scientific evidence to guide clinicians. One question has been most elusive to clinicians and researchers alike: What is the true natural history of MTBI? Fortunately, the science of MTBI has advanced more in the last decade than in the previous 50 years, and now reaches a maturity point at which the science can drive an evidence-based approach to clinical management. In particular, technological advances in functional neuroimaging have created a powerful bridge between the clinical and basic science of MTBI in humans. Collectively, findings from clinical, basic science, and functional neuroimaging studies now establish a foundation on which to build integrative theories and testable hypotheses around a comprehensive model of MTBI recovery. We review the current scientific literature on postconcussion symptom recovery, neuropsychological outcome, and neurophysiological healing after MTBI. Special emphasis is placed on how the new evidence base can help guide clinicians in the evaluation and management of military-related MTBI.*

Keywords: Brain injury; Concussion; Neuropsychological tests; Military medicine.

INTRODUCTION

Mild traumatic brain injury (MTBI) has long been considered one of the most challenging encounters for even the most skilled neuropsychologists and other

---

Address correspondence to: Michael McCrea, PhD, ABPP-CN, Executive Director, Neuroscience Center, Waukesha Memorial Hospital, 721 American Avenue, Suite 406, Waukesha, WI 53188, USA. E-mail: michael.mccrea@phci.org

clinicians throughout the neurosciences. The diagnosis of MTBI historically has been hampered by a lack of consensus around the essential, defining characteristics of injury and the limited utility of traditional methods—e.g., Glasgow Coma Scale (Teasdale & Jennett, 1974)—for detecting and classifying less severe grades of acquired brain injury (Iverson, Lange, Gaetz, & Zasler, 2007a). More recently, attempts at multidimensional definitions that incorporate information on biomechanics, acute injury characteristics, and clinical course assist clinicians in making the most accurate *diagnosis* of MTBI (Holm, Cassidy, Carroll, & Borg, 2005; Kay et al., 1993).

There remains great debate, however, about the expected recovery course after MTBI. Historically, science has not provided a sound evidence base to answer the question: *What is the true natural history of MTBI?* Thankfully, many recent breakthroughs have advanced our understanding of the biomechanics, neurophysiology, clinical presentation, and expected recovery course associated with MTBI (see reviews in Iverson et al., 2007a; McCrea, 2007). Collectively, this body of work moves us closer to a more complete understanding of the true natural history of MTBI, which also translates directly to evidence-based methods for clinical evaluation, management, and enhanced outcome.

Interestingly, the sports medicine world has been the platform for many recent advances in the science of MTBI through the prospective study of sport-related concussion. More than 20 years ago, Barth, Macciocchi, and colleagues recognized that many aspects inherent to sport-related concussion essentially create a laboratory for the study of MTBI (Barth et al., 1989; Macciocchi, Barth, Alves, Rimel, & Jane, 1996). Applying the methodological advantages first identified in Barth's Sports as a Laboratory Assessment Model (SLAM; Barth, Freeman, Broshek, & Varney, 2001; Barth, Freeman, & Winters, 2000), several studies of sport-related concussion have since not only assisted clinicians in sports medicine with respect to clinical decision making about eventual return to competition and preventing the risks of repeat injury, but also informed the broader neurosciences with new evidence on the basic and clinical science of MTBI (Belanger & Vanderploeg, 2005; Collins, Iverson, Gaetz, & Lovell, 2007; Guskiewicz et al., 2003; McCrea et al., 2003; Moser et al., 2007).

Clinicians in our armed forces now face a new set of challenges in the evaluation and management of MTBI encountered by military personnel serving in Operation Enduring Freedom (OEF) and Operation Iraqi Freedom (OIF) (Hoge et al., 2008; McCrea et al., 2008). Traumatic brain injury (TBI) has been referred to as the "signature injury" among United States military personnel involved in combat in Iraq and Afghanistan, although precise estimates of TBI incidence among U.S. military personnel have been difficult to pin down (Iverson, Langlois, McCrea, & James, 2009 this issue). Regardless of the true epidemiology, we know from direct accounts of clinicians that all echelons of care are frequently called upon to triage and manage traumatic brain injury at all severity levels, with the overwhelming majority falling into the MTBI classification. Much like managing sport-related concussion, these clinicians are called upon to make rapid, informed determinations about injury severity, level of recovery, and a warrior's fitness to return to active duty following MTBI. Measures to protect military personnel from the potentially negative or catastrophic risks associated with recurrent MTBI are also relevant in this setting.

This article is intended to summarize the relatively new evidence base that advances our scientific understanding of the true natural history of MTBI. We will specifically focus on what the scientific evidence base now tells us about the expected course of recovery in postconcussion symptoms, cognition, and neurophysiology following MTBI, ultimately integrating this information into a theoretical, comprehensive model of MTBI recovery. In keeping with the theme set forth in the series of papers stemming from the International Conference on Behavioral Health and Traumatic Brain Injury, special emphasis will be placed on how the scientific evidence base may help guide clinicians in the evaluation and management of military-related MTBI.

CLINICAL RECOVERY AFTER MTBI

Symptom recovery

In 2004 The World Health Organization (WHO) Collaborating Centre Task Force on Mild Traumatic Brain Injury published a detailed review of the literature on prognosis after MTBI. In total, 120 studies that comprised what the task force considered to be the best-evidence synthesis on prognosis after MTBI met criteria for inclusion in its critical review (Carroll et al., 2004). The WHO task force summarized the results of several studies on self-reported symptoms after MTBI, indicating that headache, blurred vision, dizziness, sleep problems, subjective memory problems, and other cognitive difficulties are the most commonly experienced symptoms after MTBI (Bazarian et al., 1999; Cline & Whitley, 1988; Garraway & Macleod, 1995; Lidvall, Linderoth, & Norlin, 1974a, 1974b; Lowdon, Briggs, & Cockin, 1989; Macciocchi et al., 1996; P. R. McCrory, Ariens, & Berkovic, 2000; Paniak, Phillips, Toller-Lobe, Durand, & Nagy, 1999; Paniak et al., 2002; Riemann & Guskiewicz, 2002). The WHO's extensive review indicated that, in both children and adults, symptoms after MTBI are typically temporary and self-limiting in nature, with resolution within days to weeks post-injury in an overwhelming majority of MTBI patients (Carroll et al., 2004). The WHO task force concluded, based on its review, that there was consistent and methodologically sound evidence that prognosis after MTBI is highly favorable, with gradual resolution of symptoms and little evidence of residual cognitive, behavioral or academic deficits (Carroll et al., 2004).

Researchers have capitalized on the methodological advantages of Barth's SLAM approach (Barth et al., 2001, 2000) to prospectively *measure* the scope and severity of symptoms beginning within minutes of injury, and plotted the time course of symptom recovery over the ensuing hours, days, and weeks (Belanger & Vanderploeg, 2005; Lovell et al., 2003; McCrea et al., 2003). These studies indicate a pattern of gradual symptom recovery within the first 1 to 2 weeks after MTBI in the overwhelming majority of cases, extending out to several weeks in some instances. Figure 1 provides results from a prospective study on the effects of sport-related concussion in a large sample of college athletes, illustrating the course of symptom recovery from time of injury to 90 days post-injury (McCrea et al., 2003). This recovery curve illustrates that: (a) symptomatology is most severe immediately following injury, (b) a pattern of symptom recovery is evident within the first

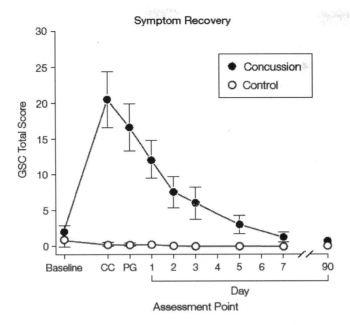

Figure 1 Symptom recovery following MTBI in college football players. GSC = Graded Symptom Checklist. Higher scores on the GSC indicate more severe symptoms; error bars indicate 95% confidence intervals; baseline is pre-injury; CC indicates time of concussion; PG, post-game/post-practice. Figure from McCrea et al., 2003.

2 hours of concussion, and (c) the pattern of symptom recovery continues on a gradual course over the first several days. There is no significant difference between the symptom scores for injured people and normal controls by day seven post-injury. Moreover, delayed onset of symptoms is a relatively rare occurrence.

Contrary to previous reports (Alexander, 1995; McLean, Temkin, Dikmen, & Wyler, 1983), a very small percentage of civilian trauma cases report symptoms 12 months after MTBI in prospective studies (Alves, Macciocchi, & Barth, 1993; Iverson, 2005). For milder injuries, such as those observed in sports, only a small percentage of cases report symptoms beyond 30 days post-injury. For example, Figure 2 categorizes the rate of symptom recovery by 635 high school and college athletes following sport-related concussion. Overall, more than 85% of injured participants reported a full symptom recovery in less than 1 week, including 21% who reportedly recovered within the first day. Fewer than 3% of participants reported symptoms beyond 1 month post injury, which is considerably lower than previous reports of persistent post-concussion syndrome incidence rates in the order of 15% (Alexander, 1995; McLean et al., 1983), but consistent with conclusions of the WHO task force.

In the case of uncomplicated MTBI with no structural injury visualized on neuroimaging, the WHO task force summarized the literature on MTBI symptom recovery by stating that there is evidence that persistent symptoms beyond the typical recovery period of several days to weeks may be attributable to factors other than MTBI (Carroll et al., 2004). Demographic (e.g., female gender,

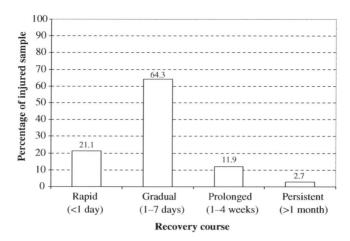

Figure 2 Distribution of post-injury symptom recovery course in 635 concussed high school and college athletes. The percentage of the injured sample recovered at each interval is based on clinical documentation from physicians and certified athletic trainers on duration of symptoms.

older age), psychosocial (e.g., unstable relationships, lack of social support system, pre-existing psychiatric problems or personality disorder, substance abuse or dependence), medical (e.g., severe associated injuries, comorbid medical or neurologic disorders, prior history of MTBI) and situational (e.g., litigation/compensation, concurrent post-traumatic stress disorder [PTSD]) factors have been implicated as predictors of prolonged symptoms after MTBI (Carroll et al., 2004; Landre, Poppe, Davis, Schmaus, & Hobbs, 2006). In more severe forms of complicated MTBI, focal, structural damage detected on head CT or brain MRI may increase the risk of slower recovery with prolonged symptoms and poorer overall outcome more consistent with that seen in moderately severe TBI (Borgaro, Prigatano, Kwasnica, & Rexer, 2003; Iverson, 2006; Kurca, Sivak, & Kucera, 2006; Williams, Levin, & Eisenberg, 1990).

Neuropsychological recovery

In our review of neuropsychological recovery after MTBI, we benefit from the combined work of prominent MTBI researchers more than a decade ago and a number of meta-analytic studies that in the last 3 years have provided a comprehensive summary of the scientific literature.

Seminal work from more than a decade ago first began to characterize neuropsychological recovery after MTBI. Dikmen and colleagues reported on what at the time was the largest prospective study of TBI patients, including a cohort of 161 MTBI patients (Dikmen, Machamer, Winn, & Temkin, 1995). Their results showed that the magnitude and pervasiveness of impairments in cognitive functioning 1 year after injury was highly dependent on TBI severity. In the MTBI sample neuropsychological performance was comparable to trauma controls 1 year post-injury, with no significant differences between the MTBI and control groups. Dikmen and colleagues concluded that their findings were consistent with other studies from that era (Dikmen, McLean, & Temkin, 1986; Levin et al., 1987) indicating that MTBI was not associated with long-term persistent neuropsychological impairments.

Separate meta-analytic studies by Larrabee (1997) and Binder, Rohling and Larrabee (1997b) later showed very small effect sizes (e.g., d statistic in the range of 0.10 to 0.20) when considering the overall neuropsychological effects of MTBI, ultimately concluding that meta-analytic data from well-conducted studies showed good long-term neuropsychological recovery for most persons after MTBI.

Several more recent meta-analytic studies have either replicated or advanced the science of neuropsychological recovery after MTBI. In 2003, Schretlen and Shapiro (2003) published a review of the effects of traumatic brain injury on cognitive functioning. This paper was a unique contribution to the literature by way of its quantitative review of cognitive functioning across the *spectrum* of TBI severity. They conducted a meta-analysis of 39 mostly cross-sectional studies of the cognitive effects of MTBI and moderate-severe TBI from the acute phase through long-term follow-up. These studies reported 48 comparisons of TBI patients ($N=1,716$) and control participants ($N=1,164$). Averaged across all follow-up periods, the effect of moderate-severe TBI (weighted mean Cohen's $d=-0.74$) was more than three times the effect of MTBI (weighted mean $d=-0.24$) on overall cognitive functioning. For MTBI, the initial weighted d of -0.41 was moderate, but the overall cognitive test performance by MTBI patients was essentially indistinguishable from that of matched controls by 1 month post-injury ($d=-0.08$). Schretlen and Shapiro concluded that overall cognitive functioning recovers most rapidly during the first few weeks following MTBI, and essentially returns to baseline within 1 to 3 months.

Belanger and colleagues (Belanger, Curtiss, Demery, Lebowitz, & Vanderploeg, 2005) published a review on factors moderating neuropsychological outcome following MTBI. They conducted a meta-analysis based on 39 studies involving 1463 MTBI patients and 1191 controls. The overall effect of MTBI on neuropsychological functioning was moderate ($d=0.54$). However, findings were moderated by cognitive domain, time since injury, patient characteristics, and sampling methods. In unselected or prospective samples the overall analysis revealed no residual neuropsychological impairments by 90 days post-injury ($d=0.04$). In contrast, clinic-based samples and samples including participants in litigation were associated with greater cognitive sequelae of MTBI ($d=0.74$ and 0.78, respectively at 3 months or greater). Litigation was actually associated with stable or worsening cognitive functioning over time. Belanger and colleagues (2005) concluded that MTBI had little to no effect on neuropsychological functioning by 3 months or greater post-injury in a MTBI population. This study also highlighted the point that sampling method (i.e., clinic-based versus unselected samples) is paramount when studying neuropsychological outcome after MTBI.

Frencham, Fox, and Maybery (2005) also conducted a meta-analytic review of neuropsychological studies of MTBI published since the previous meta-analysis by Binder and colleagues (Binder, 1997; Binder & Rohling, 1996; Binder, Rohling, & Larrabee, 1997a). Their meta-analysis revealed 17 studies that were suitable for inclusion, from which effect sizes on neuropsychological effects were aggregated. The overall effect size was $G=0.32$, but post-acute effect sizes were very small (G = 0.11). Similar to the findings of other researchers, Frencham and colleagues concluded that time since injury was found to be the most significant moderator of neuropsychological outcome after MTBI, with effect sizes approaching zero further out from MTBI.

Iverson (2005) took an innovative approach to studying the neuropsychological effects of MTBI by converting effect sizes from previous meta-analytic studies to a standard metric (i.e., the metric used for IQ scores with a mean of 100 and standard deviation of 15). This exercise illustrated that moderate and severe brain injuries have a pronounced negative effect on cognitive functioning, but MTBI has essentially no measurable effect on cognitive functioning after the acute recovery period using a metric (i.e., IQ scores) more easily understood by clinicians. Iverson also compared the overall cognitive effects of MTBI with other conditions based on a quantitative summary of hundreds of studies and thousands of patients. This approach also revealed that the effects of MTBI on cognition and memory after the acute recovery period are very small, considerably smaller than the effects of depression, bipolar disorder, ADHD, benzodiazepine use/withdrawal, litigation, and malingering (see Figure 3).

As in the general MTBI literature, studies of sport-related concussion have also revealed a rapid return to normal neuropsychological functioning in the first 2 weeks post-injury, with very small neuropsychological effect sizes further out from concussion. A 2005 meta-analysis by Belanger and Vanderploeg (2005) was conducted to determine the impact of sport-related concussion on cognitive functioning. Their analyses were based on 21 studies involving 790 cases of concussion and 2014 controls. The overall effect of concussion ($d = 0.49$) was comparable to the effect sizes cited in prior meta-analyses of the civilian trauma MTBI population, including results from the earlier meta-analysis by the same researchers which reported an overall effect size of $d = 0.54$ (Belanger et al., 2005). Belanger and Vanderploeg (2005) concluded that their meta-analysis provided compelling evidence that sport-related concussion results in no significant effect on neuropsychological functioning by 7–10 days post-injury in the athletic population at large. In tandem with their concurrent meta-analysis in civilian trauma cases (Belanger et al., 2005), this study also suggested a similar course and outcome following sport-related and non-sport related MTBI, which lends further support to the methodological advantages of the SLAM model to study MTBI in general.

In summary, several meta-analyses and prospective studies over the past decade indicate that MTBI is most often followed by a favorable course of neuropsychological recovery over a period of days to weeks, with little or no indication of permanent impairment on neuropsychological testing by 3 months post-injury in group studies. It should be acknowledged that meta-analyses represent an aggregation of effect sizes derived from multiple groups across multiple studies, but can obscure small subgroup or individual effects (Iverson, Brooks, Collins, & Lovell, 2006). Complicated MTBI characterized by structural brain damage visualized on acute neuroimaging may increase the risk for slow or incomplete recovery after MTBI, making predictions of outcome considerably less precise in this group (Borgaro et al., 2003; Iverson, 2006; Kurca et al., 2006; Williams et al., 1990).

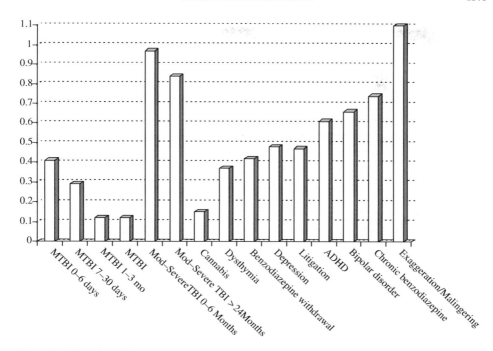

Figure 3 Effect sizes of MTBI on overall neuropsychological functioning. Effect sizes typically are expressed in pooled, weighted standard deviation units. However, across studies there are some minor variations in the methods of calculation. By convention, effect sizes of .2 are considered small, .5 medium, and .8 large. This is from a statistical, not necessarily clinical, perspective. In this figure the overall effect on cognitive or neuropsychological functioning is reported. Effect sizes less than .3 should be considered very small and difficult to detect in individual patients because the patient and control groups largely overlap. MTBI: 0–6 days, 7–30 days, 1–3 months, moderate-severe TBI 0–6 months, >24 months (all in Schretlen & Shapiro, 2003), 39 studies, $N = 1716$ TBI, $N = 1164$ controls; MTBI (Binder et al., 1997a), 11 studies, $N = 314$ MTBI, $N = 308$ controls. Cannabis (Grant, Gonzalez, Carey, Natarajan, & Wolfson, 2003): long-term regular use, 11 studies, $N = 623$ users, $N = 409$ non or minimal users. Dysthymia, depression, & bipolar disorder (Christensen, Griffiths, Mackinnon, & Jacomb, 1997): 3 comparisons for dysthymia, 97 comparisons for depression, and 15 comparisons for bipolar disorder. Benzodiazepine withdrawal (Barker, Greenwood, Jackson, & Crowe, 2004b): 10 studies, long-term follow-up, 44 comparisons. Litigation/financial incentives (Binder & Rohling, 1996): 17 studies, $N = 2,353$ total. ADHD (Frazier, Demaree, & Youngstrom, 2004): based on Full Scale IQ, 123 studies. Chronic benzodiazepine use (Barker, Greenwood, Jackson, & Crowe, 2004a): 13 studies, $N = 384$, 61 comparisons. Exaggeration/malingering (Vickery, Berry, Inman, Harris, & Orey, 2001): 32 studies published between 1985 and 1998, 41 independent comparisons. Reference: Iverson, 2005. Figure reproduced with kind permission from G. L. Iverson, Outcome from mild traumatic brain injury, *Current Opinion in Psychiatry*, *18* p. 306 © 2005, Wolters Kluwer Health. Lippincott Williams & Wilkins.

NEUROPHYSIOLOGICAL RECOVERY AFTER MTBI

Pathophysiology of MTBI

The "mild" classification range is extraordinarily broad from the perspective of pathophysiology and neurobiology. Most classification systems used by researchers and clinicians include injuries that are so mild that symptomatic recovery can occur within the same day. The person might simply have felt dazed for a brief period of time. Some degree of headache, dizziness, and cognitive slowing might have been present for a couple hours but then resolved. Thus, the person experienced a blow to the head that affected cellular physiology temporarily, with rapid return to asymptomatic status.

The other end of the mild spectrum abuts the moderate TBI classification range. These injuries can be characterized by loss of consciousness in excess of 10 minutes and many hours of post-traumatic amnesia. These injuries can be associated with macroscopic evidence of brain damage, such as a contusion visible on CT (i.e., the so-called "complicated" MTBI). Macroscopic abnormalities within brain tissue or outside the brain (i.e., extra-axial space) can be identified using neuroimaging (e.g., CT or MRI). In the most severe form of MTBI, these macroscopic injuries can include hemorrhagic contusions, non-hemorrhagic contusions, hemorrhagic or non-hemorrhagic shearing injuries, and cerebral edema evidenced on structural neuroimaging. Extra-axial manifestations of injury can include epidural hematomas, subdural hematomas, subarachnoid hemorrhage, and intraventricular hemorrhage. This represents a small percentage of MTBIs, and some clinicians and researchers are comfortable conceptualizing these injuries as "moderate."

Injuries that fall on the mild end of the MTBI spectrum ("uncomplicated" concussion with brief or no amnesia or unconsciousness) are likely associated with low levels of axonal stretching, which result in only temporary changes in neurophysiology. Giza and Hovda (2001) describe a model, conceptualized as a multilayered neurometabolic cascade, for the complex interwoven cellular and vascular changes that occur following concussive forces applied to the brain (see Figure 4). The neurobiology involves ionic shifts, abnormal energy metabolism, diminished cerebral blood flow, and impaired neurotransmission. Fortunately, for the vast majority of affected cells, there appears to be a reversible series of neurometabolic events (Giza & Hovda, 2001; Iverson, 2005; Iverson et al., 2007a)

The ultimate fate of neurons relates to the extent of traumatic axonal injury, which can culminate in secondary axotomy (see Buki & Povlishock, 2006, for a review). High intracellular Ca^{2+} levels, combined with stretch injury, can initiate an irreversible process of destruction of microtubules within axons. The disruption of the microtubular and neurofilament components contributes to axonal swelling and detachment (i.e., secondary axotomy). Some, but not all, cells that experience secondary axotomy will degenerate and die through necrotic or apoptotic mechanisms.

In general, however, most injured cells (a) do not undergo secondary axotomy and (b) appear to recover normal cellular function. In other words, for most individuals who sustain an MTBI, it appears that the brain undergoes dynamic restoration and, in due course, individuals return to a normal state of neuronal functioning (Iverson, 2005; Iverson et al., 2007a).

Influence of activity on acute physiology

When a warrior, civilian, or athlete sustains an MTBI, a decision must be made regarding return to duty, work, or play. It is widely accepted in amateur

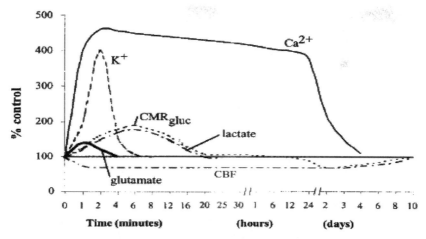

Figure 1. Neurometabolic cascade following experimental concussion. K^+, potassium; Ca^{2+}, calcium; CMRgluc, oxidative glucose metabolism; CBF, cerebral blood flow. (Reprinted with permission. Giza CC, Hovda DA. Ionic and metabolic consequences of concussion. In: Cantu RC, Cantu RI. *Neurologic Athletic and Spine Injuries*. St Louis, MO: WB Saunders Co; 2000:80–100.).

Figure 4 Neurometabolic cascade following experimental concussion in rats. Reference: Giza and Hovda, 2001 (Reprinted with permission).

athletics that athletes who sustain a concussion should not return to the practice or game in which they were injured. The now widely cited recommendation is that athletes should rest until they are asymptomatic. In general, rest means no vigorous physical activity or heavy mental exertion. From a practical perspective, this often means taking a few days off duty, work, or school.

When the athlete is asymptomatic, a return to light aerobic exercise is recommended as described in the two agreement statements following the International Concussion in Sport Conferences in Vienna (Aubry et al., 2002) and Prague (P. McCrory et al., 2005). The protocol, which is based mostly on expert consensus without empirical data, involves an athlete moving through the following exertional steps in 24-hour periods: (a) light aerobic exercise (e.g., walking or a stationary biking), (b) sport-specific training (e.g., ice skating in hockey or running in soccer), and (3) non-contact training drills (usually heavily exertional). Athletes then progress to contact or full return to play. If the athlete's previously resolved post-concussion symptoms return at any step, the athlete should return to the previous exertion level at which they were last asymptomatic.

What is less clear is whether exercising too soon can have short-, medium-, or long-term adverse effects on an injured athlete, warrior, or civilian. This, of course, is very difficult to study. Theoretically, if the brain is (a) in a state of neurometabolic crisis, and (b) using resources to try to adapt to, modify, and re-regulate, then (c) exertion, such as exercise, could worsen the neurometabolic crisis and delay recovery. Most research designs addressing these issues cannot be implemented with humans. Thus, most of the work in this area has been done with animals.

A series of interesting studies relating to exercise following MTBI have been conducted by Griesbach and colleagues. In one study, 18 rats were injured using a fluid percussion device and then they were returned to cages with or without running wheels (Griesbach, Gomez-Pinilla, & Hovda, 2004a). After a few days they were sacrificed and molecular markers of plasticity, such as Brain-Derived Neurotrophic Factor (BDNF) and Synapsin I were examined. BDNF helps regulate neuronal growth, helps with neuronal survival after injury, and facilitates synaptic function. Synapsin I is involved in synaptic vesicle clustering and release. There was an increase in molecular markers of plasticity measured at 7 days post-injury. However, if injury was followed by acute voluntary exercise, these same molecular markers were decreased. In this study early physiological stimulation through voluntary exercise reduced the capacity for plasticity in the injured rat brain.

In a larger study, Griesbach and colleagues (Griesbach, Hovda, Molteni, Wu, & Gomez-Pinilla, 2004b) administered fluid percussion brain injuries to 161 rats (mean duration of loss of consciousness = 82 seconds, $SD = 54$ seconds; mean duration of apnea = 14 seconds, $SD = 11$ seconds). Some rats were allowed to exercise immediately and some were not given access to a running wheel until 2 weeks post-injury. The rats that were given access to a running wheel immediately did not show positive molecular markers of plasticity and they performed worse on behavioral tasks. The rats that were given access to a running wheel from 14–21 days post-injury did show the positive molecular markers and they performed better on the behavioral tasks. Griesbach and colleagues (Griesbach, Gomez-Pinilla, & Hovda, 2007) utilized a similar methodology but examined both mild and moderate brain injuries. The findings for mild injury were replicated, but moderately injured rats needed to rest longer before they benefited from exercise.

In a recent study, however, Griesbach and colleagues (Griesbach, Hovda, Gomez-Pinilla, & Sutton, 2008) obtained results that ran somewhat contrary to their previous work. This study involved a different mechanism of injury (i.e., a cortical contusion injury versus a fluid percussion injury). Molecular improvement *did* occur in injured rats that exercised during the *first week*. However, they did most of their exercising in the last 3 days of that week—they exercised less than the sham rats in the initial days.

Taken together, the series of studies by Griesbach and colleagues suggests that exercise is good for the brain, even the injured brain, but there appears to be an important temporal window. That is, injured rats that exercise too soon do have suppressed molecular markers of plasticity. These studies provide basic science support for the clinical recommendation of complete rest following injury. However, these studies cannot translate directly into clinical recommendations. It is essential to appreciate that the rats first underwent neurosurgery to expose their brain, they were then rendered unconscious (and they typically stopped breathing), and upon regaining consciousness they underwent another neurosurgical procedure prior to being returned to their cages. Uninjured rats went through the same surgical procedures to control for these effects, but the point is that it is extremely difficult to use an animal model to closely approximate a mild concussion experienced in sports or in combat.

Unfortunately, due to obvious methodological and ethical issues and challenges, there is very little research on this topic with humans. Majerske and colleagues (2008) studied 95 student athletes who were retrospectively assigned into one of the following five groups based on their post-concussion activity level: (1) no school or exercise activity ($n = 35$), (2) school activity only ($n = 77$), (3) school activity and light activity at home (e.g., slow jogging, mowing the lawn; $n = 57$), (4) school activity and sports practice ($n = 26$), (5) school activity and participation in a sports game ($n = 9$). The group that seemed to function the best cognitively was #3 (school and light activity at home) and the group that functioned the worst cognitively was #5 (school and return to competition). This quasi-experimental retrospective cohort study is interesting and provocative, but does not allow causal inferences. It suggests a relation, however, between activity level and cognitive functioning acutely and post-acutely following injury.

New insights from functional imaging studies

Animal studies have described the complex neuropathological processes that come into play following even mild central nervous system (CNS) trauma (Farkas & Povlishock, 2007; Raghupathi, 2004). There have also been several reports of neuropathological findings shortly after MTBI in humans who died of other causes (Bigler, 2004; Blumbergs et al., 1994, 1995; Goodman & Mattson, 1994; Oppenheimer, 1968). Neuroimaging, however, has been the mainstay of attempts to understand the neuropathophysiology of human MTBI. A full discussion of these efforts is beyond the scope of this paper but has been detailed in recent reviews (Belanger, Vanderploeg, Curtiss, & Warden, 2007; Levine et al., 2006). Of particular interest are techniques that shed light on two groups: (a) individuals studied shortly after injury who have normal conventional structural imaging (such as CT scan or structural MRI), and (b) individuals who do not show the typical recovery pattern.

Two MRI-based techniques show particular promise: diffusion tensor imaging (DTI) and magnetization transfer imaging. DTI is of particular interest in that it is sensitive to subtle changes in white matter integrity. Arfanakis and colleagues (2002) reported that five individuals studied within 24 hours of a MTBI showed reduced fractional anisotropy (FA: a measure of white matter integrity) that was most commonly seen in the corpus callosum and internal capsule. Follow-up scans 1 month later in two of the individuals showed improvement but not complete normalization of the FA values. Inglese and colleagues (Inglese, Benedetti, & Filippi, 2005) studied 46 patients with MTBI (20 of whom within 5 days of injury) and 29 healthy controls. Both MTBI groups showed reduced FA and increased mean diffusivity in the corpus callosum, the internal capsule, and the centrum semiovale. Kraus and colleagues (2007) performed DTI in 37 individuals with a history of TBI of different severities, 20 of whom had MTBI by American Congress of Rehabilitation Medicine criteria (Kay et al., 1993). Compared to 18 healthy controls, the MTBI group showed reduced FA in three of 13 regions of interest including the cortico-spinal tract, sagittal striatum, and superior longitudinal fasciculus. Of note is that the MTBI group was studied a mean of 92.5 months after injury and had a mean loss of consciousness of about 5 minutes. Of particular interest is that FA values have been shown to correlate with cognitive performance (memory, attention, reaction time) in both healthy controls and individuals with a history of MTBI (Niogi et al., 2008a, 2008b).

Bagley and colleagues (2000) and McGowan et al. (2000) have used magnetization transfer imaging to show regional brain abnormalities following MTBI in regions consistent with known neuropathological vulnerability (corpus callosum). In both studies those individuals with persistent cognitive complaints had demonstrable abnormalities on imaging. In the Bagley study the patients were studied within 1 month of injury. In the McGowan study they were studied within "months" of their injuries and had persistent cognitive complaints.

Functional MRI (fMRI) has been used to study neural mechanisms of cognitive function after MTBI. In a fMRI study of 15 concussed high-school football athletes within 18 hours of injury, Hammeke et al. (2004) found decreased activation in the supplementary motor (SMA) and pre-SMA during a memory scanning paradigm when compared to a matched group of uninjured athletes. The decreased activation occurred largely in players who had a loss of consciousness from their injury and was related to a generalized slowing of selective reaction time. When studied 45 days following injury, the task activation pattern in the concussed players had normalized.

McAllister and colleagues (McAllister, Flashman, McDonald, & Saykin, 2006; McAllister et al., 1999, 2001) have suggested that 1 month after MTBI patients show a mismatch of activation and allocation of working memory processing resources, despite cognitive performance that is equivalent to that of healthy controls. Chen and colleagues (2004) also reported abnormal cerebral activation patterns in 16 concussed athletes studied 1–14 months after injury; 15 of the athletes were symptomatic at the time of study. Although performance on the task did not differ from controls, the concussed group showed reduced activation in frontal cortex and increased areas of activation in parietal and temporal regions relative to the controls. This group (Chen, Johnston, Petrides, & Ptito, 2008) subsequently reported on nine concussed athletes with persistent post-concussive complaints studied on two occasions; 1–9 months after injury and again 9–23 months after the first study. Compared to healthy controls ($n=6$), the concussed group initially showed reduced dorsolateral prefrontal cortical (DLPFC) activation associated with a working memory task. When reassessed, those concussed athletes whose symptoms had largely resolved ($n=4$) showed some increased left DLPFC activation relative to the unimproved group. Jantzen and colleagues (Jantzen, Anderson, Steinberg, & Kelso, 2004) found increased activation associated with cognitive tasks in four concussed athletes (compared to baseline studies and non-concussed teammates) within a week of injury. Cognitive performance was equivalent between the two groups. More recently, Lovell and colleagues (2007) also found increased medial frontal and temporo-parietal activation associated with a working memory task in 28 concussed student athletes studied about 1 week after injury. Furthermore the degree of activation in this region correlated with length of time to return to play.

In summary, inferences from the above studies must be considered tentative at best in that there are no large-scale longitudinal studies of individuals with MTBI using the most sensitive available neuroimaging techniques. Variable methods across studies also limit the ability to determine to what extent neuroimaging findings may be influenced by pre-injury differences or co-morbidities. Nevertheless, some tentative conclusions seem reasonable. The first is that with each advance in imaging technology comes an increase in the sensitivity to detect abnormalities in brain structure and function in the first days to several weeks after MTBI. For example conventional MRI demonstrates more lesions than CT scan (Bigler, 2005), and more recent MRI-based techniques are more sensitive than the initial T1 and T2 weighted images. Within the first month after injury, functional imaging, particularly PET and fMRI show changes in task-associated brain activation even in the absence of abnormal structural imaging. Studies with longer intervals between injury and assessment are more variable. Nevertheless the recent DTI studies showing increased regions of white matter abnormalities relative to non-injured controls, and correlation of performance with these white matter abnormalities in regions that are biologically plausible, suggest that some longer lasting effects of MTBI may be seen in some individuals.

Still, although interpretation of the relationship between persisting symptoms and markers of brain abnormalities noted above seems straightforward when the brain abnormalities are structural in nature (e.g., FA from DTI), more caution is needed when the brain abnormalities are derived from functional imaging techniques because the persisting symptoms may perturb the imaging signal in indirect ways (e.g., be a source of attentional distraction during the imaging study). It is also important to point out that although performance after MTBI may return to "normal," the effort required to achieve that performance may be greater than expected, giving rise to a sense of reduced cognitive capacity, and, theoretically, reduced cognitive reserve. Larger longitudinal studies are required to examine these impressions. Additional research is also needed to better understand the natural evolution of brain-related functional adaptation and compensatory mechanisms over time following injury, and to determine why some individuals have persisting brain abnormalities and others do not.

AN INTEGRATED MODEL OF MTBI RECOVERY

Our scientific understanding of MTBI has arguably progressed more in the past decade than it had in the prior 50 years, and now reaches an exciting maturity point where key findings from every corner begin to converge and ultimately bring applied value to clinical practice. Overall, the evidence base reviewed herein on the natural history of clinical and neurophysiological recovery after MTBI begins to establish the foundation for an integrated model of MTBI recovery.

As described earlier, findings from large, prospective studies now illustrate that post-concussion symptoms, cognitive dysfunction, and other functional deficits are most severe during the earliest acute period after MTBI, then follow a gradual, overlapping course of recovery beginning within hours of injury and completely resolve within days to weeks in the overwhelming majority of cases. In the case of neuropsychological recovery, meta-analytic studies demonstrate essentially undetectable effect sizes beyond roughly 2–4 weeks after MTBI.

Technological advances in functional imaging have created a powerful bridge between traditional clinical and basic science studies of MTBI. A particularly interesting picture begins to emerge when looking at the collective findings from fMRI studies of acute, subacute, and chronic MTBI. In brief, findings from functional imaging studies now begin to form a hypothesis that MTBI physiologically manifests in a pattern of decreased cerebral activation in select attention-related neural circuits during the earliest acute period (e.g., 12–24 hours post-injury) that perhaps relates to the acute physiological mechanisms of injury. Increased activation is then evident during the subacute phase (e.g., 1 month post-injury) that appears to relate to compensatory mechanisms, and there is a return to normal activation patterns further out from injury (e.g., >30 days post).

Without question, the evolution of functional imaging technologies has yielded steady gains in our understanding of the mechanisms of functional and structural abnormalities in human MTBI. Still, it should be noted that most studies to date have involved quite heterogeneous groups of MTBI patients and applied variable methods of study that make it difficult to draw global inferences across the literature.

Collectively, findings from clinical research, basic science, and functional imaging studies converge on the true natural history of single, uncomplicated MTBI across the full time course from minutes to months post-injury. Although far from conclusive at this point, these recent advances have now brought the science of MTBI to a point at which we begin to form theories and testable hypotheses around a comprehensive model of MTBI recovery (see Table 1).

At a practical level, this theoretical recovery model adds to our perspective on the direct experience of the MTBI patient. These patients often report rather severe signs and symptoms that render them largely inactive for the initial days after uncomplicated MTBI, followed by a period during which they return to school or work but feel they have to expend a great deal more mental energy to function at their customary level (which in turn may be accompanied by fatigue or diminished endurance). They then most often resume all their routine activities within 2–6 weeks after injury, without major difficulty or need for accommodations.

Admittedly, this model does not fully explain those cases that fail to follow a typical recovery course and report chronic symptoms or functional impairments after MTBI. It is known that symptoms of depression, anxiety and post-traumatic stress disorder (PTSD) are often mistaken as chronic effects of MTBI. Management strategies should focus on properly identifying and treating these conditions. Reports from systematic reviews of the treatment literature have found little evidence that neurological therapies, including drug interventions or cognitive remediation, are effective for individuals with MTBI (Borg et al., 2004; Comper, Bisschop, Carnide, & Tricco, 2005). However, there is evidence that psychological approaches to treatment, consisting of supportive or educational interventions, are effective in helping individuals to recover from MTBI and these associated conditions. Routine use of these psychological interventions early in recovery, combined with gradual but early return to normal activities following MTBI,

Table 1 Integrated model of recovery after uncomplicated MTBI

Acute Period (immediately after injury to ~5 days post):
- Symptoms and cognitive impairments can be severe and significantly disrupt normal daily function
- The brain is sufficiently injured to create a neurometabolic crisis. Functional neuroimaging studies can reveal a dysregulation of normal and consistent recruitment of neuronal resources (e.g., decreased activation)
- Exertion while the brain is in a state of neurometabolic crisis may slow down recovery and, theoretically, could have other secondary pathophysiological effects

Subacute Period (~5–30 days post)
- Symptoms and cognitive/functional impairments follow a gradual, overlapping course of improvement
- Clinically, an overwhelming majority of cases achieve full symptom and neuropsychological recovery
- Neurophysiologically, the brain continues on a course of recovery to a normal metabolic state and cerebral functioning, during which over-recruitment of neuronal resources may be required to achieve customary functional and performance standards (e.g., increased activation on functional neuroimaging)
- Once asymptomatic, a protocol of gradual, sequential exertion is appropriate, initially focusing on cardiovascular challenge before transitioning to more vigorous exercise

Chronic Period (>30 days post)
- A relatively small percentage of patients report persistent symptoms and cognitive or other complaints, which may be influenced by injury (e.g., more severe grades of complicated MTBI with abnormal structural imaging findings) or non-injury related factors (e.g., depression, PTSD, chronic pain, life stress, or secondary gain)
- The brain returns to a normal state of cerebral function (e.g., normal activation on functional neuroimaging) in the overwhelming majority of cases
- Persistent post-concussion symptoms may be observed in a small percentage (<5%) of MTBI cases, significantly influenced by non-injury-related factors
- If identified, co-morbidities (e.g., depression, anxiety, PTSD, chronic pain, etc.) should be treated. Psychological and educational interventions can be effective in improving functional outcome and reducing persistent disability from MTBI and these associated conditions

This theoretical model applies to a single, uncomplicated MTBI without focal, structural injury visualized on conventional neuroimaging (e.g., CT, MRI) and is less relevant in more severe forms of MTBI or repeat MTBI. This model does not apply to moderate or severe TBI.

---

can provide an effective means to avoiding the long-term consequences of postconcussion syndrome (Ponsford, 2006).

IMPLICATIONS FOR CLINICAL MANAGEMENT OF MILITARY-RELATED MTBI

In keeping with the theme of this special issue of *The Clinical Neuropsychologist*, our ultimate aim is to transfer the evidence base on the acute effects and true natural history of recovery after MTBI to a useful framework for the clinician charged with the challenging assignment of evaluating and managing military personnel affected by MTBI. Clearly, delivering a detailed clinical practice guideline or algorithm for management of military-related MTBI is beyond the scope and authority of this review. Likewise, it is unrealistic for us to appreciate all the military operational implications of clinical management, particularly in an austere environment.

We can, however, perhaps draw several parallels from our theoretical model of MTBI recovery to clinically useful considerations for the evaluation and management of military personnel affected by MTBI:

(1) MTBI is likely to cause significant symptoms and functional impairments during the first several days that not only negatively impact a warrior's ability to fulfill their duties, but may also place the individual at considerable risk of recurrent injury or further harm.

(2) There is basic science evidence that exercise too soon after MTBI could, at minimum, slow down the recovery process. It is less clear, but certainly possible, that vigorous exercise while the brain is in acute neurometabolic crisis could compound secondary pathophysiologies and more seriously disrupt neuroplasticity. Therefore, it is likely advisable for injured military personnel to avoid mental and physical exertion in the initial days following uncomplicated MTBI. Once asymptomatic, the injured person should begin a gradual, sequential exertion protocol focusing initially on cardiovascular challenge (e.g., stationary bike or light jogging) before transitioning to more vigorous exercise (e.g., running or supersets of pushups, situps, jumping jacks, etc.)

(3) Clinical recovery (i.e., as measured by imperfect instruments such as symptom checklists) may not fully equate to true recovery at a brain level (i.e., completely normal cerebral functioning). The main concern here is that there may be a window of neurobiological vulnerability during which the injured warrior remains functionally disadvantaged or susceptible to the ill effects of repeat concussion, even after reaching full clinical recovery. Unfortunately, we have not yet reached a point at which we have a perfect biological marker of concussion (and subsequent recovery) for clinical use. No doubt, ongoing technological advancements in neuroimaging and other areas of neuroscience show great promise, but will face unique challenges of practicality before being adopted for clinical use in the military theater. Until then, the use of standardized methods (e.g., neuropsychological testing) to *measure* recovery and to determine readiness to return to duty is recommended, rather than simply relying on a warrior's self-reported symptom recovery.

(4) The literature supports a biopsychosocial approach to the management of individuals with chronic symptoms or functional complaints reflective of postconcussion syndrome after MTBI. This is especially relevant in a military setting where post-traumatic stress disorder (PTSD), depression, anxiety, chronic pain, and other comorbidities known to complicate recovery after MTBI are highly prevalent (Hoge, Auchterlonie, & Milliken, 2006; Hoge et al., 2008). These comorbidities can mimic (or, possibly, obscure) residual effects of MTBI (see Iverson, Zasler, & Lange, 2007b, for review). Successful injury management will require attention to the diagnosis and treatment of psychological disorders in the context of MTBI.

In conclusion, major advancements in the clinical and basic science of MTBI now provide a more sound evidence base for clinical management in both civilian and military sectors. Further study is required to confirm or refute theoretical models of MTBI recovery. Much as was the case with sport-related concussion, well-planned prospective studies on the acute effects, recovery, and outcome after military-related MTBI will not only directly benefit military medicine experts, but also provide great value to the larger neurosciences by advancing the science of MTBI in the general population.

REFERENCES

Alexander, M. P. (1995). Mild traumatic brain injury: Pathophysiology, natural history, and clinical management. *Neurology, 45*(7), 1253–1260.

Alves, W., Macciocchi, S. N., & Barth, J. T. (1993). Post-concussive symptoms after uncomplicated head injury. *Journal of Head Trauma Rehabilitation, 8*, 48–59.

Arfanakis, K., Haughton, V. M., Carew, J. D., Rogers, B. P., Dempsey, R. J., & Meyerand, M. E. (2002). Diffusion tensor MR imaging in diffuse axonal injury. *AJNR American Journal of Neuroradiology, 23*(5), 794–802.

Aubry, M., Cantu, R., Dvorak, J., Graf-Baumann, T., Johnston, K. M., Kelly, J., et al. (2002). Summary and agreement statement of the 1st International Symposium on Concussion in Sport, Vienna 2001. *Clinical Journal of Sport Medicine, 12*(1), 6–11.

Bagley, L. J., McGowan, J. C., Grossman, R. I., Sinson, G., Kotapka, M., Lexa, F. J., et al. (2000). Magnetization transfer imaging of traumatic brain injury. *Journal of Magnetic Resonance Imaging, 11*(1), 1–8.

Barker, M. J., Greenwood, K. M., Jackson, M., & Crowe, S. F. (2004a). Cognitive effects of long-term benzodiazepine use: A meta-analysis. *CNS Drugs, 18*(1), 37–48.

Barker, M. J., Greenwood, K. M., Jackson, M., & Crowe, S. F. (2004b). Persistence of cognitive effects after withdrawal from long-term benzodiazepine use: A meta-analysis. *Archives of Clinical Neuropsychology, 19*(3), 437–454.

Barth, J. T., Alves, W., Ryan, T., Macciocchi, S., Rimel, R., & Jane, J. J. (1989). Mild head injury in sports: Neuropsychological sequelae and recovery of function. In H. Levin, J. Eisenberg, & A. Benton (Eds.), *Mild head injury* (pp. 257–275). New York: Oxford University Press.

Barth, J. T., Freeman, J. R., Broshek, D. K., & Varney, R. N. (2001). Acceleration–deceleration sport-related concussion: The gravity of it all. *Journal of Athletic Training, 36*(3), 253–256.

Barth, J. T., Freeman, J. R., & Winters, J. E. (2000). Management of sport-related concussions. *Dental Clinics of North America, 44*(1), 67–83.

Bazarian, J. J., Wong, T., Harris, M., Leahey, N., Mookerjee, S., & Dombovy, M. (1999). Epidemiology and predictors of post-concussive syndrome after minor head injury in an emergency population. *Brain Injury, 13*(3), 173–189.

Belanger, H. G., Curtiss, G., Demery, J. A., Lebowitz, B. K., & Vanderploeg, R. D. (2005). Factors moderating neuropsychological outcomes following mild traumatic brain injury: A meta-analysis. *Journal of the International Neuropsychological Society, 11*(3), 215–227.

Belanger, H. G., & Vanderploeg, R. D. (2005). The neuropsychological impact of sport-related concussion: A meta-analysis. *Journal of the International Neuropsychological Society, 11*(4), 345–357.

Belanger, H. G., Vanderploeg, R. D., Curtiss, G., & Warden, D. L. (2007). Recent neuroimaging techniques in mild traumatic brain injury. *Journal of Neuropsychiatry and Clinical Neurosciences, 19*(1), 5–20.

Bigler, E. D. (2004). Neuropsychological results and neuropathological findings at autopsy in a case of mild traumatic brain injury. *Journal of the International Neuropsychological Society, 10*(5), 794–806.

Bigler, E. D. (2005). Structural neuroimaging in traumatic brain injury. In J. M. Sliver, T. W. McAllister, & S. C. Yudofsky (Eds.), *Textbook of traumatic brain injury.* Washington, DC: American Psychiatric Press.

Binder, L. M. (1997). A review of mild head trauma. Part II: Clinical Implications. *Journal of Clinical and Experimental Neuropsychology, 19*(3), 432–457.

Binder, L. M., & Rohling, M. L. (1996). Money matters: A meta-analytic review of the effects of financial incentives on recovery after closed-head injury. *American Journal of Psychiatry, 153*(1), 7–10.

Binder, L. M., Rohling, M. L., & Larrabee, G. J. (1997a). A review of mild head trauma. Part I: Meta-analytic review of neuropsychological studies. *Journal of Clinical and Experimental Neuropsychology, 19,* 421–431.

Binder, L. M., Rohling, M. L., & Larrabee, G. J. (1997b). A review of mild head trauma. Part I: Meta-analytic review of neuropsychological studies. *Journal of Clinical and Experimental Neuropsychology, 19*(3), 421–431.

Blumbergs, P. C., Scott, G., Manavis, J., Wainwright, H., Simpson, D. A., & McLean, A. J. (1994). Staining of amyloid precursor protein to study axonal damage in mild head injury. *Lancet, 344*(8929), 1055–1056.

Blumbergs, P. C., Scott, G., Manavis, J., Wainwright, H., Simpson, D. A., & McLean, A. J. (1995). Topography of axonal injury as defined by amyloid precursor protein and the sector scoring method in mild and severe closed head injury. *Journal of Neurotrauma, 12*(4), 565–572.

Borg, J., Holm, L., Peloso, P. M., Cassidy, J. D., Carroll, L. J., von Holst, H., et al. (2004). Non-surgical intervention and cost for mild traumatic brain injury: Results of the WHO Collaborating Centre Task Force on Mild Traumatic Brain Injury. *Journal of Rehabilitation Medicine, 43*(Suppl), 76–83.

Borgaro, S. R., Prigatano, G. P., Kwasnica, C., & Rexer, J. L. (2003). Cognitive and affective sequelae in complicated and uncomplicated mild traumatic brain injury. *Brain Injury, 17*(3), 189–198.

Buki, A., & Povlishock, J. T. (2006). All roads lead to disconnection? Traumatic axonal injury revisited. *Acta Neurochirurgica (Wien), 148*(2), 181–193; discussion 193–184.

Carroll, L. J., Cassidy, J. D., Peloso, P. M., Borg, J., von Holst, H., Holm, L., et al. (2004). Prognosis for mild traumatic brain injury: Results of the WHO Collaborating Centre Task Force on Mild Traumatic Brain Injury. *Journal of Rehabilitation Medicine, 43*(Suppl), 84–105.

Chen, J. K., Johnston, K. M., Frey, S., Petrides, M., Worsley, K., & Ptito, A. (2004). Functional abnormalities in symptomatic concussed athletes: An fMRI study. *Neuroimage, 22*(1), 68–82.

Chen, J. K., Johnston, K. M., Petrides, M., & Ptito, A. (2008). Recovery from mild head injury in sports: Evidence from serial functional magnetic resonance imaging studies in male athletes. *Clinical Journal of Sport Medicine, 18*(3), 241–247.

Christensen, H., Griffiths, K., Mackinnon, A., & Jacomb, P. (1997). A quantitative review of cognitive deficits in depression and Alzheimer-type dementia. *Journal of the International Neuropsychological Society, 3*(6), 631–651.

Cline, D. M., & Whitley, T. W. (1988). Observation of head trauma patients at home: A prospective study of compliance in the rural south. *Annals of Emergency Medicine, 17*(2), 127–131.

Collins, M. W., Iverson, G. L., Gaetz, M., & Lovell, M. (2007). Sport-related concussion. In N. Zasler, D. Katz, & R. Zafonte (Eds.), *Brain injury medicine: Principles and practice* (pp. 407–421). New York: Demos Medical Publishing.

Comper, P., Bisschop, S. M., Carnide, N., & Tricco, A. (2005). A systematic review of treatments for mild traumatic brain injury. *Brain Injury, 19*(11), 863–880.

Dikmen, S., Machamer, J., Winn, H. R., & Temkin, N. (1995). Neuropsychological outcome at one-year post head injury. *Neuropsychology, 9*, 80–90.

Dikmen, S., McLean, A., & Temkin, N. (1986). Neuropsychological and psychosocial consequences of minor head injury. *Journal of Neurology, Neurosurgery and Psychiatry, 49*(11), 1227–1232.

Farkas, O., & Povlishock, J. T. (2007). Cellular and subcellular change evoked by diffuse traumatic brain injury: A complex web of change extending far beyond focal damage. *Progress in Brain Research, 161*, 43–59.

Frazier, T. W., Demaree, H. A., & Youngstrom, E. A. (2004). Meta-analysis of intellectual and neuropsychological test performance in attention-deficit/hyperactivity disorder. *Neuropsychology, 18*(3), 543–555.

Frencham, K. A., Fox, A. M., & Maybery, M. T. (2005). Neuropsychological studies of mild traumatic brain injury: A meta-analytic review of research since 1995. *Journal of Clinical and Experimental Neuropsychology, 27*(3), 334–351.

Garraway, M., & Macleod, D. (1995). Epidemiology of rugby football injuries. *Lancet, 345*(8963), 1485–1487.

Giza, C. C., & Hovda, D. A. (2001). The neurometabolic cascade of concussion. *Journal of Athletic Training, 36*(3), 228–235.

Goodman, Y., & Mattson, M. P. (1994). Staurosporine and K-252 compounds protect hippocampal neurons against amyloid beta-peptide toxicity and oxidative injury. *Brain Research, 650*(1), 170–174.

Grant, I., Gonzalez, R., Carey, C. L., Natarajan, L., & Wolfson, T. (2003). Non-acute (residual) neurocognitive effects of cannabis use: A meta-analytic study. *Journal of the International Neuropsychological Society, 9*(5), 679–689.

Griesbach, G. S., Gomez-Pinilla, F., & Hovda, D. A. (2004a). The upregulation of plasticity-related proteins following TBI is disrupted with acute voluntary exercise. *Brain Research, 1016*(2), 154–162.

Griesbach, G. S., Gomez-Pinilla, F., & Hovda, D. A. (2007). Time window for voluntary exercise-induced increases in hippocampal neuroplasticity molecules after traumatic brain injury is severity dependent. *Journal of Neurotrauma, 24*(7), 1161–1171.

Griesbach, G. S., Hovda, D. A., Gomez-Pinilla, F., & Sutton, R. L. (2008). Voluntary exercise or amphetamine treatment, but not the combination, increases hippocampal brain-derived neurotrophic factor and synapsin I following cortical contusion injury in rats. *Neuroscience, 154*(2), 530–540.

Griesbach, G. S., Hovda, D. A., Molteni, R., Wu, A., & Gomez-Pinilla, F. (2004b). Voluntary exercise following traumatic brain injury: Brain-derived neurotrophic factor upregulation and recovery of function. *Neuroscience, 125*(1), 129–139.

Guskiewicz, K. M., McCrea, M., Marshall, S. W., Cantu, R. C., Randolph, C., Barr, W., et al. (2003). Cumulative effects associated with recurrent concussion in collegiate football players: The NCAA Concussion Study. *JAMA, 290*(19), 2549–2555.

Hammeke, T., McCrea, M., Verber, M., Durgerion, S., Olsen, G., Leo, P., et al. (2004). Functional magnetic resonance imaging after acute sports concussion. *Journal of the International Neuropsychological Society, 18*, 168.

Hoge, C. W., Auchterlonie, J. L., & Milliken, C. S. (2006). Mental health problems, use of mental health services, and attrition from military service after returning from deployment to Iraq or Afghanistan. *JAMA, 295*(9), 1023–1032.

Hoge, C. W., McGurk, D., Thomas, J. L., Cox, A. L., Engel, C. C., & Castro, C. A. (2008). Mild traumatic brain injury in U.S. warriors returning from Iraq. *New England Journal of Medicine, 358*(5), 453–463.

Holm, L., Cassidy, J. D., Carroll, L. J., & Borg, J. (2005). Summary of the WHO Collaborating Centre for Neurotrauma Task Force on Mild Traumatic Brain Injury. *Journal of Rehabilitation Medicine, 37*(3), 137–141.

Inglese, M., Benedetti, B., & Filippi, M. (2005). The relation between MRI measures of inflammation and neurodegeneration in multiple sclerosis. *Journal of Neurological Science, 233*(1–2), 15–19.

Iverson, G. L. (2005). Outcome from mild traumatic brain injury. *Current Opinion in Psychiatry, 18*(3), 301–317.

Iverson, G. L. (2006). Complicated vs uncomplicated mild traumatic brain injury: Acute neuropsychological outcome. *Brain Injury, 20*(13–14), 1335–1344.

Iverson, G. L., Brooks, B. L., Collins, M. W., & Lovell, M. R. (2006). Tracking neuropsychological recovery following concussion in sport. *Brain Injury, 20*(3), 245–252.

Iverson, G. L., Lange, R. T., Gaetz, M., & Zasler, N. D. (2007a). Mild TBI. In N. D. Zasler, D. I. Katz, & R. D. Zafonte (Eds.), *Brain injury medicine: Principles and practice* (pp. 333–371). New York: Demos Medical Publishing.

Iverson, G. L., Langlois, J. A., McCrea, M., & James, K. P. (2009). Challenges associated with post-deployment screening for mild traumatic brain injury in military personnel. *The Clinical Neuropsychologist, 23*(8), 1299–1314.

Iverson, G. L., Zasler, N. D., & Lange, R. T. (2007b). Post-concussive disorder. In N. D. Zasler, D. I. Katz, & R. D. Zafonte (Eds.), *Brain injury medicine: Principles and practice* (pp. 373–405). New York: Demos Medical Publishing.

Jantzen, K. J., Anderson, B., Steinberg, F. L., & Kelso, J. A. (2004). A prospective functional MR imaging study of mild traumatic brain injury in college football players. *AJNR American Journal of Neuroradiology, 25*(5), 738–745.

Kay, T., Harrington, D. E., Adams, R. E., Anderson, T. W., Berrol, S., Cicerone, K., et al. (1993). Definition of mild traumatic brain injury: Report from the Mild Traumatic Brain Injury Committee of the Head Injury Interdisciplinary Special Interest Group of the American Congress of Rehabilitation Medicine. *Journal of Head Trauma Rehabilitation, 8*(3), 86–87.

Kraus, M. F., Susmaras, T., Caughlin, B. P., Walker, C. J., Sweeney, J. A., & Little, D. M. (2007). White matter integrity and cognition in chronic traumatic brain injury: A diffusion tensor imaging study. *Brain, 130*(Pt 10), 2508–2519.

Kurca, E., Sivak, S., & Kucera, P. (2006). Impaired cognitive functions in mild traumatic brain injury patients with normal and pathologic magnetic resonance imaging. *Neuroradiology, 48*(9), 661–669.

Landre, N., Poppe, C. J., Davis, N., Schmaus, B., & Hobbs, S. E. (2006). Cognitive functioning and postconcussive symptoms in trauma patients with and without mild TBI. *Archives of Clinical Neuropsychology, 21*(4), 255–273.

Larrabee, G. J. (1997). Neuropsychological outcome, post concussion symptoms, and forensic considerations in mild closed head trauma. *Seminars in Clinical Neuropsychiatry, 2*(3), 196–206.

Levin, H. S., Mattis, S., Ruff, R. M., Eisenberg, H. M., Marshall, L. F., Tabaddor, K., et al. (1987). Neurobehavioral outcome following minor head injury: A three-center study. *Journal of Neurosurgery, 66*(2), 234–243.

Levine, B., Fujiwara, E., O'Connor, C., Richard, N., Kovacevic, N., Mandic, M., et al. (2006). In vivo characterization of traumatic brain injury neuropathology with structural and functional neuroimaging. *Journal of Neurotrauma, 23*(10), 1396–1411.

Lidvall, H. F., Linderoth, B., & Norlin, B. (1974a). Causes of the post-concussional syndrome. *Acta Neurologica Scandinavica, 56*(Suppl), 3–144.

Lidvall, H. F., Linderoth, B., & Norlin, B. (1974b). Causes of the post-concussional syndrome: IX. Psychological tests. *Acta Neurologica Scandinavica, 50*, 64–71.

Lovell, M. R., Collins, M. W., Iverson, G. L., Field, M., Maroon, J. C., Cantu, R., et al. (2003). Recovery from mild concussion in high school athletes. *Journal of Neurosurgery, 98*(2), 296–301.

Lovell, M. R., Pardini, J. E., Welling, J., Collins, M. W., Bakal, J., Lazar, N., et al. (2007). Functional brain abnormalities are related to clinical recovery and time to return-to-play in athletes. *Neurosurgery, 61*(2), 352–359; discussion 359–360.

Lowdon, I. M., Briggs, M., & Cockin, J. (1989). Post-concussional symptoms following minor head injury. *Injury, 20*(4), 193–194.

Macciocchi, S. N., Barth, J. T., Alves, W., Rimel, R. W., & Jane, J. A. (1996). Neuropsychological functioning and recovery after mild head injury in collegiate athletes. *Neurosurgery, 39*(3), 510–514.

Majerske, C. W., Mihalik, J. P., Ren, D., Collins, M. W., Reddy, C. C., Lovell, M. R., et al. (2008). Concussion in sports: Postconcussive activity levels, symptoms, and neurocognitive performance. *Journal of Athletic Training, 43*(3), 265–274.

McAllister, T. W., Flashman, L. A., McDonald, B. C., & Saykin, A. J. (2006). Mechanisms of working memory dysfunction after mild and moderate TBI: Evidence from functional MRI and neurogenetics. *Journal of Neurotrauma, 23*(10), 1450–1467.

McAllister, T. W., Saykin, A. J., Flashman, L. A., Sparling, M. B., Johnson, S. C., Guerin, S. J., et al. (1999). Brain activation during working memory 1 month after mild traumatic brain injury: A functional MRI study. *Neurology, 53*(6), 1300–1308.

McAllister, T. W., Sparling, M. B., Flashman, L. A., Guerin, S. J., Mamourian, A. C., & Saykin, A. J. (2001). Differential working memory load effects after mild traumatic brain injury. *Neuroimage, 14*(5), 1004–1012.

McCrea, M. (2007). *Mild traumatic brain injury and post-concussion syndrome: The new evidence base for diagnosis and treatment.*. New York: Oxford University Press.

McCrea, M., Guskiewicz, K. M., Marshall, S. W., Barr, W., Randolph, C., Cantu, R. C., et al. (2003). Acute effects and recovery time following concussion in collegiate football players: The NCAA Concussion Study. *JAMA, 290*(19), 2556–2563.

McCrea, M., Pliskin, N., Barth, J., Cox, D., Fink, J., French, L., et al. (2008). Official position of the military TBI task force on the role of neuropsychology and rehabilitation psychology in the evaluation, management, and research of military veterans with traumatic brain injury. *Clinical Neuropsychology, 22*(1), 10–26.

McCrory, P., Johnston, K., Meeuwisse, W., Aubry, M., Cantu, R., Dvorak, J., et al. (2005). Summary and agreement statement of the 2nd International Conference on Concussion in Sport, Prague 2004. *British Journal of Sports Medicine, 39*(4), 196–204.

McCrory, P. R., Ariens, T., & Berkovic, S. F. (2000). The nature and duration of acute concussive symptoms in Australian football. *Clinical Journal of Sport Medicine, 10*(4), 235–238.

McGowan, J. C., Yang, J. H., Plotkin, R. C., Grossman, R. I., Umile, E. M., Cecil, K. M., et al. (2000). Magnetization transfer imaging in the detection of injury associated with mild head trauma. *AJNR American Journal of Neuroradiology, 21*(5), 875–880.

McLean Jr, A., Temkin, N. R., Dikmen, S., & Wyler, A. R. (1983). The behavioral sequelae of head injury. *Journal of Clinical Neuropsychology, 5*(4), 361–376.

Moser, R. S., Iverson, G. L., Echemendia, R. J., Lovell, M. R., Schatz, P., Webbe, F. M., et al. (2007). Neuropsychological evaluation in the diagnosis and management of sport-related concussion. *Archives of Clinical Neuropsychology, 22*(8), 909–916.

Niogi, S. N., Mukherjee, P., Ghajar, J., Johnson, C. E., Kolster, R., Lee, H., et al. (2008a). Structural dissociation of attentional control and memory in adults with and without mild traumatic brain injury. *Brain, 131*(Pt 12), 3209–3221.

Niogi, S. N., Mukherjee, P., Ghajar, J., Johnson, C., Kolster, R. A., Sarkar, R., et al. (2008b). Extent of microstructural white matter injury in postconcussive syndrome correlates with impaired cognitive reaction time: A 3T diffusion tensor imaging study of mild traumatic brain injury. *AJNR American Journal of Neuroradiology, 29*(5), 967–973.

Oppenheimer, D. R. (1968). Microscopic lesions in the brain following head injury. *Journal of Neurology, Neurosurgery and Psychiatry, 31*(4), 299–306.

Paniak, C., Phillips, K., Toller-Lobe, G., Durand, A., & Nagy, J. (1999). Sensitivity of three recent questionnaires to mild traumatic brain injury-related effects. *Journal of Head Trauma Rehabilitation, 14*(3), 211–219.

Paniak, C., Reynolds, S., Phillips, K., Toller-Lobe, G., Melnyk, A., & Nagy, J. (2002). Patient complaints within 1 month of mild traumatic brain injury: A controlled study. *Archives of Clinical Neuropsychology, 17*(4), 319–334.

Ponsford, J. (2006). Rehabilitation interventions after mild head injury. *Current Opinions in Neurology, 18*, 692–697.

Raghupathi, R. (2004). Cell death mechanisms following traumatic brain injury. *Brain Pathology, 14*(2), 215–222.

Riemann, B. L., & Guskiewicz, K. M. (2002). Effects of mild head injury on postural stability as measured through clinical balance testing. *Journal of Athletic Training, 35*, 19–25.

Schretlen, D. J., & Shapiro, A. M. (2003). A quantitative review of the effects of traumatic brain injury on cognitive functioning. *International Review of Psychiatry, 15*(4), 341–349.

Teasdale, G., & Jennett, B. (1974). Assessment of coma and impaired consciousness; a practical scale. *Lancet, 2*, 81–84.

Vickery, C. D., Berry, D. T., Inman, T. H., Harris, M. J., & Orey, S. A. (2001). Detection of inadequate effort on neuropsychological testing: A meta-analytic review of selected procedures. *Archives of Clinical Neuropsychology, 16*(1), 45–73.

Williams, D. H., Levin, H. S., & Eisenberg, H. M. (1990). Mild head injury classification. *Neurosurgery, 27*(3), 422–428.

THE NEW NEUROSCIENCE FRONTIER: PROMOTING NEUROPLASTICITY AND BRAIN REPAIR IN TRAUMATIC BRAIN INJURY

Philip DeFina[1], Jonathan Fellus[2], Mary Zemyan Polito[1], James W. G. Thompson[1], Rosemarie Scolaro Moser[3], and John DeLuca[4]

[1]International Brain Research Foundation, Edison, NJ, [2]Kessler Institute for Rehabilitation, West Orange, NJ, [3]RSM Psychology Center, LLC, Lawrenceville, NJ, and [4]Kessler Foundation Research Center, West Orange, NJ, USA

Increased awareness of traumatic brain injury (TBI) in the military, a persistent call for evidence-based treatment, and recent government funding have revealed new research opportunities in neuroscience. This paper describes a relatively new frontier for research: that of the facilitation or enhancement of neuroplasticity and brain repair in TBI using novel treatment protocols. Such protocols, algorithmically introduced, may be tailored to the individual through the matching of neuromarkers with specific interventions. Examples of neuromarkers and interventions employed for the purpose of neuromodulation are reported. Problems with lack of controlled studies and inferring causation in correlational research are noted. Healthy skepticism and open-minded creativity are needed so that we can think in unorthodox ways, create partnerships, harness available knowledge and expertise, and ultimately develop effective treatments.

Keywords: Neuroplasticity; Neuromarkers; Neuromodulation.

INTRODUCTION

Frontiers in science and medicine are not uncommon, as they are the introduction and extension of any new, untapped field of learning or thought. The purpose of the present article is to indeed present a new frontier in neuroscience, which invites systematic investigation, empirical research, and standardized methods: the facilitation or optimization of neuroplasticity and brain cell repair in traumatic brain injury (TBI). Urgently spurred on by the needs of wounded military personnel and their families, and by the calls of the "Report of the International Conference on Behavioral Health and Traumatic Brain Injury" (2008) and the Congressional Task Force on Traumatic Brain Injury (see Pascrell, 2009

Address correspondence to: James W. G. Thompson, Ph.D., IBRF, 100 Menlo Park, Suite 412, Edison, NJ 08837, USA. E-mail: JThompson@IBRFinc.org

© 2009 Psychology Press, an imprint of the Taylor & Francis group, an Informa business

this issue) we, as neuroscientists, face an unprecedented opportunity to substantially advance our knowledge and treatment of brain injury.

Frontiers are often precipitated by major cultural or world events. The field of neuropsychology was so unleashed by the serendipitous experience of Alexander Luria's work with brain-injured soldiers for the Soviet military in World War II. As with all new scientific frontiers, skepticism and resistance may hinder the integration of novel schemata and anecdotal case studies into contemporary theoretical frameworks. Skepticism, applied in science, is a valuable attribute that provides safeguards. Luria and his mentor Lev Vygotsky, although restricted by the political philosophy of their times, inevitably challenged the psychological arenas of their era, moving from an introspective psychology to a new frontier that considered the sociocultural influences on cognition, and brain–behavior relationships (see Cole & Cole, 1979).

Similarly, in the 1940s Jerzy Konorski, a Polish neurophysiologist, forged the concept of brain "plasticity," suggesting that the brain has the ability to modify, strengthen, and create, as well as eliminate, synaptic connections in response to stimuli and life events (Zielinski, 2006). Hebb (1949) developed this concept further, describing "use-induced plasticity" of the nervous system, thus heralding a new frontier in brain science which resulted in the later discoveries of the importance of enriched environments on the developing brain (Rosenzweig & Bennett, 1996). The property of plasticity results from the broad connectional organization of the cortex and the capacity for activity-driven synaptic strength changes (Sanes & Donoghue, 2000). Plasticity can occur via four processes. First, unmasking can occur whereby neural pathways that had been kept dormant by inhibition are made functional by the removal of the inhibitory signal (Jacobs & Donoghue, 1991). Second, a strengthening or weakening of existing synapses can occur through the process of long-term potentiation (LTP) or long-term depression (LTD) (Hess, Aizenman, & Donoghue, 1996). Third, there can be a change in neuronal membrane excitability (Halter, Carr, & Wolpaw, 1995). Fourth, anatomical changes can occur such as the sprouting of new axon terminals or the formation of new synapses (Toni, Buchs, Nikonenko, Bron, & Muller, 1999). Currently, brain plasticity training and interventions are being developed in an effort to combat the downward spiral of negative plastic changes that occur in age-related functional decline (Mahncke, Bronstone, & Merzenrich, 2006). The idea that one might be similarly able to manipulate the brain's external and internal environments and affect neuroplasticity in patients with TBI follows logically and thus appears promising.

The current paper presents a glimpse of this concept of neuroplasticity and its role in a new frontier, healing injured brain cells. This new frontier will challenge our thinking and may require us to table some old notions, at least for now, in order to consider the possibility of being able to prevent neuroplasticity degradation that follows TBI and to promote recovery of injured brain cells through novel treatments.

A CALL FOR RESEARCH AND TREATMENT

The wars in Iraq and Afghanistan are major world events that currently provide an increased awareness of the enduring and devastating effects of TBI. Medical and health care advances have decreased the rate of mortality in trauma cases. Whereas it was an average of 45 days before a soldier wounded in the Vietnam conflict returned to the continental United States for medical treatment, a soldier wounded in Iraq may arrive at the Landstuhl trauma center in Germany in as little as 12 hours and then be transported home to the United States within a period of 3 days (Hyer, 2006). Survival rate for the Vietnam conflict is documented at 76% compared to the rate for the current wars in Iraq and Afghanistan, which is at 90.5% (Hyer, 2006).

With improved trauma care, those individuals who survive the most serious injuries are left to manage neurological disorders and impairment. For cases of mild TBI that do not resolve, the effects may not seem readily visible but are nonetheless far-reaching, affecting loved ones, family, friends, and community, and often resulting in chronic unemployment, increased hospitalizations, homelessness, substance abuse, and suicide (Kube & Johnson, 2009). Similarly, the opposite end of the severity spectrum of TBI, comprised of severe disorders of consciousness (SDOC), traumatizes family members, drains the hospital care system, and tears at the fabric of our greater society.

Injuries sustained by military service members in Operation Enduring Freedom and Operation Iraqi Freedom have prompted the United States Congress and the Department of Defense to take swift action, searching for effective evidence based treatments for traumatic brain injury (see Department of Defense, 2009). With millions of dollars allocated toward the assessment and treatment of wounded warriors and their families, frustration has been mounting as to whether scientists, clinicians, technologists, and others are truly able to provide answers, "cures," and deliverables. The pressure is on the scientific community, whether the military, private, or non-profit sectors, to generate innovative, novel approaches that are scientifically validated and maximally effective. Recently, scientists have the prospect of unprecedented access to government funding sources to facilitate breakthroughs and conduct research that will lead us down new treatment pathways and render benefits for all those who suffer from TBI.

The International Conference on Behavioral Health and Traumatic Brain Injury provided a think-tank platform for the presentation of state-of-the-art, forward thinking about ways to address the problems of TBI, not only in the military, but also in the large civilian community. The creation of this venue was in part fueled by families and loved ones of wounded warriors who are desperate to access the products of translational research in their search for hope, and who are often willing to try any reasonable treatment possibility.

There are many experimental treatments being employed to address the entire spectrum of brain injury, from severe disorders of consciousness and acute injury to mild TBI/concussion. What is currently needed is to validate the clinical and translational work on neuroplasticity that is being conducted globally, so that we can expedite treatment in an evidence-based manner. We are called to build this bridge, starting with anecdotal, variably controlled, small research or case studies and treatments (see Whyte et al., 2005). The goal is to create a menu of operationalized and standardized treatment algorithms. This bridge, however, requires a theoretical framework from which to draw hypotheses. One such framework is that of the identification of a spectrum of neuromarkers to guide treatment, and the utilization of a complex menu of neuromodulation and other interventions, to normalize brain functions and promote neuroplasticity and brain cell repair: the new neuroscience frontier.

A NOVEL TREATMENT FRAMEWORK

How can we facilitate recovery of neuroplasticity in TBI? We assume that we cannot bring back the function of dead brain cells. However, is it possible to normalize the brain environment, electrochemically and metabolically? Perhaps by establishing a more normalized environment, the brain may be better able to reorganize itself, resulting in quicker recovery, decreased cell death, and the re-emergence of lost functions. The idea is to (1) identify neuromarkers, such as specific neurotransmitters or hormones, for example, that are directly related to the biochemical cascade of TBI, (2) validate specific interventions, such as neuromodulation (e.g., use of electromagnetic stimulation), cognitive rehabilitation, off-label pharmaceuticals (that target neurotransmitters), nutraceuticals (such as vitamins, minerals, proteins, amino acids), median nerve stimulation, and neurofeedback, which might be effective in normalizing those neuromarkers within the brain environment, and (3) determine the safety, efficacy and affordability of these new treatment protocols through controlled, blinded studies. Thus, treatment would consist of identifying/quantifying neuromarkers in the injured brain, and then individualizing multimodal interventions that would normalize the brain environment so that it would maximize natural healing, in turn facilitating rehabilitation and neuromodulation.

The concept of tailoring treatments to patient characteristics is gaining great attention internationally (Gordon, 2007; The Royal Society, 2005) especially in the arena of pharmacogenomics, in which pharmaceutical treatments are matched to the patient's genetic traits via identification and use of biomarkers. However, it has been difficult to conduct well-controlled studies on individualized treatments, as each patient may possess a different set of traits and thus receive a unique set of applied interventions.

The use of markers to identify and guide treatment is a relatively new approach in the history of medicine, beginning with the focus on single biomarkers and specifically applied pharmacotherapy intervention, such as in the case of the antibody drug breast-cancer treatment for women who exhibit the overly expressed human epidermal growth factor receptor 2 (HER2) (Gordon, 2007). What is novel about the treatment approach presented here is that it builds on our more recent knowledge of the brain chemical cascade, focuses on TBI, and proposes to integrate numerous diagnostic, cutting edge tools to guide new innovative, advanced diagnostic and treatment protocols that are currently being developed (Dingfelder, 2009).

Identifying neuromarkers

The seminal work regarding the relationship between the apolipoprotein E (APOE) allele and the risk of developing Alzheimer's disease helped to usher in the concept that we can identify genetic brain markers that may predict cognitive disorders (Saunders et al., 1993). Building on that discovery, there is evidence that the use of functional magnetic resonance imaging (fMRI) technology and the identification of APOE (3 and 4 alleles) may predict memory decline in individuals (Bookheimer et al., 2000). The latter authors reported that "Patterns of brain activation during tasks requiring memory differ depending on the genetic risk of Alzheimer's disease and may predict a subsequent decline in memory" (p. 450). The identification of neuromarkers has also been demonstrated by single photon emission computed tomography (SPECT) and positron emission tomography (PET) measurements of neurotransmitters for the differential diagnosis of Parkinson's disease (Ilgin, 1998). Similarly, the attention deficit hyperactivity disorder (ADHD) research abounds with searches for brain patterns that may serve as diagnostic markers. Hermens and his coauthors (2005) documented correlations between specific electroencephalographic indices (resting EEG theta activity) and accuracy/reaction time on cognitive tasks that differentiated children with and without ADHD. The more recent discovery that (cerebrospinal fluid) CSF tau may predict the post-1 year outcome of those patients with severe TBI is groundbreaking (Ost et al., 2006). Not surprisingly, it has been posited that it could lead to a "routine clinical test" as a biochemical predictor of brain trauma severity, noted by James Kelly, MD (Goodman, 2008).

We have come to understand the chemical cascade of TBI (Giza & Hovda, 2001) that reveals a disturbance of the potassium, sodium, and calcium ion balance, as well as the occurrence of hyperglycolosis, glutamate alterations, decreased oxygen, and apoptosis. This astute, methodical research imposed a paradigmatic shift in our thinking about TBI. It now provides the foundation for identifying relevant neuromarkers and discovering treatments to prevent and repair traumatically induced damage. Once theoretical questions are now yielding to action-oriented translational research aimed at improving CNS bloodflow, oxygenation, and nutritional blood supply. Current and future studies will focus on this metabolic cascade, whether trying to prevent it, halt it, or reverse it by targeting neuromarkers with novel interventions to facilitate neurorecovery.

Nevertheless, accurately identifying neuromarkers and determining their sensitivity and specificity is a formidable challenge. For example, the problem of identifying neurofibrillary tangles and senile plaques in Alzheimer's disease is well known. Imaging techniques are hampered by the lack of suitable agents that can cross the blood brain barrier (Backsai & Klunk, 2002). Identifying brain activation patterns is replete with methodological issues when using MRI measures: scanner sensitivity, accuracy of signal measure, movement of the individual (Bookheimer et al., 2000).

Despite these difficulties, in the last couple of decades we have become better at identifying and measuring biomarkers. We can measure O_2, glucose consumption, neurotransmitters, and electro-chemical and spectral brain activity. We also have advanced technologies that provide us with extensive data that still may not be well understood or explained by standard theoretical frameworks. The brain can be assessed in a multitude of ways that go beyond the scope of the present article: PET, SPECT, magnetic resonance spectroscopy (MRS), quantitative magnetic resonance imaging (MRI), diffusion tensor imaging (DTI), functional MRI, magnetoencephalography (MEG), evoked and event-related potentials, near infra-red spectroscopy, autonomic nervous system (ANS) mapping, and bispectral index (BIS) monitoring, as well as by cognitive rating scales and neuropsychological testing. Importantly, neuromarkers identify preserved functions, and if accurately defined, may be able to guide us to develop prescriptive interventions.

Identifying interventions

Many of the myriad interventions mentioned above have been used to facilitate neuroplasticity and remediate CNS dysfunction both in published studies (Boggio et al., 2007; Liepert, 2005; Reis et al., 2008), as well as in studies that have been underway over the past few years (P. DeFina & J. Fellus, personal communication, April 20, 2009). Understandably, those interventions that are non-invasive tend to exhibit many advantages over those that are invasive. Non-invasive techniques tend to be easier to implement, with less physical risk and fewer liability concerns, less arduous IRB clearance, and lower cost than, for example, deep brain stimulation. Such techniques have already demonstrated value in the recovery of motor functions related to stroke. There is promising evidence that non-invasive transcranial magnetic stimulation (TMS) improves motor recovery (Liepert, 2003), and may have other applications (Silvanto & Pascual-Leone, 2008). Transcranial direct current stimulation (tDCS) has shown promise in motor improvement in post stroke cases (Boggio et al., 2007). This approach to motor recovery may guide the development of an application for cognitive recovery.

Non-invasive techniques such as quantitative EEG (QEEG) and MEG, which provide indices of amplitude, phase lag (speed of signal), frequency, and coherence, can be employed not only in the identification of neuromarkers but also to help guide non-invasive interventions. Yet the lack of rigorous controls in this area of electrical research is problematic. For example, in a study of participants with mild TBI or ADHD who received 20 sessions of cognitive retraining and EEG biofeedback, positive results were reported on measures of attention and response accuracy employing the Intermediate Visual and Auditory Continuous Response Test (Tinius & Tinius, 2000). Yet this study's serious limitations include lack of a placebo condition, and the inability to differentiate the individual efficacy of each intervention. However, recent work using randomized controlled research is promising in the validation of the effectiveness of EEG biofeedback, and overcoming the shortfalls of previous, mainly clinical, findings (Gevensleben et al., 2009).

In their review of the literature on transcranial magnetic stimulation and cortical mechanisms of motor control, Reis and her co-authors (2008, p. 354) elucidate some of the common pitfalls in the published research:

> ...the specific relationship between physiological changes and motor behavior remains elusive...more work is needed to prove that the associations between specific functional interactions and behavior represent more than mere epiphenomena of the specific behavior. The design of these types of experiments represents one of the crucial challenges ahead of us.

Indeed, McCallister (2009 this issue) has posed the dilemma of using correlational indicators or markers for the psychopharmacotherapy of TBI and post traumatic stress disorder (PTSD). We may choose medications in an effort to alter the indicators or markers of a disorder, but that does not necessarily mean that we are altering the patient's outcome or functions. Simply put, causality is difficult to determine.

Facing the frontier

Partnerships and consortia around the world, from Charlottesville to Tokyo, are addressing the most severe disorders of consciousness with advanced treatment protocols (Cooper & Cooper, 2008). Such creative, scientific partnerships are also needed to address the entire spectrum of TBI, from mild to most severe. There are TBI treatment protocols and advanced algorithms currently being implemented based on the framework of neuromodulation of neuromarkers (P. DeFina & J. Fellus, personal communication, April 20, 2009). These protocols and algorithms remain in their infancy. Since these novel algorithms are in their early stages of development, clinicians may disregard them as scientifically unvalidated. But what is needed is to harness the relevant global knowledge and expertise to rigorously test such protocols. The Department of Defense and Congress are ready to support such scientific, collaborative ventures (Department of Defense, 2009; Report of the International Conference on Traumatic Brain Injury and Behavioral Health, 2008). Importantly, no one discipline or technology can do this. With sophisticated modes of communication, scientists and laboratories do not need to be isolated in their clinical trials. We can bring together multidisciplinary teams of scientists: neuropsychologists, neurologists, neurosurgeons, physiatrists, physicists, mathematicians, chemists, engineers, and others to develop an interdisciplinary approach to the treatment of TBI and to the facilitation of neuroplasticity. In working with international partners we will need to be culturally sensitive to, and respectful of, different ways of conducting research, and different ways of thinking and taking risks.

We are at a neuroscience crossroad. Do we continue to be bound to a routine, linear paradigm or do we consider novel, experimental, and simultaneous, multimodal ideas? Can we balance our skepticism with open-mindedness to an algorithm buttressed by creativity and solution generation? We bear a serious responsibility to our wounded military service members and their families who search for hope, but who should not be led on by interventions that have no evidence base. We need to better understand the mechanisms and parameters of brain function, derive specific data to guide evidence-based treatment, and more accurately predict outcomes. The current opportunities for research and development of new treatments, within this burgeoning frontier, will serve to improve the lives of all those who suffer from brain injury.

REFERENCES

Bacskai, B. J., & Klunk, W. E. (2002). Imaging amyloid-beta deposits *in vivo*. *Journal of Cerebral Blood Flow Metabolism, 22*(9), 1035–1041.

Boggio, P. S., Nunes, A., Rigonatti, S. P., Nitsche, M. A., Pascual-Leone, A., & Fregni, F. (2007). Repeated sessions of non-invasive brain DC stimulation is associated with motor function improvement in stroke patients. *Restorative Neurology and Neuroscience, 25*(2), 123–129.

Bookheimer, S. Y., Strojwas, M. H., Cohen, M. S., Saunders, A. M., Pericak-Vance, M. A., Mazziotta, J. C., et al. (2000). Patterns of brain activation in people at risk for Alzheimer's disease. *The New England Journal of Medicine, 343*(7), 450–455.

Cole, M., & Cole, S. (Eds.). (1979). *The making of mind: A personal account of Soviet psychology, A. R. Luria.* Cambridge, MA: Harvard University Press.

Cooper, E., & Cooper, B. (2008). *Right median nerve stimulation for treatment of coma states.* Unpublished manuscript, North Carolina, USA. [www.headwayhomes.org]

Department of Defense (2009). *A new era of responsibility: Funding highlights.* Washington, DC: http://www.whitehouse.gov/omb/assets/fy2010_new_era/Department_of_Defense.pdf

Dingfelder, S. F. (2009). From the research lab to the operating room. *Monitor on Psychology*, March, 40–43.

Gevensleben, H., Holl, B., Albrecht, B., Vogel, C., Schlamp, D., Kratz, O., et al. (2009). Is neurofeedback an efficacious treatment for ADHD? A randomized controlled clinical trial. *The Journal of Child Psychology and Psychiatry, 50*(7), 780–789.

Giza, C. C., & Hovda, D. A. (2001). The neurometabolic cascade of concussion. *Journal of Athletic Training, 36*(3), 228–235.

Goodman, A. (2008). CSF brain tau predicts outcome in severe traumatic brain injury. *Neurology Today.* Retrieved November 21, 2008 from http://www.neurotodayonline.com/pt/re/neurotoday/fulltext.00132985-200611210-00008.html

Gordon, E. (2007). Personalized medicine. *Future Medicine, 4*(2), 201–215.

Halter, J. A., Carp, J. S., & Wolpaw, J. R. (1995). Operantly conditioned motoneuron plasticity: Possible role of sodium channels. *Journal of Neurophysiology, 73*, 867–871.

Hebb, D. O. (1949). *The organization of behavior.* New York: Wiley.

Hermens, D. F., Soei, E. X. C., Clarke, S. D., Kohn, M. R., Gordon, E., & Williams, L. M. (2005). Resting EEG theta activity predicts cognitive performance in attention-deficit hyperactivity disorder. *Pediatric Neurology, 34*(4), 248–256.

Hess, G., Aizenman, C. D., & Donoghue, J. P. (1996). Conditions for the induction of longterm potentiation in layer II/III horizontal connections of the rat motor cortex. *Journal of Neurophysiology, 75*, 1765–1778.

Hyer, R. (March 27, 2006). Iraq and Afghanistan producing new pattern of extremity war injuries. *MedScape Medical News.* Available from http://www.medscape.com/viewarticle/528624

Ilgin, N. (1998). Functional imaging of neurotransmitter systems in movement disorders. *Quarterly Journal of Nuclear Medicine, 42*(3), 179–192.

Jacobs, K. M., & Donoghue, J. P. (1991). Reshaping the cortical motor map by unmasking latent intracortical connections. *Science, 251*, 944–947.

Kube, C., & Johnson, A. (2009). *Suicides continue alarming rise in military.* Retrieved January 29, 2009 from http://www.msnbc.msn.com/id/28895624

Liepert, J. (2003). TMS in Stroke. *Supplements of Clinical Neurophysiology, 56*, 368–380.

Liepert, J. (2005). Transcranial magnetic stimulation in neurorehabilitation. *Acta Neurochirurgica, 93*, 71–74.

Mahncke, H. W., Bronstone, A., & Merzenich, M. M. (2006). Brain plasticity and functional losses in the aged: Scientific bases for a novel intervention. *Progress in Brain Research, 157*, 81–109.

McCallister, T. (2009). Psychopharmacological issues in the treatment of mild TBI and PTSD. *The Clinical Neuropsychologist, 23*(8), 1338–1367.

Ost, M., Nylen, K., Ohrfelt, A. O., Tullberg, M., Wikkelson, C., Nellgard, P., et al. (2006). Initial CSF total tau correlates with 1-year outcome in patients with traumatic brain injury. *Neurology, 67*, 1600–1604.

Pascrell, B. (2009). Introduction to the report of the international conference on behavioral health and traumatic brain injury. *The Clinical Neuropsychologist*, *23*(8), 1281–1290.

Reis, J., Swayne, O. B., Vandermeeren, Y., Camus, M., Dimyan, M. A., Harris-Love, M., et al. (2008). Contribution of transcranial magnetic stimulation to the understanding of cortical mechanisms involved in motor control. *The Journal of Physiology*, *586*(2), 325–351.

Report of the International Conference on Traumatic Brain Injury and Behavioral Health (November 19, 2008). Paterson, NJ: St. Joseph's Regional Medical Center.

Rosenzwieg, M. R., & Bennett, E. L. (1996). Psychobiology of plasticity: Effects of training and experience on brain and behavior. *Behavioural Brain Research*, *78*(1), 57–65.

Sanes, J. N., & Donoghue, J. P. (2000). Plasticity and primary motor cortex. *Annual Review of Neuroscience*, *23*, 393–415.

Saunders, A. M., Strittmatter, W. J., Schmechel, D., St. George-Hyslop, P. H., Pericak-Vance, M. A., Joo, S. H., et al. (1993). Association of apolipoprotein E allele epsilon 4 with late-onset familial and sporadic Alzheimer's disease. *Neurology*, *43*, 1467–1472.

Silvanto, J., & Pascual-Leone, A. (2008). State-dependency of transcranial magnetic stimulation. *Brain Topography*, *21*(1), 1–10.

The Royal Society (2005). *Personalised medicine: Hopes and realities*. London: The Royal Society. www.royalsoc.ac.uk/displaypagedoc.asp?id=15874

Tinius, T., & Tinius, K. (2000). Changes after EEG biofeedback and cognitive retraining in adults with mild traumatic brain injury and attention deficit disorder. *Journal of Neurotherapy*, *4*(2), 27–44.

Toni, N., Buchs, P. A., Nikonenko, I., Bron, C. R., & Muller, D. (1999). LTP promotes formation of multiple spine synapses between a single axon terminal and a dendrite. *Nature*, *402*, 421–425.

Whyte, J., Katz, D., Long, D., DiPasquale, M. C., Polansky, M., Kalmar, K., et al. (2005). Predictors of outcome in prolonged posttraumatic disorders of consciousness and assessment of medication effects: A multicenter study. *Archives of Physical Medicine Rehabilitation*, *86*, 453–462.

Zielinski, K. (2006). Jerzy Konorski on brain associations. *Acta Neurobiologiae Experimentalis*, *66*, 75–90.

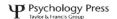

THE INTERACTION BETWEEN PSYCHOLOGICAL HEALTH AND TRAUMATIC BRAIN INJURY: A NEUROSCIENCE PERSPECTIVE

Stuart W. Hoffman[1] and Catherine Harrison[2]

[1]Henry M. Jackson Foundation for the Advancement of Military Medicine Defense and Veterans Brain Injury Center–Johnstown, PA and [2]Air Force Research Laboratory, Wright Patterson Air Force Base, OH, USA

The occurrence of traumatic brain injury (TBI) and psychological health issues in the current theater of military operations has become a major factor in planning for the long-term healthcare of our wounded warriors. Post-traumatic stress disorder (PTSD) can co-exist with brain injury in military members who have been exposed to blasts. Specific areas of the brain may be more susceptible to damage from blasts. In particular, damage to the prefrontal cortex can lead to disinhibition of cerebral structures that control fear and anxiety. Reactive systemic inflammatory processes related to TBI may also impair psychological health. Impaired psychological health may lead to increased psychological distress that impedes brain repair due to the release of stress-related hormones. Since the external environment has been shown to exert a significant influence on the internal environment of the organism, enriching the external environment may well reduce anxiety and facilitate the neuroplasticity of brain cells, thus promoting recovery of function after TBI.

Keywords: Brain injury; Post-traumatic stress disorder; Depression; Enriched environment; Inflammation.

INTRODUCTION

Psychological illnesses can be defined as behavioral manifestations of underlying disorders in physiological processes of the brain and/or endocrine systems. Jamesian theory posits that emotions are the mind's interpretation of internal physiological conditions that have resulted in reaction to a provocative external stimulus (Ellsworth, 1994). Thus, according to Jamesian theory, fear is not simply elicited by the sight of a ferocious bear. Rather the sight of the bear evokes a physiological response, which we subsequently interpret as fear. Our experience of fear arises from our interpretation of the internal physical sensations we experience: elevated adrenaline level, heartbeat, rapid breathing, etc. (Ellsworth, 1994).

Importantly, under some conditions, such as traumatic brain injury (TBI), the process by which we cognitively perceive our physiological states may become impaired so that even a minor change in a physiological state can produce an overly

---

Address correspondence to: Stuart W. Hoffman, Ph.D., Research Director, DVBIC–Johnstown, 109 Sunray Drive, Johnstown, PA 15905, USA. E-mail: shoffman@dvbic-lh.org

© 2009 Psychology Press, an imprint of the Taylor & Francis group, an Informa business

heightened emotional response. Such may be the case in the development of post-traumatic stress disorder (PTSD) in individuals who have suffered a TBI. Emotional responses, such as fear, are generated from some of the same brain and endocrine systems that are often affected by TBI (L. M. Williams et al., 2006). Proper functioning of these systems may be critical to recovery of both brain function and psychological health. Recovery of normal brain function and psychological health is complicated when conditions, such as PTSD, cause excessive and inappropriate activation of these systems, resulting in exaggerated emotional arousal and cognitive misperception (L. M. Williams et al., 2006). Interestingly, the timeline for the development of psychological symptoms appears to be different in TBI patients with PTSD compared to non-TBI patients with PTSD. Non-TBI patients have reported greater anxiety and more intrusive memories. Furthermore, the rate of intrusions decreased over time in non-TBI patients, but increased in those who had sustained a TBI (Bryant, 2001b).

Traumatic brain injury and psychological health issues within the current theater of military operations has become a major factor in planning for the long-term healthcare of our warriors. The present article will explore four topic areas related to TBI and psychological health:

(1) PTSD may be related to the type of brain injury sustained. There are areas of the brain that are more susceptible to damage from a blast. This is particularly true for cortical areas, such as those near the orbital sockets and nasal sinuses. Since the role of cortical areas is to inhibit subcortical structures and to integrate information, damage to susceptible cortical areas, in particular to the prefrontal cortex, can lead to disinhibition of the brain structures that regulate fear and anxiety responses.
(2) The systemic effects of TBI may create chronic conditions that affect psychological health. For example, chronic inflammatory processes in the brain may result in the presentation of depression.
(3) Endocrine responses to stress may directly impact reparative processes and psychological health.
(4) Environmental experiences may serve an important role in both the protection and repair of the brain and in maintenance of psychological health.

INJURY TO BRAIN STRUCTURES MAY RESULT IN PTSD

The role of physical damage to the central nervous system (CNS) in precipitating psychological health difficulties has been a controversial topic (Kennedy et al., 2007). Some believe TBI has the potential to mediate or even cause psychiatric conditions even without psychological trauma or environmental factors that are typically required to produce the conditions (Lux, 2007). Others believe that brain injury plays no direct causative role in the formation of, severity of, or persistence of psychological health issues (Meares et al., 2008). This dichotomous picture as to the role of brain injury in psychological health, presented by scientific literature, reflects a significant clash in points of view. Research on brain injury and psychological health supports the observation that both brain injury and psychological disorders are associated with common brain and endocrine system functioning (Beer, John, Scabini, & Knight, 2006; Jorge et al., 2004; Liston, McEwen, & Casey, 2009; Lux, 2007; Roberts et al., 2004).

In current military operations the wide use of improvised explosive devices (IEDs) and advancements in body armor have allowed personnel to survive situations that were not previously survivable (Martin, Lu, Helmick, French, & Warden, 2008). Blast wave energy hitting and penetrating the head can be focused by the structure of the skull (e.g., by the orbital sockets and sinuses) through to the underlying cortex (Saljo, Arrhen, Bolouri, Mayorga, & Hamberger, 2008; Taylor & Ford, 2008). Shearing forces at the interface of brain, dura mater, bone, and gray/white matter border can cause both localized and diffuse brain injury (D. F. Moore et al., 2009). In the area of the orbital frontal cortex blast forces can be focused by the orbital sockets and nasal sinuses to produce impairments associated with orbitofrontal cortex injury, including executive dysfunction and loss of inhibition.

Damage to the brain caused by TBI, including blast-related TBI, is not limited to the gray matter. Shearing can cause damage along the borders where white matter interfaces with gray matter (D. F. Moore et al., 2009). The loss of white matter structure can be seen in diffuse tensor imaging (DTI) (Niogi et al., 2008). DTI has revealed white matter loss in the frontal cortex of long-term survivors of TBI (Salmond et al., 2006). DTI performed on those suffering from post-concussive syndrome (PCS) indicates similar findings to those found in blast-related TBI, revealing fiber tracts that have relatively high diffusivity and low anisotrophy (Niogi et al., 2008). The relatively high diffusivity and low anisotrophy suggests that the myelin sheaths on these fiber tracts have lost their integrity, allowing water to diffuse equally in all directions, (such as occurs in gray matter fibers), rather than in distinct channels (as occurs in white matter fibers). This loss of fiber tract integrity impairs the connections from the orbitofrontal cortex to the subcortical structures, such as the amygdala. This results in a significant impairment of the healthy system by which an intact orbitofrontal cortex is able to monitor emotional signals from the amygdala and provide appropriate inhibitory and regulatory feedback.

In addition, damage to the prefrontal cortex can lead to disinhibition of responses to irrelevant stimuli (Beer et al., 2006; Roberts et al., 2004). Such prefrontal cortex damage can result in deficits in working memory, impairments in attention, and decreased inhibition of the amygdala, leading to emotional volatility and confabulation (Beer, Heerey, Keltner, Scabini, & Knight, 2003; Elzinga & Bremner, 2002; Metcalf, Langdon, & Coltheart, 2007). In PTSD similar deficits have been found (e.g., failure to inhibit irrelevant memories, working memory impairment, disinhibition of emotions, intrusive memories, and decreased ability in attention and concentration; van der Kolk, 2001).

Prefrontal cortex appears to play a central role in the processing of fear and anxiety (Sotres-Bayon, Cain, & LeDoux, 2006), with rich connections between prefrontal cortex and the amygdala (Alvarez, Biggs, Chen, Pine, & Grillon, 2008; Figueiredo, Bodie, Tauchi, Dolgas, & Herman, 2003). Prefrontal cortex hypoactivity and amygdala hyperactivity, as determined by fMRI and PET, has been found to occur in those individuals with PTSD-like symptoms. In animal models of PTSD there is hypotrophy of the dendritic trees of neurons found in the prefrontal cortex and hypertrophy of dendrites located in the amygdala. Roberts and colleagues (2004) discovered that lesions caused by trauma to the orbital prefrontal exhibit a significantly increased reactivity to unanticipated acoustic startle stimuli.

Thus, considering that a blast wave can be concentrated through the orbits and sinuses and onto the orbitofrontal cortex, a blast wave that is non-injurious to the body's exterior could conceivably be focused enough by the skull to injure the orbitofrontal cortex (Saljo et al., 2008; Taylor & Ford, 2008). The orbitofrontal cortex is critical to processing and inhibiting fear, and if damaged may produce psychological symptoms that are similar to PTSD, or that may aggravate or complicate recovery from PTSD. Thus it is problematic to study TBI in isolation of, or separately from, PTSD.

Clinicians have reasoned that PTSD can only exist when memories of the event are intact. However, there is an emerging literature suggesting that when the injury is severe enough to cause amnesia of the event, PTSD-like symptoms can still develop (Greenspan, Stringer, Phillips, Hammond, & Goldstein, 2006). Although loss of consciousness appears to have protective effects against the development of PTSD because the memory of the traumatic event does not exist (Bryant, 2001a), there are studies that have demonstrated that PTSD still occurs in some cases despite amnesia (Greenspan et al., 2006; Williams, Evans, Needham, & Wilson, 2002).

In a study by Glaesser, Neuner, Lutgehetmann, Schmidt, and Elbert (2004), no differences in levels of depression were reported between a group that had experienced loss of consciousness and a group that had not. The conscious group, however, reported greater levels of anxiety than did the group that had been unconscious. Furthermore, in a study by Bryant (2001b), in cases of suspected TBI, PTSD symptoms became apparent, and stronger over time, often months after the event. In cases in which the TBI was severe and accompanied by post-traumatic amnesia, the development of PTSD occurred over time and became more severe. In particular, cases of TBI with post-traumatic amnesia exhibited more PTSD symptoms than individuals who possessed a memory of the injury (Greenspan et al., 2006).

Although PTSD-like symptoms develop less frequently in severe as opposed to mild TBI, the presence of PTSD-like symptoms even when memories of the event are absent suggests that the psychological distress may be a direct result of physical injury to the brain (Metcalf et al., 2007). In milder forms of TBI a disruption of the inhibitory role of the prefrontal cortex in regulating the amygdala may produce PTSD symptoms, as previously described above (Kennedy et al., 2007). In more severe TBI, when post-traumatic amnesia occurs, the individual may unwittingly engage in cognitive confabulation that effectively fills the gaps in memories of the traumatic event.

There is an extensive literature concerning psychiatric disorders that develop after TBI (Ashman et al., 2004; Jorge et al., 2004; Lux, 2007; Metcalf et al., 2007; Tanielian & Jaycox, 2008). Major depressive and general anxiety disorders are two frequently cited psychiatric conditions that have been associated with TBI. Nevertheless, there are ongoing disagreements regarding whether (1) mild TBI and PTSD co-occur following a concussive injury, (2) PTSD requires conscious exposure to a psychological trauma, (3) TBI and PTSD are unrelated in etiology, (4) a mild TBI with post-concussive syndrome causes the symptoms of PTSD, or (5) the symptoms of post-concussive syndrome are actually caused by PTSD. These disagreements cannot be settled simply and require more targeted research, the discussion of which is beyond the scope of the present article.

CHRONIC INFLAMMATORY PROCESSES AND PSYCHOLOGICAL HEALTH

Traumatic brain injury can be considered an inflammatory disease process. Even a minor perturbation of brain tissue results in an immune response and the release of inflammatory agents that initiate additional injury beyond the primary site of damage (Holmin et al., 1997). The result of this inflammation is a function of the intensity and type of the injury. In cases of diffuse injury in children or contusions in adults, the inflammatory response precipitates brain edema, the primary cause of the morbidity and mortality related to TBI (Bullock et al., 2006; Kochanek, 2006).

Neuroinflammation in TBI has been well characterized in the acute stage (i.e. the first 72 hours post-injury; Stahel et al., 2000). Both animal and clinical observations have demonstrated that activated immune cells and the inflammatory agents released by these cells cause secondary injury to brain tissue (Keel & Trentz, 2005; Morganti-Kossmann, Rancan, Stahel, & Kossmann, 2002; Zhang, Artelt, Burnet, Trautmann, & Schluesener, 2006). However, eliminating post-injury inflammation may also have adverse effects on brain repair and recovery of function (Lenzlinger, Morganti-Kossmann, Laurer, & McIntosh, 2001) as shown in mice that were engineered to lack a certain pro-inflammatory cytokine, the result of which was an initial decrease in inflammation followed by impaired recovery.

TBI has also been shown to promote a more systemic inflammatory immune response, with activated immune cells invading major organs after injury. These activated immune cells subsequently release cytokines, complement factors, and other inflammatory agents (Lu et al., 2009). Such systemic inflammatory exposure leads to cachexia, a condition resulting in severe weight loss, with loss of appetite, that can occur after severe TBI (Falconer, Fearon, Plester, Ross, & Carter, 1994). Cachexia is often experienced in advanced stage cancer patients. These cancer patients have activated immune cells that systematically release various pro-inflammatory cytokines that are associated with cachexia (Falconer et al., 1994). Importantly, depression, which is often severe, frequently occurs co-morbidly with cachexia (Myers, 2008).

Specifically, systemic inflammation has been found to be strongly associated with clinical depression (Dantzer, O'Connor, Freund, Johnson, & Kelley, 2008). Neuroscientists have long known that neurons and glia have cytokine receptors and that cytokines elicit responses in both of these neural cell types (Abbadie et al., 2009). Similarly, immune cells carry receptors for various neurotransmitters and can therefore be modulated by neural or hormonal inflammatory status (Carnevale, De Simone, & Minghetti, 2007; Castagnetta et al., 2002). After TBI, interleukin 1-beta and tumor necrosis factor alpha, two cytokines involved in the inflammatory process, are upregulated and highly expressed during the acute period of injury (Lenzlinger et al., 2001). Although the intensity of inflammatory factor release diminishes after the first 72 hours post-injury, there is evidence that there is a second peak of cytokine release that is followed by a chronic elevated level, particular of the pro-inflammatory cytokine interleukin-6 (Holmin et al., 1997).

Interleukin-6 is a pro-inflammatory cytokine that keeps immune cells ready for response to another injury, as well as a chemoattractant, or chemical substance that attracts peripheral immune cells. The release of interleukin-6 by immune cells in the injured CNS keeps the migrating extrinsic macrophages, or defensive white blood cells, primed (Morganti-Kossmann, Satgunaseelan, Bye, & Kossmann, 2007). This chronic inflammatory state has been demonstrated to exist up to 20 years post-injury (Gentleman et al., 2004). The impact such inflammatory cells may have on long-term outcome is not clear. However, the fact that these abnormal cells exist long after a TBI, and evidence that the brain continues to atrophy after injury, suggests that TBI can be considered a chronic inflammatory disorder.

Research indicates that certain brain areas are more sensitive to the emotionally depressive effects of cytokines on metabolism. These areas include the prefrontal and temporal cortices, which are also frequently areas of primary injury in TBI (Dantzer et al., 2008). Strong evidence from brain-imaging studies indicates that these cortical areas typically exhibit lower metabolic activity in depressed people than is seen in people who do not report depressive symptoms (Jorge et al., 2004). Thus brain metabolism, site of injury, and inflammatory response are three factors that result in disordered physiological processes, and as a result impact psychological health.

Since inflammation appears to have an important role over the long term of TBI, it is likely that pharmacological modulation of the level of immune response is preferred over the complete inhibition of the immune response. In fact, it has been observed that the total suppression of the immune response worsens brain repair (Lenzlinger et al., 2001). Nevertheless, cautiously treating inflammation in the *acute* phase after TBI seems to have positive effects on recovery in both pre-clinical and clinical studies (Pettus, Wright, Stein, & Hoffman, 2005; Wright et al., 2007). Further research is needed to ascertain the efficacy of modulating the microenvironments in the *chronic* phase of TBI, years or decades post-injury, in order to improve physiological and psychological outcomes.

THE ROLE OF ENDOCRINE STRESS RESPONSES IN BRAIN REPAIR AND PSYCHOLOGICAL HEALTH

The effect of physiological stress, precipitated by psychogenic trauma, on brain repair and emotional well-being has drawn significant attention in the research literature. Military service members are being exposed to extremely stressful situations, which often differ drastically from what they experienced during training (Everly, Welzant, & Jacobson, 2008; Figueiredo et al., 2003). Recent, well-publicized increases in suicide rates in both active-duty and returning veterans indicate that military service has resulted in severe clinical depression. The effects of behavioral stress on brain function have been well investigated by McEwen (2000) and others (Liston et al., 2006; Radley et al., 2006; Sotres-Bayon et al., 2006). Research indicates that chronic stress, corticosteroids, and corticotrophin releasing hormone (CRH), a neurotransmitter involved in the stress response, work in combination to decrease brain metabolism in prefrontal and temporal cortices

(Liston et al., 2009). Psychogenic stressors can also have adverse effects on both brain resilience and brain repair. Chronic psychogenic stress can weaken the resilience of brain tissue by increasing levels of corticosteroids and CRH (Sorrells & Sapolsky, 2007). Corticosteroids impair the ability of neurons to respond metabolically to an insult that may occur from excitatory amino acids, hypoxia/ischemia, oxidative stress, or mediators of inflammation (Sorrells & Sapolsky, 2007). Much of this weakening or impairment of neurons results from opposing actions of corticosteroids on glucose uptake, which limits ATP production needed for protective or reparative actions in the injured brain (Tombaugh & Sapolsky, 1992).

Contrary to popular scientific thought, chronic high levels of corticosteroids activate, rather than suppress, inflammation in the central nervous system (Sorrells & Sapolsky, 2007). Chronically elevated levels of corticosteroids lead to greater extravasation, or leakage, of peripheral immune cells across the blood–brain barrier in response to injury. In fact, the microglial and astroglial inflammatory response is accelerated and increased when there has been chronic pre-injury exposure to corticosteroids.

The physiological result of depressed metabolism is the reduction in the potential for neuroplasticity and brain repair. Psychogenic stress evidences detrimental effects on dendritic structure that can "deactivate" regions of the brain (Liston et al., 2006; Radley et al., 2006). Studies have shown that neurons in the frontal and temporal cortices in animals that have been exposed to a chronic stressor exhibit atrophy of their dendritic arborizations (Liston et al., 2006; Radley et al., 2006). This loss of dendritic density is correlated with decreased cognitive ability in several animal models of stress (Liston et al., 2006). Dendritic pruning has been associated with changes in neurotransmitter receptors due to shifts in glutamate receptors that are expressed on the dendrites (McEwen, Magarinos, & Reagan, 2002; M. Roy & Sapolsky, 2003). The loss of dendrites due to excessive exposure to corticosteroids and CRH results in a loss of synapses; this synaptic loss is a physiological outcome, which can also occur in TBI, clinical depression, and PTSD.

Furthermore, chronic stress leads to an interruption of neurogenesis (Schloesser, Manji, & Martinowich, 2009). Neurogenesis has been shown to be correlated with recovery of function after neural insult (Urrea et al., 2007). The new neural cells can develop into neurons, which integrate into the neuronal circuits of the brain, or can differentiate into glial cells, e.g., oligodendrocytes, which repair neuronal connections by remyelinating axons of injured neurons (Horner, Thallmair, & Gage, 2002; Sun et al., 2007). The suppression of normal cell replacement, or neurogenesis, over the long term not only impairs the recovery process but also accelerates the aging process (Ekdahl, Claasen, Bonde, Kokaia, & Lindvall, 2003; McEwen, 2000). Recent research suggests that these brain changes, such as thinning of frontal cortical areas in chronically depressed patients, precede the development of Alzheimer's disease (Geerlings, den Heijer, Koudstaal, Hofman, & Breteler, 2008; Peterson et al., 2009). Together these findings support the idea that injured brains, and/or the brains of people with psychological health problems, tend to age at a faster rate than do the uninjured brains of people with intact psychological health. The overlap of behavioral symptoms and physiological/metabolic manifestations suggests that brain deactivation and diminished neuroplasticity may be common dysfunctions that result from TBI, psychogenic stress, and/or psychological health problems.

ENVIRONMENTAL EXPERIENCES MAY PROTECT AND REPAIR THE BRAIN AND MAINTAIN PSYCHOLOGICAL HEALTH

Pharmacological treatment of psychological health disorders is greatly complicated when these disorders are accompanied by a TBI, primarily because many pharmaceutical therapies for anxiety conditions, such as PTSD, are contraindicated when there is a brain injury. Benzodiazepines and other anti-anxiety drugs have been used in the treatment of PTSD, with the rationale that these drugs reduce anxiety and suppress the cycle of intrusive memories. However, the brain repair and recovery of function literature indicates that drugs that have a sedating effect also have an accompanying effect of blocking the reparative processes (Jones & Schallert, 1992; Schallert, Hernandez, & Barth, 1986; Schallert, Jones, & Lindner, 1990). Investigators have additionally shown that agents that inhibit the formation of new synapses circumvent the recovery process by preventing the neuroplasticity needed for brain repair.

The problem of pharmacological treatment in these co-morbid disorders suggests that other modes of therapy need to be developed and identified. The interaction of the internal environment of the person with their external environment is often ignored in the treatment of people with TBI and/or psychological health issues, despite the abundance of the pre-clinical literature. One such therapy that has been shown to enhance neuroplasticity, improve recovery of function, and increase brain resilience to injury, while reducing stress and anxiety, is Environmental Enrichment (EE) therapy (Harrison & Choeiri, 2006; B. Will, Galani, Kelche, & Rosenzweig, 2004).

Promoting recovery from brain injury by enriching the environment is derived from the concept of EE that is found in the pre-clinical animal literature. Decades of animal research have demonstrated that EE, a term describing an environment that encourages visuo-spatial, cognitive, social, and skilled motor exploration, promotes recovery of function across a variety of domains after traumatic brain injury (B. Will et al., 2004). Although researchers have discussed implications of this work for human rehabilitation, no randomized controlled studies have yet sought to establish whether specific analogs to the enrichments used with animals will have similar effectiveness in humans. In fact, most TBI therapies have evolved from clinical best practices in use before the revolution in neuroscience that has taken place over the past 15 years.

Extensive animal research using EE, which consists of enhanced opportunities to explore a complex multi-sensory three-dimensional space (Chapillon, Patin, Roy, Vincent, & Caston, 2002; Rosenzweig, Bennett, Hebert, & Morimoto, 1978), indicates that EE promotes recovery from traumatic brain injury (Manosevitz & Pryor, 1975). EE induces morphological, neurobiological, and behavioral changes (Greenough & Volkmar, 1973; Larsson, Winblad, & Mohammed, 2002; Rosenzweig & Bennett, 1996; van Praag, Kempermann, & Gage, 2000; B. E. Will, Rosenzweig, Bennett, Hebert, & Morimoto, 1977), and not only protects against but also has been shown to reverse the negative effects of the psychogenic and neurogenic stresses that lead to PTSD and TBI (Benaroya-Milshtein et al., 2004; Escorihuela, Tobena, & Fernandez-Teruel, 1994; Francis, Diorio, Plotsky, & Meaney, 2002; Klein, Lambert, Durr, Schaefer, & Waring, 1994). Enriched environments in the animal literature have been documented as promoting the voluntary exploration of complex and multi-sensory environments, stimulating learning and memory of rewarding areas within the explored space, and enhancing self-regulation of stress through utilization of shelters or stimulating microenvironments. EE has also been shown to increase total brain and cortical weight (Henderson, 1970; Rosenzweig, Bennett, & Diamond, 1972) with an increase in (1) neuronal density, i.e., gray matter density (Kempermann, Kuhn, & Gage, 1997), (2) dendritic branches (Greenough & Volkmar, 1973), (3) synapses (Turner & Greenough, 1985), and (4) growth factor expressions such as neuronal growth factor (Pham, Soderstrom, Winblad, & Mohammed, 1999). All these EE-induced morphological and physiological alterations may mediate the effect on stress.

It is possible that EE-induced cognitive recovery in mutant mice or injured animals is mediated by brain circuits that have not been damaged (Chapillon et al., 2002). This hypothesis may apply to behavioral recovery. Behavioral improvements following brain injury may be accounted for by compensation from other unaffected brain circuitry (Kolb, 1999).

On an endocrinological level, EE may decrease emotional reactivity by lowering stress hormone levels such as ACTH and corticosterone. Corticosteroids are good physiological indicators of stress level (Jost, 1966). However, there is some ambiguity as to the specific effects, if any, of EE on corticosterone. While some studies have found that EE decreases corticosterone levels at baseline (Belz, Kennell, Czambel, Rubin, & Rhodes, 2003) or following exposure to stress (Francis et al., 2002; V. Roy, Belzung, Delarue, & Chapillon, 2001), others have found that, at baseline, enriched animals do not differ from non-enriched (Devenport, Dallas, Carpenter, & Renner, 1992; Pham et al., 1999; V. Roy et al., 2001; Van de Weerd, Van Loo, Van Zutphen, Koolhaas, & Baumans, 1997) or have relatively higher baseline levels of that hormone to begin with (Benaroya-Milshtein et al., 2004; de Jong et al., 2000; Moncek, Duncko, Johansson, & Jezova, 2004). High baseline corticosterone levels may be related to the continual mild stress induced by repetitive exposure to new objects (Benaroya-Milshtein et al., 2004). Nevertheless, EE does seem to lower baseline ACTH levels (Belz et al., 2003).

Behavioral/cognitive researchers explain the positive effect of EE on stress in terms of the organism's ability to gain a greater sense of control over the environment. Enrichment provides animals with opportunities to structure and organize their environments, giving them a sense of control over their surroundings (Chamove, 1989; Van de Weerd et al., 1997, 2002). Thus a greater ability to make choices and control one's environment has been shown to reduce stress levels in animals (Wiepkema & Koolhaas, 1993).

IMPLICATIONS FOR RESEARCH AND TREATMENT OF CO-MORBID TBI AND PSYCHOLOGICAL HEALTH ISSUES

The importance of anxiety and stress reduction in military service members who suffer from both emotional distress and TBI cannot be underestimated.

However, differential diagnosis and accurate identification of these co-occurring conditions is critical for proper treatment to occur. We know that PTSD is identified co-morbidly with traumatic brain injury (TBI) in up to 33% of TBI cases (Ashman et al., 2004; Bryant, 2001a, 2001b; Bryant, Marosszeky, Crooks, & Gurka, 2004; Ohry, Rattok, & Solomon, 1996; Sojka, Stalnacke, Bjornstig, & Karlsson, 2006; W. H. Williams et al., 2002), although some still question the existence of co-morbidity (E. L. Moore, Terryberry-Spohr, & Hope, 2006). Change in consciousness at the time of the trauma does not fully identify cases of co-morbidity (Greenspan et al., 2006), as 3% to 27% of TBI patients with altered consciousness and/or amnesia for the event develop PTSD (Glaesser et al., 2004). We also know that symptoms of PTSD and mild to moderate TBI overlap sufficiently so as to render accurate diagnosis of TBI problematic. Thus some cases of mild TBI may be missed among patients who initially present with stress disorders from combat. As noted above, treatment by way of pharmacological intervention is often difficult and ineffective as medications that improve one disorder may actually hinder improvement of the other disorder.

The co-morbid occurrence of PTSD and TBI, the overlap of symptoms, and the fact that, regardless of cause, these disorders involve many of the same brain and endocrine systems, raises the possibility that common underlying brain mechanisms could cause these conditions to aggravate one another. A better understanding of this possibility may provide specific guidance in the treatments we choose for individuals suffering from the effects of psychological and/or physical trauma to the brain, and help us to develop new, integrative therapies, such as EE.

To quote a passage from a recent book by Alva Noë, "We need to turn our attention to the way brain, body, and world together maintain living consciousness" (Noë, 2009, p. 42). The implications of animal research on enriched environments for the rehabilitation of brain-injured humans are significant. EE offers treatment that does not involve risk of negative drug side-effects, and that takes advantage of the fact that the brain is constantly interacting with the environment and has the ability, indeed the proclivity, to reconfigure itself in response to that interaction. Rehabilitation of individuals with TBI, or with psychological health issues and co-occurring physiological conditions, should deliberately utilize and integrate the individual's environmental surroundings as a significant component of his/her therapy.

DISCLAIMER

The views expressed in this paper are those of the authors and do not reflect the views of the US Department of Defense or the Henry Jackson Foundation.

REFERENCES

Abbadie, C., Bhangoo, S., De Koninck, Y., Malcangio, M., Melik-Parsadaniantz, S., & White, F. A. (2009). Chemokines and pain mechanisms. *Brain Research Reviews, 60*(1), 125–134.

Alvarez, R. P., Biggs, A., Chen, G., Pine, D. S., & Grillon, C. (2008). Contextual fear conditioning in humans: Cortical-hippocampal and amygdala contributions. *Journal of Neuroscience, 28*(24), 6211–6219.

Ashman, T. A., Spielman, L. A., Hibbard, M. R., Silver, J. M., Chandna, T., & Gordon, W. A. (2004). Psychiatric challenges in the first 6 years after traumatic brain injury: Cross-sequential analyses of Axis I disorders. *Archives of Physical Medicine and Rehabilitation, 85*(4 Suppl 2), S36–42.

Beer, J. S., Heerey, E. A., Keltner, D., Scabini, D., & Knight, R. T. (2003). The regulatory function of self-conscious emotion: Insights from patients with orbitofrontal damage. *Journal of Personality and Social Psychology, 85*(4), 594–604.

Beer, J. S., John, O. P., Scabini, D., & Knight, R. T. (2006). Orbitofrontal cortex and social behavior: Integrating self-monitoring and emotion–cognition interactions. *Journal of Cognitive Neuroscience, 18*(6), 871–879.

Belz, E. E., Kennell, J. S., Czambel, R. K., Rubin, R. T., & Rhodes, M. E. (2003). Environmental enrichment lowers stress-responsive hormones in singly housed male and female rats. *Pharmacology Biochemistry and Behavior, 76*(3–4), 481–486.

Benaroya-Milshtein, N., Hollander, N., Apter, A., Kukulansky, T., Raz, N., Wilf, A., et al. (2004). Environmental enrichment in mice decreases anxiety, attenuates stress responses and enhances natural killer cell activity. *European Journal of Neuroscience, 20*(5), 1341–1347.

Bryant, R. A. (2001a). Post-traumatic stress disorder and mild brain injury: Controversies, causes and consequences. *Journal of Clinical and Experimental Neuropsychology, 23*(6), 718–728.

Bryant, R. A. (2001b). Post-traumatic stress disorder and traumatic brain injury: Can they co-exist? *Clinical Psychology Reviews, 21*(6), 931–948.

Bryant, R. A., Marosszeky, J. E., Crooks, J., & Gurka, J. A. (2004). Elevated resting heart rate as a predictor of post-traumatic stress disorder after severe traumatic brain injury. *Psychosomatic Medicine, 66*(5), 760–761.

Bullock, M. R., Chesnut, R., Ghajar, J., Gordon, D., Hartl, R., Newell, D. W., et al. (2006). Surgical management of traumatic parenchymal lesions. *Neurosurgery, 58*(3 Suppl), S25–46; discussion Si–iv.

Carnevale, D., De Simone, R., & Minghetti, L. (2007). Microglia–neuron interaction in inflammatory and degenerative diseases: Role of cholinergic and noradrenergic systems. *CNS & Neurological Disorders Drug Targets, 6*(6), 388–397.

Castagnetta, L., Granata, O. M., Traina, A., Cocciadiferro, L., Saetta, A., Stefano, R., et al. (2002). A role for sex steroids in autoimmune diseases: A working hypothesis and supporting data. *Annals of the New York Academy Sciences, 966*, 193–203.

Chamove, A. S. (1989). Cage design reduces emotionality in mice. *Laboratory Animal, 23*(3), 215–219.

Chapillon, P., Patin, V., Roy, V., Vincent, A., & Caston, J. (2002). Effects of pre- and postnatal stimulation on developmental, emotional, and cognitive aspects in rodents: A review. *Developmental Psychobiology, 41*(4), 373–387.

Dantzer, R., O'Connor, J. C., Freund, G. G., Johnson, R. W., & Kelley, K. W. (2008). From inflammation to sickness and depression: When the immune system subjugates the brain. *Nature Reviews. Neuroscience, 9*(1), 46–56.

de Jong, I. C., Prelle, I. T., van de Burgwal, J. A., Lambooij, E., Korte, S. M., Blokhuis, H. J., et al. (2000). Effects of environmental enrichment on behavioral responses to novelty, learning, and memory, and the circadian rhythm in cortisol in growing pigs. *Physiology Behavior, 68*(4), 571–578.

Devenport, L., Dallas, S., Carpenter, C., & Renner, M. J. (1992). The relationship between adrenal steroids and enrichment-induced brain growth. *Behavioral Neural Biology, 58*(1), 45–50.

Ekdahl, C. T., Claasen, J. H., Bonde, S., Kokaia, Z., & Lindvall, O. (2003). Inflammation is detrimental for neurogenesis in adult brain. *Proceedings of the National Academy of Sciences of the United States of America, 100*(23), 13632–13637.

Ellsworth, P. C. (1994). William James and emotion: Is a century of fame worth a century of misunderstanding? *Psychological Review, 101*(2), 222–229.

Elzinga, B. M., & Bremner, J. D. (2002). Are the neural substrates of memory the final common pathway in post-traumatic stress disorder (PTSD)? *Journal of Affective Disorders, 70*(1), 1–17.

Escorihuela, R. M., Tobena, A., & Fernandez-Teruel, A. (1994). Environmental enrichment reverses the detrimental action of early inconsistent stimulation and increases the beneficial effects of postnatal handling on shuttlebox learning in adult rats. *Behavioral Brain Research, 61*(2), 169–173.

Everly, G. S. Jr., Welzant, V., & Jacobson, J. M. (2008). Resistance and resilience: The final frontier in traumatic stress management. *International Journal of Emergency Mental Health, 10*(4), 261–270.

Falconer, J. S., Fearon, K. C., Plester, C. E., Ross, J. A., & Carter, D. C. (1994). Cytokines, the acute-phase response, and resting energy expenditure in cachectic patients with pancreatic cancer. *Annals of Surgery, 219*(4), 325–331.

Figueiredo, H. F., Bodie, B. L., Tauchi, M., Dolgas, C. M., & Herman, J. P. (2003). Stress integration after acute and chronic predator stress: Differential activation of central stress circuitry and sensitization of the hypothalamo-pituitary-adrenocortical axis. *Endocrinology, 144*(12), 5249–5258.

Francis, D. D., Diorio, J., Plotsky, P. M., & Meaney, M. J. (2002). Environmental enrichment reverses the effects of maternal separation on stress reactivity. *Journal of Neuroscience, 22*(18), 7840–7843.

Geerlings, M. I., den Heijer, T., Koudstaal, P. J., Hofman, A., & Breteler, M. M. (2008). History of depression, depressive symptoms, and medial temporal lobe atrophy and the risk of Alzheimer disease. *Neurology, 70*(15), 1258–1264.

Gentleman, S. M., Leclercq, P. D., Moyes, L., Graham, D. I., Smith, C., Griffin, W. S., et al. (2004). Long-term intracerebral inflammatory response after traumatic brain injury. *Forensic Science International, 146*(2–3), 97–104.

Glaesser, J., Neuner, F., Lutgehetmann, R., Schmidt, R., & Elbert, T. (2004). Post-traumatic stress disorder in patients with traumatic brain injury. *BMC Psychiatry, 4*, 5.

Greenough, W. T., & Volkmar, F. R. (1973). Pattern of dendritic branching in occipital cortex of rats reared in complex environments. *Experimental Neurology, 40*(2), 491–504.

Greenspan, A. I., Stringer, A. Y., Phillips, V. L., Hammond, F. M., & Goldstein, F. C. (2006). Symptoms of post-traumatic stress: Intrusion and avoidance 6 and 12 months after TBI. *Brain Injury, 20*(7), 733–742.

Harrison, C., & Choeiri, C. (2006). Interaction of pre- and post-injury environmental enrichment on recovery from traumatic brain injury. *Society for Neuroscience* (Vol. 18.6.2006), Washington, DC.

Henderson, N. D. (1970). Brain weight increases resulting from environmental enrichment: A directional dominance in mice. *Science, 169*(947), 776–778.

Holmin, S., Schalling, M., Hojeberg, B., Nordqvist, A. C., Skeftruna, A. K., & Mathiesen, T. (1997). Delayed cytokine expression in rat brain following experimental contusion. *Journal of Neurosurgery, 86*(3), 493–504.

Horner, P. J., Thallmair, M., & Gage, F. H. (2002). Defining the NG2-expressing cell of the adult CNS. *Journal of Neurocytology, 31*(6–7), 469–480.

Jones, T. A., & Schallert, T. (1992). Subcortical deterioration after cortical damage: Effects of diazepam and relation to recovery of function. *Behavioral Brain Research, 51*(1), 1–13.

Jorge, R. E., Robinson, R. G., Moser, D., Tateno, A., Crespo-Facorro, B., & Arndt, S. (2004). Major depression following traumatic brain injury. *Archives of General Psychiatry*, *61*(1), 42–50.

Jost, A. (1966). Anterior pituitary function in foetal life. In G. W. Harris & B. T. Donovan (Eds.), *The pituitary gland* (p. 3 v.). London: Butterworths.

Keel, M., & Trentz, O. (2005). Pathophysiology of polytrauma. *Injury*, *36*(6), 691–709.

Kempermann, G., Kuhn, H. G., & Gage, F. H. (1997). More hippocampal neurons in adult mice living in an enriched environment. *Nature*, *386*(6624), 493–495.

Kennedy, J. E., Jaffee, M. S., Leskin, G. A., Stokes, J. W., Leal, F. O., & Fitzpatrick, P. J. (2007). Post-traumatic stress disorder and post-traumatic stress disorder-like symptoms and mild traumatic brain injury. *Journal of Rehabilitation Research and Development*, *44*(7), 895–920.

Klein, S. L., Lambert, K. G., Durr, D., Schaefer, T., & Waring, R. E. (1994). Influence of environmental enrichment and sex on predator stress response in rats. *Physiology and Behavior*, *56*(2), 291–297.

Kochanek, P. M. (2006). Pediatric traumatic brain injury: Quo vadis? *Developmental Neuroscience*, *28*(4–5), 244–255.

Kolb, B. (1999). Synaptic plasticity and the organization of behavior after early and late brain injury. *Canadian Journal of Experimental Psychology*, *53*(1), 62–75.

Larsson, F., Winblad, B., & Mohammed, A. H. (2002). Psychological stress and environmental adaptation in enriched vs. impoverished housed rats. *Pharmacology, Biochemistry, and Behavior*, *73*(1), 193–207.

Lenzlinger, P. M., Morganti-Kossmann, M. C., Laurer, H. L., & McIntosh, T. K. (2001). The duality of the inflammatory response to traumatic brain injury. *Molecular Neurobiology*, *24*(1–3), 169–181.

Liston, C., McEwen, B. S., & Casey, B. J. (2009). Psychosocial stress reversibly disrupts prefrontal processing and attentional control. *Proceedings of the National Academy of Sciences of the United States of America*, *106*(3), 912–917.

Liston, C., Miller, M. M., Goldwater, D. S., Radley, J. J., Rocher, A. B., Hof, P. R., et al. (2006). Stress-induced alterations in prefrontal cortical dendritic morphology predict selective impairments in perceptual attentional set-shifting. *Journal of Neuroscience*, *26*(30), 7870–7874.

Lu, J., Goh, S. J., Tng, P. Y., Deng, Y. Y., Ling, E. A., & Moochhala, S. (2009). Systemic inflammatory response following acute traumatic brain injury. *Frontiers of Bioscience*, *14*, 3795–3813.

Lux, W. E. (2007). A neuropsychiatric perspective on traumatic brain injury. *Journal of Rehabilitation Research and Development*, *44*(7), 951–962.

Manosevitz, M., & Pryor, J. B. (1975). Cage size as a factor in environmental enrichment. *Journal of Comparative and Physiological Psychology*, *89*, 648–654.

Martin, E. M., Lu, W. C., Helmick, K., French, L., & Warden, D. L. (2008). Traumatic brain injuries sustained in the Afghanistan and Iraq wars. *The American Journal of Nursing*, *108*(4), 40–47.

McEwen, B. S. (2000). The neurobiology of stress: From serendipity to clinical relevance. *Brain Research*, *886*(1–2), 172–189.

McEwen, B. S., Magarinos, A. M., & Reagan, L. P. (2002). Structural plasticity and tianeptine: Cellular and molecular targets. *The Journal of the Association of European Psychiatrists*, *17*(Suppl 3), 318–330.

Meares, S., Shores, E. A., Taylor, A. J., Batchelor, J., Bryant, R. A., Baguley, I. J., et al. (2008). Mild traumatic brain injury does not predict acute postconcussion syndrome. *Journal of Neurology, Neurosurgery, and Psychiatry*, *79*(3), 300–306.

Metcalf, K., Langdon, R., & Coltheart, M. (2007). Models of confabulation: A critical review and a new framework. *Cognitive Neuropsychology, 24*(1), 23–47.

Moncek, F., Duncko, R., Johansson, B. B., & Jezova, D. (2004). Effect of environmental enrichment on stress related systems in rats. *Journal Neuroendocrinology, 16*(5), 423–431.

Moore, D. F., Jerusalem, A., Nyein, M., Noels, L., Jaffee, M. S., & Radovitzky, R. A. (2009). Computational biology: Modeling of primary blast effects on the central nervous system. *Neuroimage, 47*(Suppl. 2), T10–T20.

Moore, E. L., Terryberry-Spohr, L., & Hope, D. A. (2006). Mild traumatic brain injury and anxiety sequelae: A review of the literature. *Brain Injury, 20*(2), 117–132.

Morganti-Kossmann, M. C., Rancan, M., Stahel, P. F., & Kossmann, T. (2002). Inflammatory response in acute traumatic brain injury: A double-edged sword. *Current Opinion in Critical Care, 8*(2), 101–105.

Morganti-Kossmann, M. C., Satgunaseelan, L., Bye, N., & Kossmann, T. (2007). Modulation of immune response by head injury. *Injury, 38*(12), 1392–1400.

Myers, J. S. (2008). Proinflammatory cytokines and sickness behavior: Implications for depression and cancer-related symptoms. *Oncology Nursing Forum, 35*(5), 802–807.

Niogi, S. N., Mukherjee, P., Ghajar, J., Johnson, C., Kolster, R. A., Sarkar, R., et al. (2008). Extent of microstructural white matter injury in postconcussive syndrome correlates with impaired cognitive reaction time: A 3T diffusion tensor imaging study of mild traumatic brain injury. *American Journal Neuroradiology, 29*(5), 967–973.

Noë, A. (2009). *Out of our heads: Why you are not your brain, and other lessons from the biology of consciousness* (1st ed.). New York: Hill & Wang.

Ohry, A., Rattok, J., & Solomon, Z. (1996). Post-traumatic stress disorder in brain injury patients. *Brain Injury, 10*(9), 687–695.

Peterson, B. S., Warner, V., Bansal, R., Zhu, H., Hao, X., Liu, J., et al. (2009). Cortical thinning in persons at increased familial risk for major depression. *Proceedings of the National Academy of Sciences of the United States of America, 106*(15), 6273–6278.

Pettus, E. H., Wright, D. W., Stein, D. G., & Hoffman, S. W. (2005). Progesterone treatment inhibits the inflammatory agents that accompany traumatic brain injury. *Brain Research, 1049*(1), 112–119.

Pham, T. M., Soderstrom, S., Winblad, B., & Mohammed, A. H. (1999). Effects of environmental enrichment on cognitive function and hippocampal NGF in the non-handled rats. *Behavioral Brain Research, 103*(1), 63–70.

Radley, J. J., Rocher, A. B., Miller, M., Janssen, W. G., Liston, C., Hof, P. R., et al. (2006). Repeated stress induces dendritic spine loss in the rat medial prefrontal cortex. *Cereberal Cortex, 16*(3), 313–320.

Roberts, N. A., Beer, J. S., Werner, K. H., Scabini, D., Levens, S. M., Knight, R. T., et al. (2004). The impact of orbital prefrontal cortex damage on emotional activation to unanticipated and anticipated acoustic startle stimuli. *Cognitive, Affective & Behavioral Neuroscience, 4*(3), 307–316.

Rosenzweig, M. R., & Bennett, E. L. (1996). Psychobiology of plasticity: Effects of training and experience on brain and behavior. *Behavioral Brain Research, 78*(1), 57–65.

Rosenzweig, M. R., Bennett, E. L., & Diamond, M. C. (1972). Cerebral effects of differential experience in hypophysectomized rats. *Journal of Comparative Physiological Psychology, 79*(1), 56–66.

Rosenzweig, M. R., Bennett, E. L., Hebert, M., & Morimoto, H. (1978). Social grouping cannot account for cerebral effects of enriched environments. *Brain Research, 153*(3), 563–576.

Roy, M., & Sapolsky, R. M. (2003). The exacerbation of hippocampal excitotoxicity by glucocorticoids is not mediated by apoptosis. *Neuroendocrinology, 77*(1), 24–31.

Roy, V., Belzung, C., Delarue, C., & Chapillon, P. (2001). Environmental enrichment in BALB/c mice: Effects in classical tests of anxiety and exposure to a predatory odor. *Physiology and Behavior, 74*(3), 313–320.

Saljo, A., Arrhen, F., Bolouri, H., Mayorga, M., & Hamberger, A. (2008). Neuropathology and pressure in the pig brain resulting from low-impulse noise exposure. *Journal of Neurotrauma, 25*(12), 1397–1406.

Salmond, C. H., Menon, D. K., Chatfield, D. A., Williams, G. B., Pena, A., Sahakian, B. J., et al. (2006). Diffusion tensor imaging in chronic head injury survivors: Correlations with learning and memory indices. *Neuroimage, 29*(1), 117–124.

Schallert, T., Hernandez, T. D., & Barth, T. M. (1986). Recovery of function after brain damage: Severe and chronic disruption by diazepam. *Brain Research, 379*(1), 104–111.

Schallert, T., Jones, T. A., & Lindner, M. D. (1990). Multilevel transneuronal degeneration after brain damage: Behavioral events and effects of anticonvulsant gamma-aminobutyric acid-related drugs. *Stroke, 21*(11 Suppl), III143–146.

Schloesser, R. J., Manji, H. K., & Martinowich, K. (2009). Suppression of adult neurogenesis leads to an increased hypothalamo-pituitary-adrenal axis response. *Neuroreport, 20*(6), 553–557.

Sojka, P., Stalnacke, B. M., Bjornstig, U., & Karlsson, K. (2006). One-year follow-up of patients with mild traumatic brain injury: Occurrence of post-traumatic stress-related symptoms at follow-up and serum levels of cortisol, S-100B and neuron-specific enolase in acute phase. *Brain Injury, 20*(6), 613–620.

Sorrells, S. F., & Sapolsky, R. M. (2007). An inflammatory review of glucocorticoid actions in the CNS. *Brain, Behavior, and Immunity, 21*(3), 259–272.

Sotres-Bayon, F., Cain, C. K., & LeDoux, J. E. (2006). Brain mechanisms of fear extinction: Historical perspectives on the contribution of prefrontal cortex. *Biological Psychiatry, 60*, 329–336.

Stahel, P. F., Shohami, E., Younis, F. M., Kariya, K., Otto, V. I., Lenzlinger, P. M., et al. (2000). Experimental closed head injury: Analysis of neurological outcome, blood–brain barrier dysfunction, intracranial neutrophil infiltration, and neuronal cell death in mice deficient in genes for pro-inflammatory cytokines. *Journal of Cereberal Blood Flow Metabolism, 20*(2), 369–380.

Sun, D., McGinn, M. J., Zhou, Z., Harvey, H. B., Bullock, M. R., & Colello, R. J. (2007). Anatomical integration of newly generated dentate granule neurons following traumatic brain injury in adult rats and its association to cognitive recovery. *Experimental Neurology, 204*(1), 264–272.

Tanielian, T. L., & Jaycox, L. (2008). *Invisible wounds of war: Psychological and cognitive injuries, their consequences, and services to assist recovery*. Santa Monica, CA: RAND Corporation.

Taylor, P., & Ford, C. C. (2008). *Simulation of blast-induced, early-time intracranial wave physics leading to traumatic brain injury*. Paper presented at the 83rd Regional Meeting of the American Association for the Advancement of Science Southwestern and Rocky Mountain Division, Albuquerque, New Mexico.

Tombaugh, G. C., & Sapolsky, R. M. (1992). Corticosterone accelerates hypoxia- and cyanide-induced ATP loss in cultured hippocampal astrocytes. *Brain Research, 588*(1), 154–158.

Turner, A. M., & Greenough, W. T. (1985). Differential rearing effects on rat visual cortex synapses. I. Synaptic and neuronal density and synapses per neuron. *Brain Research, 329*(1–2), 195–203.

Urrea, C., Castellanos, D. A., Sagen, J., Tsoulfas, P., Bramlett, H. M., & Dietrich, W. D. (2007). Widespread cellular proliferation and focal neurogenesis after traumatic brain injury in the rat. *Restorative Neurology and Neuroscience, 25*(1), 65–76.

Van de Weerd, H. A., Aarsen, E. L., Mulder, A., Kruitwagen, C. L., Hendriksen, C. F., & Baumans, V. (2002). Effects of environmental enrichment for mice: Variation in experimental results. *Journal of Applied Animal Welfare Science*, *5*(2), 87–109.

Van de Weerd, H. A., Van Loo, P. L., Van Zutphen, L. F., Koolhaas, J. M., & Baumans, V. (1997). Preferences for nesting material as environmental enrichment for laboratory mice. *Laboratory Animals*, *31*(2), 133–143.

van der Kolk, B. A. (2001). The assessment and treatment of complex PTSD. In R. Yehuda (Ed.), *Traumatic stress*. Washington, DC: American Psychiatric Press.

van Praag, H., Kempermann, G., & Gage, F. H. (2000). Neural consequences of environmental enrichment. *Nature Reviews: Neuroscience*, *1*(3), 191–198.

Wiepkema, P. R., & Koolhaas, J. M. (1993). Stress and animal welfare. *Animal Welfare*, *2*, 195–218.

Will, B., Galani, R., Kelche, C., & Rosenzweig, M. R. (2004). Recovery from brain injury in animals: Relative efficacy of environmental enrichment, physical exercise or formal training (1990–2002). *Progress in Neurobiology*, *72*(3), 167–182.

Will, B. E., Rosenzweig, M. R., Bennett, E. L., Hebert, M., & Morimoto, H. (1977). Relatively brief environmental enrichment aids recovery of learning capacity and alters brain measures after postweaning brain lesions in rats. *Journal of Comparative Physiological Psychology*, *91*(1), 33–50.

Williams, L. M., Kemp, A. H., Felmingham, K., Barton, M., Olivieri, G., Peduto, A., et al. (2006). Trauma modulates amygdala and medial prefrontal responses to consciously attended fear. *Neuroimage*, *29*(2), 347–357.

Williams, W. H., Evans, J. J., Needham, P., & Wilson, B. A. (2002). Neurological, cognitive and attributional predictors of post-traumatic stress symptoms after traumatic brain injury. *Journal of Traumatic Stress*, *15*(5), 397–400.

Wright, D. W., Kellermann, A. L., Hertzberg, V. S., Clark, P. L., Frankel, M., Goldstein, F. C., et al. (2007). ProTECT: A randomized clinical trial of progesterone for acute traumatic brain injury. *Annals of Emergency Medicine*, *49*(4), 391–402.

Zhang, Z., Artelt, M., Burnet, M., Trautmann, K., & Schluesener, H. J. (2006). Early infiltration of CD8+ macrophages/microglia to lesions of rat traumatic brain injury. *Neuroscience*, *141*(2), 637–644.

BEYOND DIAGNOSIS: UNDERSTANDING THE HEALTHCARE CHALLENGES OF INJURED VETERANS THROUGH THE APPLICATION OF THE INTERNATIONAL CLASSIFICATION OF FUNCTIONING, DISABILITY AND HEALTH (ICF)

Mark A. Sandberg[1], Shane S. Bush[2], and Thomas Martin[3]
[1]Private Practice, Smithtown, NY, [2]Long Island Neuropsychology, PC, and [3]University of Missouri, Columbia, MO, USA

Psychiatric and neurological disorders brought about by exposure to combat can create serious obstacles to community reintegration. Effective therapeutic and rehabilitative methods designed to address disorders that arise from combat are available. Yet there continues to be a need to develop both a deeper understanding of veterans' needs and best-practice methods to alleviate distress and facilitate community participation. Awareness of these needs served as the catalyst for the **International Conference on Behavioral Health and Traumatic Brain Injury** and is the basis for developing numerous new programs and service refinements across government and non-government organizations. Despite advances, community reintegration remains a complicated endeavor for many veterans returning home who are experiencing traumatic brain- and stress-related disorders. Accurately conceptualizing and codifying symptoms and barriers to community participation, beyond impairment analysis and diagnostic inclusion, is necessary to guide treatment planning and inform programmatic refinements. The International Classification of Function, Disability and Health (ICF) offers a useful taxonomic tool that can assist in refining an understanding of the challenges confronting our returning veterans. In turn, resources can be appropriately allocated, and neuropsychological therapies and other rehabilitation interventions, which assist veterans to resume productive and satisfying lives, will more likely be developed and implemented.

Keywords: Neuropsychology; Rehabilitation; Classification.

INTRODUCTION

Prolonged exposure to combat and blast-related injuries have contributed to an unprecedented number of veterans who meet criteria for various psychiatric conditions (e.g., PTSD) and/or traumatic brain injury (TBI). Estimates by the Rand Corporation indicate that of the 1.64 million U.S. troops deployed for Operations Enduring Freedom and Iraqi Freedom (OEF/OIF) in Afghanistan and Iraq, approximately 320,000 (19.5%) have sustained a TBI and another 300,000 meet criteria for PTSD (18.3%). Other studies have supported the high prevalence of mental health problems after deployment. Hoge, Auchterlonic,

---

Address correspondence to: Mark A. Sandberg, Ph.D., ABPP, 50 Karl Avenue, Smithtown, NY 11787, USA. E-mail: MASPSY@Verizon.net

and Milliken (2006) studied more than 200,000 Army soldiers and Marines using a brief post-deployment health assessment form and found that approximately 20% of active duty service members screened positive for one of the mental health concerns, and 31% of veterans had at least one outpatient mental health care visit within the first year after returning home from Iraq or Afghanistan. Seal, Bertenthal, Miner, Sen, and Marmar (2007) reviewed cases of more than 100,000 returning veterans treated at VA facilities and found that 25% received mental health diagnoses, with 56% of those veterans receiving two or more mental health diagnoses.

Although liberal diagnostic criteria for mild TBI may inflate injury estimates somewhat, the injury estimates reported in those studies also may not reflect "delayed" onset or reluctant reporting of mild TBI, PTSD, or other mental health conditions, and they do not take into account the reality that conflicts are ongoing and new injuries are incurred continually. Evidence suggests that the psychological toll of OEF/OIF deployments may be disproportionately greater than the toll of physical injuries sustained during combat (Karney, Ramchand, Osilla, Caldarone, & Burns, 2008). Because of these epidemiological considerations, TBI and PTSD have been referred to as "signature" injuries associated with OEF and OIF. These disorders can have staggering effects on veterans' quality of life, social functioning, and capacity to resume satisfying roles within the community. These consequential realities served as the basis for convening the *International Conference on Behavioral Health and Traumatic Brain Injury* and represent the impetus for continuing efforts toward identifying best practice approaches within medical, mental health, and rehabilitation systems. The purpose of the present article is to facilitate best-practice efforts in neuropsychological assessment and treatment by integrating the International Classification of Functioning, Disability and Health (ICF) into neuropsychological and interdisciplinary rehabilitation case conceptualization.

DIAGNOSTIC DETERMINATION

Diagnosis of psychiatric and many neurological disorders is based on a process of clinical analysis utilizing a polythetic model of clinical feature selection. In the case of PTSD the most current psychiatric nomenclature (i.e., DSM-IV-TR) is based on a core etiological assumption that the person meeting criteria has been exposed to a traumatic event that involved actual or threatened death or serious injury, or a threat to the physical integrity of self or others, and that the person's response involved intense fear, helplessness, or horror (American Psychiatric Association, 2000). More than most other life circumstances, deployment to a theater of war lays the groundwork for meeting this criterion. Additional defining clinical characteristics include persistent re-experiencing of the trauma, avoidance behaviors, and hyperarousal, with facets of each dimension variably present among those diagnosed, leading to heterogeneity among similarly diagnosed veterans (i.e., polythetic model).

Like PTSD, the diagnosis of TBI also has a central inclusion criterion, which is an acute change in brain neurophysiology secondary to mechanically induced disruption as immediately evidenced by a loss or alteration of consciousness and/or a period of post-traumatic amnesia (American Congress of Rehabilitation

Medicine, 1993). Although diagnosis of TBI is based on the characteristics of the injury (e.g., post-traumatic amnesia, loss of consciousness), at the "mild" end of the injury continuum there often exists ambiguity as to whether a person actually sustained a concussive injury. Ascertaining residual impairment, even with sensitive neuropsychological measures, can be a complex process, particularly when developmental conditions, such as learning and attention disorders, co-exist with TBI. Furthermore, diagnostic complexity also coincides with the fact that many patients inevitably portray features of multiple disorders at any one time, with few prototypically showing all of the characteristics of a particular condition. Co-occurring disorders (e.g., chronic pain, alcohol or substance abuse) are common among individuals who have sustained a TBI and/or meet diagnostic criteria for depression or PTSD, and often result in more adverse outcomes than any of the disorders alone (Taber & Hurley, 2009).

Another level of diagnostic complexity corresponds with knowing that unequivocal neurophysiological changes brought about by mechanical forces (e.g., certain loss of consciousness) offers little to no clarity as to presence or nature of residual impairment, functional disturbance, or prognosis for restoration. A positive history of TBI should not automatically imply residual neurologically based impairments. A TBI is something that one *sustains* at a given point in time; it is not something one *has* months or years after an injury-causing event. Likewise, identification of residual TBI impairments does not naturally inform the evaluation team as to reasons for activity restrictions, nor does that information translate clearly into specific treatment methods or neurorehabilitation objectives. A critical reason for making diagnoses is to understand prognosis and inform treatment. Commonly employed diagnostic systems, particularly in the spheres of mental health and rehabilitation, frequently fail to meet these objectives.

Neuropsychological assessment is an important tool available within the interdisciplinary clinical arena. Results of neuropsychological assessment serve multiple purposes including assisting with diagnostic decision making, clarifying the presence and prominence of cognitive and executive skill impairment, ascertaining residual strengths that can be harnessed in rehabilitation endeavors, and assisting veterans and their families to understand the impact of injury. Neuropsychological assessment is a useful diagnostic method for persons with acquired neurological and psychological disorders in military and civilian settings. Psychometric data, while beneficial in promoting an understanding of the veteran with known or suspected brain disorders, predominantly rely on tests designed to measure ability at the body function level. Although interview data and personality/emotional assessment (e.g., MMPI-2) in many cases complement neuropsychological test findings leading to a more biopsychosocial synthesis, a gap often exists between delineation of impairments (and strengths) and knowing why someone is not living his/her life as fully as possible.

The benefits of augmenting the medical model of health care, which traditionally prioritized diagnosis with a system that understands disability as a complex construct reflecting the interaction between the individual and environment, has been clearly articulated (WHO, 2001). For many veterans returning from Vietnam, societal attitudes shaped greatly their disability experience. In this example, to solely consider diagnosis (e.g., PTSD) without weighing the experiential influence of environmental factors depletes our understanding and our potential to offer the most targeted assistance. Even when diagnosis is determined with a high degree of certainty, clinicians often know little about levels of functioning. For example, knowing the correct diagnosis does not predict work performance (Gatchel, Polatin, Mayer, & Garcy, 1994)), length of hospitalization (McCrone & Phelan, 1994), and degree of social integration (Ormel, Oldehinkel, Brilman, & vanden Brink, 1993), among other functional outcomes (Sbordone & Long, 1996). A different framework is called for which appreciates the many relevant facets of human functioning that could potentially be affected by neurological or psychiatric trauma. The attributes of this type of framework are present in the ICF. A unique classificatory framework developed by the World Health Organization (WHO, 2001), the ICF offers a system of collecting fundamental biopsychosocial data in a consistent and internationally comparable manner, and is a useful classification system that can complement other data sources including etiology (i.e., ICD-10) (available at www.who.int/classifications/icfbrowser/).

ICF: A BIOPSYCHOSOCIAL MODEL

The ICF was devised to "provide a unified and standard language and framework for the description of health and health-related states" (WHO, 2001, p. 3). At its foundation is a basic tenet positing that medical classification of diagnoses alone, although necessary, is insufficient for purposes of health planning. The ICF offers a fresh perspective that examines human function and dysfunction through a codified taxonomic system. It is not intended to classify people as, for example, the DSM-IV and ICD-10 are designed to do. Rather, its focus is descriptive, examining a person's unique health circumstances, which are viewed as a dynamic assemblage of physiological (including psychological/neuropsychological) functions and body structures, actions, and activities, all of which are experienced within a particular context.

The ICF was not conceived to exclusively measure disability; health and health-associated states are also within its visionary scope. Health is defined by the ICF in terms of the spectrum of well-being, encompassing dimensions commonly focused on by health care practitioners (e.g., hearing and walking), as well as other critical domains that are less commonly attended to in traditional health care (e.g., access to entitlements, employment, family support) (Peterson, 2005; Peterson & Rosenthal, 2005). Acknowledging the caveat that an interrelationship between aspects of functioning and disability are complex and prone to misinterpretation, Figure 1 depicts an illustrative factorial diagram which serves as a representation of the model of disability that is the basis for the ICF (WHO, 2001). What is most important and highlighted in the diagram is that an individual's functioning and disability are seen as an interactive picture, representing a flow between disability, underlying health conditions, and other contextual factors. Therefore impairment (e.g., impaired auditory-verbal memory) does not automatically imply an activity limitation (e.g., inability to succeed in school). Likewise, a person can be restricted in his or her ability to participate in an activity when there is little or no evidence for impairment (e.g., the untoward influence that stigma associated with a particular personal attribute might create).

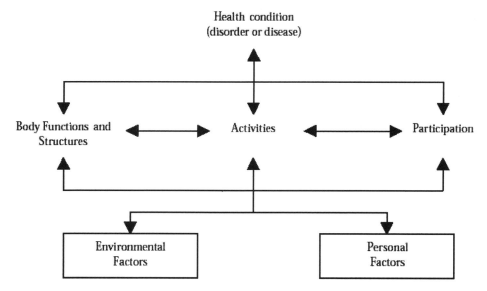

Figure 1 Interactions between the components of the ICF. From *International Classification of Functioning, Disability and Health: ICF.* World Health Organization, 2001, Geneva: WHO. Copyright 2001 by the World Health Organization. Reprinted with permission.

A core ICF precept is that health care can be contemporized by an appreciation of the dynamic interplay between physiological, environmental, and personal influences and that a full picture of a person's health and identification of how to best minimize disability is not available merely by knowing diagnosis. For example, consider the diagnosis of TBI (e.g., ICD-10 category 854.X). Beyond the fuzziness of diagnostic inclusion that exists at the milder levels, there is the reality that even among those who unequivocally meet criteria for having sustained a TBI, there is very little known about how the person functions or why deficits in activity participation might be present. For example, diagnosis offers information at the level of *Body Structure* (e.g., ICD-10 intracranial injury) or *Body Function* (e.g., ICD-10 Memory Loss), but without knowing more about activity limitations or participation restrictions, or without having discerned other relevant contextual details, understanding the veteran's true, unique situation is difficult and hinders the design of effective interventions. Through the ICF lens, disability is not a static condition but rather a state that fluidly exists within the context of various factors—these factors are recognized, operationalized and systematically coded by the ICF.

ICF STRUCTURE

Although initially appearing onerous, the detailed layout of the ICF taxonomy is logically arranged and consists of two parts: (1) Functioning and Disability and (2) Contextual Factors, with each part comprised of two components. Within *Functioning and Disability* the two components are a body component and an activities and participation component. The body component describes how the body is anatomically structured (referred to as *Body Structures*) and how it physiologically and psychologically functions (referred to as *Body Functions*). Impairments in body structures and functions are expressed as either non-problematic or as disabling through the use of Likert-scale qualifiers (0 through 4, with 8 and 9 qualifiers representing "not specified" and "not applicable," respectively) denoting the presence of a deviation or loss.

The *Activities and Participation* component addresses functional domains that are viewed from the perspectives of the individual and society. Included are a range of activities from basic to complex which describe a person's ability to live in a socially integrated and independent fashion. *Activity* is described as the execution of a task or action by an individual (e.g., preparing meals, doing homework) and *Participation* is defined as involvement in a life situation (e.g., work and employment, arts and culture). Qualifiers within this section offer information as to participation restrictions (i.e., the degree to which a person experiences problems participating) and activity limitations (the extent to which a person experiences difficulty executing an activity). Additional qualifiers are used to describe *performance* (the person's actual performance of a task or action) and *capacity* (the person's ability to execute a task or action).

The second ICF part, *Contextual Factors*, describes the extent to which background factors influence human functioning. The two components of this part are *environmental factors* (including physical and attitudinal) and *personal factors* (including lifestyles and education). Although the personal factors are considered in the analyses of the contextual aspects of a person's life, they are not currently classified by the ICF; however, it has been suggested that fully appreciating a person's experience of disability requires reporting of this dimension (Jelsma, 2009). Coding of the environmental factors is augmented by qualifiers that serve to denote whether the factor serves as a hindrance or as a facilitator to functioning.

Figure 2 offers details about the four primary ICF classifications ("chapters") and their respective classification components. Each chapter (i.e., Body Function, Body Structure, Activities and Participation, Environmental Factors) begins at a relatively generic level and unfolds into layers that offer greater functional specificity as might be called for depending on clinical need. For example, within the Body Function chapter (labeled by the letter *b*) are eight components; the first-level classification, for instance, addresses *Mental Functions* and is assigned the alphanumeric label *b*1. Classificatory precision continues to be enhanced through a detailed unfolding of defining characteristics. Within *Mental Functions* are *Specific Mental Functions* (alphanumerically coded *b*140 through *b*189). Within this array are found the *Emotional Functions* (alphanumerically coded *b*152), which in turn subsumes a menu of emotional features including those describing appropriateness (*b*1520), regulation (*b*1521), and range (*b*1522).

To illustrate, consider a clinical interview with a veteran for whom it is determined that difficulty exists in exhibiting a full range of emotional expressiveness. That is, emotions tend to be tightly controlled, and the veteran appears unrelaxed, joyless, and reluctant to express warm feelings. Coding of this emotional feature would follow its clinical identification. The clinician would browse through the appropriate ICF section (i.e., specific mental functions) where the best-fitting descriptor would be identified. In this case it would be (*b*1522) *Range of emotion*,

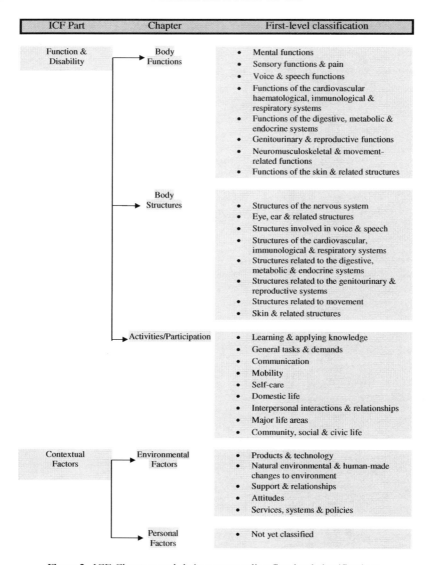

Figure 2 ICF Chapters and their corresponding first-level classifications.

described by the ICF as "Mental functions that produce the spectrum of experience of arousal of affect or feelings such as love, hate, anxiousness, sorrow, joy, fear and anger." As is evident by the numerical coding schema offered in this example ($b \rightarrow b1 \rightarrow b140-b189 \rightarrow b152 \rightarrow b1522$), more detailed features share the attributes of the lesser-detailed features that include them (Peterson, 2005). Once a classification unit is selected, a qualifier is then chosen to describe the degree to which that attribute disrupts functioning. Range of emotion is a body function, and qualifiers applicable for this section range from 0 (no impairment—there is no problem present) through 4 (complete impairment—present 95% of the time, totally disrupting the person's day-to-day life).

Categories and units of classification comprising the ICF are mutually exclusive such that multiple codes can be used to describe an individual's functional picture. Additional classifications in one or more of the four primary ICF chapters would be chosen with the goal of capturing the veteran's full clinical picture using standardized terminology that aptly describes the consequences of identified conditions (diagnoses).

ADOPTION OF THE ICF

In May of 2001 the ICF was approved by 191 countries as the international standard for the classification of health and health-related states (Bruyere & Peterson, 2005). In addition to its international status, the ICF also has interdisciplinary appeal. In June 2008 the American Physical Therapy Association (APTA) House of Delegates officially endorsed the ICF, and its use has been identified as an assistive tool in the management of disorders including chronic low back pain (Rundell, Davenport, & Wagner, 2009) and flexor tendon rehabilitation (Oltman, Neises, Scheible, Mehrtens, & Grüneberg, 2008), and as a conceptual framework for guiding ergonomic intervention (Leyshon & Shaw, 2008). Kearney and Pryor (2004) supported the ICF's application as conceptual scaffold for broadening nurses' awareness of the multi-factorial nature of disability.

The American Speech and Hearing Association (ASHA) adopted the ICF as the framework for assessment and intervention in the *2001 Scope of Practice in Speech-Language Pathology* (ASHA, 2001). The ICF has been found helpful in informing clinical practices, such as in alaryngeal speech rehabilitation (Eadie, 2003) and in discerning change in function following language therapy (Thomas-Stonell, Oddson, Robertson, & Rosenbaum, 2009). Its utility has also been recognized in identifying functional communication outcomes in persons diagnosed with traumatic brain injury (Larkins, Worrall, & Hickson, 2008). Barrow (2006) suggested that the ICF has good potential for social work classification and assessment, given that it prioritizes the social model of disability.

The ICF was also used in a pilot study designed to understand the challenges faced by OEF and OIF veterans as they reintegrate into the community (Resnik & Allen, 2007). The authors recognized that the combined prevalence of TBI and PTSD among OEF/OIF veterans places them at greater risk for experiencing poor community reintegration. Using qualitative data collected from OEF/OIF service members, family members, and clinicians, they concluded that "the ICF framework of participation provided a comprehensive lens through which to understand the challenges in role participation faced by injured veterans as they reintegrate into the community" (p. 1003). Understanding the needs of OEF/OIF veterans can be enhanced through the appropriate use of ICF taxonomic categories.

Coinciding with the ICF's descriptive breadth is an unwieldy quality, which makes difficult the efficient assimilation into clinical practice. A barrier to its everyday application stems from the fact that in its original form the ICF is comprised of more than 1400 categories. Although it is a comprehensive reference, making it more "user-friendly" is necessary to facilitate more widespread use in the healthcare setting. Recognizing that its breadth can be a barrier, brief and comprehensive disease specific *core sets* are now being developed. Core sets represent a selection of categories from the whole classification, which can adequately describe patients' functioning and disability when used conjointly with ICF qualifiers. They have been developed for a variety of health conditions including spinal cord injury (Biering-Sørensen et al., 2006), multiple sclerosis (Kesselring et al., 2008), bipolar disorder (Vieta et al., 2007), metabolic disorders and other chronic conditions (Cieza et al., 2004), and more recently TBI (Bernabeu et al., 2009).

The American Psychological Association (APA), in collaboration with other professional associations, is preparing a publication entitled *Procedural Manual and Guide for a Standardized Application of the ICF: A Manual for Health Professionals* (http://icf.apa.org/). The manual is designed to make application of the ICF, in various clinical settings, easy and efficient.

BENEFITS OF THE ICF

Since its inception in 2001 the ICF has had a major impact on how disability is conceptualized and measured, and its use is growing within the United States and internationally (Jelsma, 2009). Reasons to consider its use exist at multiple levels (WHO, 2001). At the person-centered level, prioritizing the functional consequences of health problems allows for more targeted and personally relevant treatment planning and outcome measurement. To know what functions and activities a person can perform, rather than only knowing the true diagnosis, helps clinicians identify interventions that are best suited, thus promoting desired outcomes (Ustun, Chatterji, Bickenbach, Kostanjsek, & Schneider, 2003).

At the organizational level the functional language embedded within the ICF can help to enhance communication and team collaboration and can serve as a guide to performance improvement initiatives. At the societal level the ICF offers a mechanism for collecting population-level data that can be used to guide policy decisions and to improve the quality of rehabilitation services for veterans.

ICF AS A MEANS OF CODING PRE- AND POST-DEPLOYMENT HEALTH

The ICF's multidimensional coding scheme can be employed to create a valuable summary of an individual's health at the outset of military service, with ratings acquired at specified intervals and following events that have the potential to disrupt functioning and participation. Pre and post deployment would be critical times during which ICF health updates could be gathered. Specific methods of health assessment would need to be identified, including those focusing on neurocognitive functions.

The Automated Neuropsychological Assessment Metrics (ANAM) is one such measure that has recently been implemented by the armed forces as a pre-deployment screening (U.S. Government Accountability Office, 2008). However, in accordance with the biopsychosocial framework of the ICF, a more complete and holistic data set would need to be gathered for the purpose of informing the treatment team on how the course of recovery might be influenced. Relevant dimensions have been shown to predict injury outcome and can be effectively coded using the ICF system. Such dimensions include pre-injury productivity (Keyser-Marcus et al., 2002), level of educational attainment (Stulemeijer, van der Werf, Borm, & Vos, 2008), pre-existing psychological problems (Robertson, Rath, Fournet, Zelhart, & Estes, 1994), and social support (Ergh, Rapport, Coleman, & Hanks, 2002), as well as other personal health details. Consideration should also be given to developing core sets similar to those devised for other conditions and settings. The challenge on this front would be to identify pertinent measures that directly assess ICF dimensions and classification.

Reed and colleagues (2005) discussed the intricacies of matching assessment findings to the ICF, recognizing that assessment data tend to be far more detailed and imperfectly aligned with ICF units of classification. Perhaps the clearest example of the differences between assessment data and the ICF is in the transposition of neuropsychological findings. Although shades of nuance in cognitive and executive functioning are gleaned through neuropsychological assessment, the richness of these results is not matched by an equally sensitive set of classification units. Yet the right blend of psychometric analysis, clinical interview, self-report, and observational data can be identified, offering a reasonably complete picture of functioning and health, the results of which can be translated to ICF codes. The ICF also supports the use of evaluation methods that are closely linked to the selection of treatment goals and therapeutic techniques (Bickenbach, Chatterji, Bradley, & Ustin, 1999). Transforming neuropsychological results to more functionally described assets and limitations may offer many advantages, including the development of ecologically relevant interventions to address cognitive dysfunction. Treatment effectiveness should not be measured by the degree to which a test score has risen, but rather by the extent to which an injured person can increasingly perform a desired real-world activity. This level of outcome measurement may be more easily captured by the ICF than a cognitive measure. The discrepancy between psychometric analysis and real-life function is an area ripe for neuropsychological research investigation.

ICF AS THE POLYTRAUMA REHABILITATION FOUNDATION

Accompanying the serious injuries facing veterans is the reality that recovery is likely to involve creating a new sense of self and purpose beyond the limits of the impairments that for many will inevitably persist over time. This challenge is particularly relevant when veterans face what has been termed "polytrauma" which, according to the Veterans Health Administration, involves injury to the brain (traumatic brain injury; TBI) and to other body parts or systems, resulting in multifaceted impairments and functional disability (Dept of Veterans Affaris, Veterans Health Administration, 2005). Rehabilitation in these cases should be qualitatively different from less-complex injury cases in that recovery following polytrauma is rarely a linear process of improvement. "Polytrauma rehabilitation" tends to progress as a series of small steps (some likely to be backwards) whereby a person learns to accept and overcome the challenges brought about by a disability. The infrastructure of a polytrauma rehabilitation program, which is prepared to address these complex issues, can be more easily developed through the language and conceptual essence of the ICF.

Although partitioning a dimension as complex as polytrauma rehabilitation can result in oversimplification, Table 1 outlines attributes essential to "polytrauma rehabilitation," which we contrast with traditional features of a more conventional rehabilitation therapy. The *scope* of the polytrauma rehabilitation model recognizes that community reintegration subsumes maximum body functioning. Although maximizing anatomical functioning will always be a treatment priority, functional gains in daily life do not naturally spring from reductions in impairment, and body structure and function are not the most decisive indicators of how a person will ultimately function in his or her daily life (Reed et al., 2005). This view is philosophically aligned with the structural values of the ICF, which espouses the measurement of societal functioning, regardless of why impairments exist and advocates to assist those served take advantage of their individual strengths to the fullest possible degree (WHO, 2001).

Similarly, *identified goals* of polytrauma rehabilitation should be defined in terms of regaining valued life skills; living life autonomously, social assimilation, and engagement in productive and meaningful life roles within the community (i.e., community reintegration). The effectiveness of rehabilitation should therefore be measured in amounts of reduction in disability experienced by the patient (e.g., improved ability to independently prepare meals; resumed ability to participate in religious services). The taxonomic language of the ICF, in particular those attributes comprising the dimension of *activity* and *participation*, appear to be appropriate for describing and measuring the progression toward community reintegration (Ustun et al., 2003).

The *veteran's experience* and the *role of the family* are also important dimensions to consider as polytrauma rehabilitation programs are developed to meet the needs of returning veterans. Historically, medical experts treated patients as passive recipients of services that were delivered until such time as a "plateau" in recovery was reached. Fortunately times have changed and a different view of rehabilitation has emerged, capturing the active role of patients and their families in the rehabilitation process and defining recovery beyond return of body functions. These changes have critical implications for how patients and their families are encouraged to participate. Clinicians are challenged to equip patients and their families to become the "experts," and it is the role of the polytrauma rehabilitation team to assist in developing that expertise. This movement is consistent with the biopsychosocial model on which the ICF is based and the ethical provisions it incorporates.

Representing individuals through alphanumeric descriptions can potentially be dehumanizing; as such, the ICF offers ethical guidelines that are designed to inform health care classifications (Peterson & Threats, 2005). Two of those guidelines directly promote the involvement of the persons served and their families. For example, within clinical use, "the person whose level of functioning is being classified, or the person's advocate, should have the opportunity to participate, and in particular to challenge or affirm the appropriateness of the category being used and the assessment assigned" (Peterson & Threats, 2005, p. 131). With regard to the ICF's social use, the user is guided to employ the ICF information "to the greatest extent feasible, with the collaboration of individuals to enhance their choices and their control over their lives" (WHO, 2001, pp. 244–245).

Table 1 Traditional versus comprehensive polytrauma rehabilitation models

Rehabilitation feature	"Traditional" model	Comprehensive "Polytrauma" model
Scope	Rehabilitation is conceived as reparatory treatment designed to restore or maintain maximum possible functioning to anatomical damage. Remains focused on what can be done to remedy impairment as much as possible.	Rehabilitation is seen as a process not only of maximizing organ function but also of helping persons to develop new skills to compensate for losses and open up new areas of meaningful life. Maximum participation in the community subsumes maximum body function.
Identified goals	Goals are defined as improved functioning in specific areas of impairment (e.g., increase range of motion, improve ability to memorize list of words).	Goals are defined in terms of regaining the life skills that are needed in order to function optimally in life roles (e.g., get to work, go shopping, care for children). Focuses from the start on the veteran's reintegration into home and community including compensating for impairments that cannot be remedied.
Patient's experience	Patients come to therapy to be treated by experts.	Veteran and family become experts together with the team in defining and achieving new life goals.
Role of family	Family involvement is not systematically included.	Family involvement is considered a vital element in the success of the rehabilitation.
Integration of treatment	Not an essential issue.	Staff professionals constantly interacting, co-treating, addressing goals from several perspectives, and jointly assessing results, etc.
Applicability	Suitable for veterans whose disabling condition will not significantly disrupt their life course.	Suitable for all rehabilitation patients, particularly those whose rehabilitation will entail developing and accepting altered life roles.

The *integration of treatment* is also an essential component of polytrauma rehabilitation. By integration, the team's style (team includes patients and their families) and values are emphasized, with recognition that optimal outcomes occur when group members are identified as equally important, capable of collaborating, developing cooperative goals, and building trusting relationships to achieve shared goals (Kouzes & Pozner, 1987). Historically, rehabilitation was delivered in a discipline-specific fashion, with goals formulated by each professional using terminology that minimized fuzziness between professional boundaries (i.e., a multidisciplinary approach). Gradually there has been a move toward greater professional synergism whereby the collective expertise of professionals is combined and brought to bear toward the goal of promoting functional change (i.e., an interdisciplinary approach). This integration movement is continuing within polytrauma rehabilitation. Team members are increasingly sharing roles and crossing over discipline-specific boundaries while simultaneously orienting their efforts around the valued outcomes and perspectives of the consumer (i.e., a transdisciplinary approach). The ICF language is patient-centered and thus emphasizes the potential contributions of each rehabilitation team member. In turn, the goal of promoting optimal patient functioning within the context of his/her environments, and based on valued preferences, is more likely to emerge.

Studies examining the benefit of the ICF, as it promotes the rehabilitation team process, have been reported. For example, Rentsch et al. (2003) found that implementing the ICF classification resulted in improved work processes and promoted a more systematic approach to interdisciplinary rehabilitation activities. Tempest and McIntyre (2006) studied the utility of the ICF in clarifying team roles and clinical reasoning in stroke rehabilitation. Their findings demonstrated that the ICF is useful in aiding communication and structuring the provision of services, and that it offers guidance in clarifying team roles especially when there appears to be role overlap. Darzins, Fone, and Darzins (2006) offered a similar viewpoint, noting that the ICF can "help guide clinical reasoning about clinical assessments and interventions to provide optimal client-centered care and, ultimately, to help us edge nearer to an 'ideal' health-care system" (p. 127). These authors helped clarify the clinical value of the ICF. This initial evidence of the ICF's value serves as a basis for adopting the ICF in polytrauma rehabilitation of OEF and OIF veterans. Neuropsychologists, by education, training, and experience, are well positioned to play significant roles in the comprehensive conceptualization and care of veterans receiving polytrauma rehabilitation.

CONCLUSIONS

The primary objective of the present article was to highlight the relevance of the International Classification of Functioning, Disability and Health (ICF), for neuropsychological assessment and treatment in the context of polytrauma rehabilitation. The ICF, a comprehensive and systematic biopsychosocial classification model of health and disability, possesses a strong potential to improve the delivery of health care to veterans returning from Iraq and Afghanistan who have experienced neurological and/or psychiatric trauma. The overarching conceptual framework of the ICF offers many potential benefits, from enhancing communication to shaping contemporary rehabilitation programs to serving as a guide to health policy design and implementation. Although the ICF is an imperfect taxonomic system, it holds considerable promise for promoting a comprehensive understanding of patients. Traditional neuropsychological assessment that is based on an ICF foundation will maximize the ultimate goal of helping veterans maximize functioning and quality of life. In the absence of a common conceptual framework, development of effective therapeutic systems will be hindered (Steiner et al., 2002).

As neuropsychologists, health care professionals, and citizens we bear a commitment to serve those who have served us. Doing so starts with a personal commitment to use the methods that best allow us, as health care givers, to know those whom we are called to serve, beyond diagnosis, in a manner that provides an understanding of health concerns and their functional ramifications. The ICF has the potential to assist the health care community to reduce suffering, and to promote participation in healthcare rehabilitation and recovery in the most effective and benevolent manner possible.

REFERENCES

American Congress of Rehabilitation Medicine, Head Injury Interdisciplinary Special Interest Group. (1993). Definition of mild traumatic brain injury. *Journal of Head Trauma Rehabilitation, 8*, 86–87.

American Psychiatric Association. (2000). *Diagnostic and Statistical Manual of Mental Disorders, 4th Edition, Text Revision*. Washington, DC: American Psychiatric Association.

American Speech and Hearing Association. (2001). *Scope of practice in speech-language pathology*. Posted online and retrieved March 24, 2009 from: http://www.asha.org/docs/html/SP2007-00283.html

Barrow, F. H. (2006). The International Classification of Functioning, Disability and Health (ICF), a new tool for social workers. *Journal of Social Work in Disability and Rehabilitation, 5*, 65–73.

Bernabeu, M., Laxe, S., Lopez, R., Stucki, G., Ward, A., Barnes, M., et al. (2009). Developing core sets for persons with traumatic brain injury based on the International Classification of Functioning, Disability and Health. *Neurorehabilitation and Neural Repair Online*. Posted online at http://nnr.sagepub.com/cgi/content/abstract/1545968308328725v1 February 12, 2009.

Bickenbach, J., Chatterji, S., Bradley, E. M., & Ustin, T. B. (1999). Models of disablement, universalism, and the International Classification of Impairments, Disabilities and Handicaps. *Social Science Medicine, 48*, 1173–1187.

Biering-Sørensen, F., Scheuringer, M., Baumberger, M., Charlifue, S. W., Post, M. W., Montero, F., et al. (2006). Developing core sets for persons with spinal cord injuries based on the International Classification of Functioning, Disability and Health as a way to specify functioning. *Spinal Cord, 44*, 541–546.

Bruyere, S. M., & Peterson, D. B. (2005). Introduction to the special section on the International Classification of Functioning, Disability and Health: Implications for rehabilitation psychology. *Rehabilitation Psychology, 50*, 103–104.

Cieza, A., Ewert, T., Ustün, T. B., Chatterji, S., Kostanjsek, N., & Stucki, G. (2004). Development of ICF Core Sets for patients with chronic conditions. *Journal of Rehabilitation Medicine, 44*(supplement), 9–11.

Darzins, P., Fone, S., & Darzins, S. (2006). The International Classification of Functioning, Disability and Health can help to structure and evaluate therapy. *Australian Occupational Therapy Journal, 53,* 127–131.

Department of Veterans Affairs, Veterans Health Administration. (2005). *Directive 2005-024: Polytrauma Rehabilitation Centers.* Washington, DC: Author. Retrieved 2/22/09 from www1.va.gov/vhapublications/ViewPublication.asp?pub_ID=1274

Eadie, T. (2003). The ICF: A proposed framework for comprehensive rehabilitation of individuals who use alaryngeal speech. *American Journal of Speech-Language Pathology, 12,* 189–197.

Ergh, T. C., Rapport, L. J., Coleman, R. D., & Hanks, R. A. (2002). Predictors of caregiver and family functioning following traumatic brain injury: Social support. *Journal of Head Trauma Rehabilitation, 17*(2), 155–174.

Gatchel, R. J., Polatin, P. B., Mayer, T. G., & Garcy, P. D. (1994). Psychopathology and the rehabilitation of patients with chronic low back pain disability. *Archives of Physical Medicine and Rehabilitation, 75,* 666–670.

Hoge, C. W, Auchterlonic, J. L., & Milliken, C. (2006). Mental health problems, use of mental health services, and attrition from military service after returning from deployment to Iraq or Afghanistan. *Journal of the American Medical Association, 295,* 1023.

Jelsma, J. (2009). Use of the International Classification of Functioning, Disability and Health: A literature survey. *Journal of Rehabilitation Medicine, 41,* 1–12.

Karney, B. R., Ramchand, R., Osilla, K. C., Caldarone, L. B., & Burns, R. M. (2008). *Invisible wounds: Predicting the immediate and long-term consequences of mental health problems in veterans of Operation Enduring Freedom and Operation Iraqi Freedom. Rand–Center for Military Health Policy Research.* Document No. WR-546-CCF. Retrieved 2/22/09 from: http://www.rand.org/pubs/working_papers/WR546/

Kearney, P., & Pryor, J. (2004). The international classification of functioning, disability and health and nursing. *Journal of Advanced Nursing, 46,* 162–170.

Kesselring, J., Coenen, M., Cieza, A., Thompson, A., Kostanjsek, N., & Stucki, G. (2008). Developing the ICF Core Sets for multiple sclerosis to specify functioning. *Multiple Sclerosis, 14,* 252–254.

Keyser-Marcus, L. A., Bricout, J. C., Wehman, P., Campbell, L. R., Cifu, D. X., Englander, J., et al. (2002). Acute predictors of return to employment after traumatic brain injury: A longitudinal follow-up. *Archives of Physical Medicine & Rehabilitation, 83*(5), 635–641.

Kouzes, J. M., & Posner, B. Z. (1987). *The leadership challenge: How to get extraordinary things done in organizations.* San Francisco: Jossey-Bass.

Larkins, B., Worrall, L., & Hickson, L. (2008). Developing a traumatic brain injury index for social and vocational communication outcomes (SAVCO). *Brain Injury, 9,* 247–266.

Leyshon, R. T., & Shaw, L. E. (2008). Using the ICF as a conceptual framework to guide ergonomic intervention in occupational rehabilitation. *Work, 31,* 47–61.

McCrone, P., & Phelan, M. (1994). Diagnosis and length of psychiatric in-patient stay. *Psychological Medicine, 24,* 1025–1030.

Oltman, R., Neises, G., Scheible, D., Mehrtens, G., & Grüneberg, C. (2008). ICF components of corresponding outcome measures in flexor tendon rehabilitation – a systematic review. *BMC Musculoskeletal Disorders, 9,* 139.

Ormel, J., Oldehinkel, T., Brilman, E., & vanden Brink, W. (1993). Outcome of depression and anxiety in primary care: A three wave 3/12 year study of psychopathology and disability. *Archives of General Psychiatry, 50,* 759–766.

Peterson, D. B. (2005). International classification of functioning, disability and health: An introduction for rehabilitation psychologists. *Rehabilitation Psychology, 50,* 105–112.

Peterson, D. B., & Rosenthal, D. A. (2005). The international Classification of Functioning: Disability and Health (ICF): A primer for rehabilitation educators. *Rehabilitation Education, 19*(2/3), 81–94.

Peterson, D. B., & Threats, T. (2005). Introduction to the special issue of Rehabilitation Education: The International Classification of Functioning, Disability and Health (ICF). *Rehabilitation Education, 19,* 75–80.

Reed, G. M., Lux, J. B., Bufka, L. F., Trask, C., Peterson, D. B., Stark, S., et al. (2005). Operationalizing the international classification of functioning, disability and health in clinical settings. *Rehabilitation Psychology, 50,* 122–131.

Rentsch, H. P., Bucher, P., Dommen-Nyffeler, I., Wolf, C., Hefti, H., Fluri, E., et al. (2003). The implementation of the international classification of functioning, disability and health (ICF) in daily practice of neurorehabilitation: An international project at the Kantonsspital of Lucerne, Switzerland. *Disability and Rehabilitation, 25,* 411–421.

Resnik, L. J., & Allen, S. M. (2007). Using International Classification of Functioning, Disability and Health to understand challenges in community reintegration of injured veterans. *Journal of Rehabilitation Research and Development, 44,* 991–1006.

Robertson, E., Rath, B, Fournet, G., Zelhart, P., & Estes, R. (1994). Assessment of mild brain trauma: A preliminary study of the influence of premorbid factors. *The Clinical Neuropsychologist, 8,* 69–74.

Rundell, S. D., Davenport, T. E., & Wagner, T. (2009). Physical therapist management of acute and chronic low back pain. *Physical Therapy, 89,* 82–90.

Sbordone, R. J., & Long, C. J. (1996). *Ecological validity of neuropsychological testing.* Boca Raton, FL: CRC Press.

Seal, K. H., Bertenthal, D., Miner, C. R., Sen, S., & Marmar, C. (2007). Bringing the war back home: Mental health disorders among 103788 US veterans returning from Iraq and Afghanistan seen at Department of Veterans Affairs facilities. *Archives of Internal Medicine, 167,* 476–482.

Steiner, W. A., Ryser, L., Huber, E., Uebelhart, D., Aeschlimann, A., & Stucki, G. (2002). Use of the ICF model as a clinical problem-solving tool in physical therapy and rehabilitation medicine. *Physical Therapy, 82,* 1098–1107.

Stucki, G., Ewert, T., & Cieza, A. (2003). Value and application of the ICF in rehabilitation medicine. *Disability and Rehabilitation, 25,* 628–634.

Stulemeijer, M., van der Werf, S., Borm, G. F., & Vos, P. E. (2008). Early predictions of favourable recovery 6 months after mild traumatic brain injury. *Journal of Neurology, Neurosurgery and Psychiatry, 79,* 936–942.

Taber, K. H., & Turley, R. A. (2009). PTSD and combat-related injuries: Functional neuroanatomy. *The Journal of Neuropsychiatry and Clinical Neurosciences, 21,* 1–5.

Tempest, S., & McIntyre, A. (2006). Using the ICF to clarify team roles and demonstrate clinical reasoning in stroke rehabilitation. *Disability and Rehabilitation, 28,* 663–667.

Thomas-Stonell, N., Oddson, B., Robertson, B., & Rosenbaum, P. (2009). Predicted and observed outcomes in preschool children following speech and language treatment: Parent and clinician perspectives. *Journal of Communication Disorders, 42,* 29–42.

United States Government Accountability Office. (2008). *DOD Health Care: Mental health and traumatic brain injury screening efforts implemented but consistent pre-deployment medical record review policies needed. May GAO-08-615.* Retrieved 3/1/09 from: www.gao.gov/new.items/d08615.pdf

Ustun, T. B., Chaterji, S., Bickenbach, J., Kastanjsek, N., & Schneider, M. (2003). The International Classification of Functioning, Disability and Health: A new tool for understanding disability and health. *Disability and Rehabilitation, 25,* 565–571.

Vieta, E., Cieza, A., Stucki, G., Chatterji, S., Nieto, M., Sanchez-Moreno, J., et al. (2007). Developing core sets for persons with bipolar disorder based on the International Classification of Functioning, Disability and Health. *Bipolar Disorders, 9*, 16–24.

World Health Organization. (2001). *International Classification of Functioning, Disability and Health.* Geneva: WHO.

INSTRUCTIONS FOR AUTHORS

The Clinical Neuropsychologist (TCN) provides in-depth discussions of matters germane to the practicing clinical neuropsychologist. Clinical neuropsychology is a rapidly expanding field, there is a need for airing of empirical data, models, concepts, and positions pertaining to educational, clinical, and professional issues. *TCN* is designed to provide a forum for such presentation and discussions.

Submission

Manuscripts must be submitted through the journal's Scholar One website, http://mc.manuscriptcentral.com/ntcn. Questions for the editor may be addressed to: Russell M. Bauer at **rbauer@phhp.ufl.edu** or to Jerry J. Sweet at **jerrysweet@uchicago.edu**

Each manuscript must be accompanied by a statement that it has not been published elsewhere and that it has not been submitted simultaneously for publication in another source. Authors are responsible for obtaining permission to reproduce copyrighted material from other sources and are required to sign an agreement for the transfer of copyright to the publisher. All accepted manuscripts, artwork, and photographs become the property of the publisher. Authors are responsible for disclosing any funding sources and financial interests that could create a potential conflict of interest (see volume 18, page 1). All parts of the manuscript should be typewritten, double-spaced, with margins of at least one inch on all sides. Authors should also supply a shortened version of the title suitable for the running head, not exceeding 50 character spaces. Each article should be summarized in an abstract of not more than 120 words. Avoid abbreviations, diagrams, and reference to the text in the abstract.

Before uploading your final accepted manuscript authors must check the following:

- The first page of the article contains all author(s) contact details.
- The number of tables is the same as the number of table legends, table and figure numbers are consecutive and figures are numbered.
- Journal titles in text or references must not be abbreviated. Please supply full journal names.
- You must supply your accepted manuscript in document format, not as a pdf.

References

Cite in the text by author and date (Smith, Jones, & Brown, 1983). Prepare reference list in accordance with the APA Publication Manual, 5th ed. Examples:

Journal: Tsai, M., & Wagner, N. N. (1978). Therapy groups for women sexually molested as children. *Archives of Sexual Behaviour, 7*(6), 417–427.

Book: Millman, M. (1980). *Such a pretty face*. New York: W. W. Norton.

Contribution to a Book: Hartley, J. T., & Walsh, D. A. (1980). Contemporary issues in adult development of learning. In L. W. Poon (Ed.), *Ageing in the 1980s* (pp. 239–252). Washington, DC: American Psychological Association.

Illustrations

Illustrations submitted (line drawings, halftones, photos, photomicrographs, etc.) should be clean originals or digital files. Digital files are recommended for highest quality reproduction and should follow these guidelines:

- 300 dpi or higher
- Sized to fit on journal page
- JPEG or TIFF format only
- Submitted as separate files, not embedded in text files

Color illustrations will be considered for publication; however, the author will be required to bear the full cost involved in their printing and publication. The charge for the first page with color is $900.00. The next three pages with color are $450.00 each. A custom quote will be provided for color art totaling more than 4 journal pages. Good-quality color prints should be provided in their final size. The publisher has the right to refuse publication of color prints deemed unacceptable.

Tables and Figures

Tables and figures (illustrations) should not be embedded in the text, but should be included as separate sheets or files. A short descriptive title should appear above each table with a clear legend and any footnotes suitably identified below. All units must be included. Figures should be completely labeled, taking into account necessary size reduction. Captions should be typed, double-spaced, on a separate sheet. All original figures should be clearly marked in pencil on the reverse side with the number, author's name, and top edge indicated.

Proofs

Page proofs are sent to the designated author using Taylor & Francis' EProof system. They must be carefully checked and returned within 48 hours of receipt.

Offprints/Reprints

The corresponding author will receive 25 reprints of their article upon registration with Rightslink, our authorized reprint provider. Authors will need to create a unique account and register with Rightslink for this free service. The link is provided at the time of page proof review. Complimentary reprints are not available post publication.

Grand Rounds in Clinical Neuropsychology

Overview

Grand Rounds in Clinical Neuropsychology, a new section in *TCN*, is devoted to case presentations of interesting, timely, important, or unusual cases. Cases of interest to be considered may represent unusual presentations of well-known disorders/syndromes, rarely seen disorders, 'classic' or prototypical neuropsychological syndromes (text-book presentations), or other cases of distinction. Adult and child cases will be considered. Criteria for publication include a well-documented history of the patient, medical/neurologic/psychiatric findings, neuroimaging (*preferred, but not required*), neuropsychological evaluation, discussion, and conclusions. Cases should be instructive and focus on the contributions that competent neuropsychological assessment makes in terms of:

(1) elucidating brain-behavior relationships;
(2) determining the functional status of patients; and
(3) instructing intervention, treatment, rehabilitation, education, etc.

TCN Grand Rounds in Clinical Neuropsychology, unlike the aims and scope of *Neurocase*, a sister publication of T&F, will not focus on elucidating theoretical aspects of brain-behavior relations, but instead will focus on well-known and documented aspects of "behavioral geography" particularly as illustrated in neurological or neuropsychiatric conditions.

Format

Two general formats will be utilized:

(1) The traditional case presentation format, where the diagnosis/syndrome/disorder known in advance, usually in the title, and
(2) clinical problem-solving cases, where the diagnosis/syndrome/disorder is not revealed until the conclusion, similar in organization to the Grand Rounds Presentations of the Massachusetts General Hospital in the *New England Journal of Medicine*.

Page Limitations

A maximum of 35 pages, **double spaced**, inclusive of references. Allowances will be made for slight departures, dependent on the case.

Neuropsychological Testing

Neuropsychological assessment may follow a flexible or fixed battery approach, as long as the referral question is appropriately and fully answered. Truncated or focused assessment batteries may be acceptable in specific cases; comprehensive testing is not always indicated or necessarily appropriate. Authors are encouraged to present cases that illustrate assessment skills and clinical knowledge at an advanced level, illustrative of strong clinical judgment skills.

Literature Review

Sufficient review of the literature regarding the syndrome is necessary, but this should not be overly elaborated and detailed. Where presented findings are congruent or at odds with 'classic' cases, this should be so noted and appropriately referenced. Presentations of a relatively 'pure' prototypical disorder should reference the original article (e.g., a circumscribed Gerstmann's syndrome).

Neuroimaging

Authors are encouraged to present CT/MRI when available, documenting the relationship between neuropsychological test findings and cerebral abnormalities. Where definitive "diagnoses" have been made in a neurological or other medical venue, confirmatory evidence must be presented. These may include neuroimaging where available (this is preferred; we will publish b&w CT/MRI), scans, pathology reports, inclusive of examination by board certified medical specialists.

Types of Cases

The editor(s) will consider most types of clinical cases. These may include well-known and documented neurological conditions, low base rate (rarer or unusual) disorders, and common disorders with an unusual presentation or neuropsychological findings (e.g., a large cerebral neoplasm with a paucity of neuropsychological test abnormalities), neurodevelopmental conditions (in the case of a pediatric presentation), and disorders of controversial etiology (e.g., CFS). Cases involving poor effort, frank malingering, factitious disorders and the like must include appropriate use of SVTs and documentation of a lack of medical evidence. Some psychiatric conditions with known or putative CNS abnormalities may be appropriate (e.g., schizophrenia) at the discretion of the editor(s).

Grand Rounds in Clinical Neuropsychology is an exciting new section in *TCN*. As part of one of neuropsychology's leading journal publications, the highest professional standards of practice and publication are expected.

Queries relating to the '**Grand Rounds**' Section should be addressed to Joel Morgan at **joelmor@comcast.net**

Enhance your clinical judgment with the new WAIS-IV

- Obtain the data you need for making clinical decisions quicker due to *a shortened administration time*.
- Address the needs of your older clients with items and tasks that are more *developmentally appropriate*.
- Be confident in the data presented for your clients with special needs using *new special group studies*.

Find out about more enhancements at WAIS-IV.com.

Change you can count on

- Older Adult Battery, focus on visual memory, and improved floors *address the needs of Older Adults*.
- Gain insight with the *Brief Cognitive Status Exam (BCSE)*.
- Stay abreast of changing demographics with studies on *new clinical groups*.

Find out about more enhancements at WMS-IV.com

If WAIS-IV or WMS-IV is where you start your evaluation—ACS will help you take it to the next level

- Additional data for special applications such as *Pre-morbid IQ and Demographically Adjusted Norms*.
- Social Perception, Effort/Motivation and Executive Function are *new subsets and measures*.
- For in-depth analysis of special clients see Additional Clinical groups such as *MCI, TBI, Temporal Lobe Epilepsy, Schizophrenia, Dementia, Autism, and Asperger's*.

To order, or for more information please contact us today.

PEARSON   800.627.7271 | PsychCorp.com

AUTHOR SERVICES

Publish With Us

  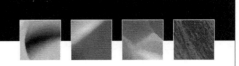

The Taylor & Francis Group Author Services Department aims to enhance your publishing experience as a journal author and optimize the impact of your article in the global research community. Assistance and support is available, from preparing the submission of your article through to setting up citation alerts post-publication on **informa**world[TM], our online platform offering cross-searchable access to journal, book and database content.

Our Author Services Department can provide advice on how to:

- direct your submission to the correct journal
- prepare your manuscript according to the journal's requirements
- maximize your article's citations
- submit supplementary data for online publication
- submit your article online via Manuscript Central[TM]
- apply for permission to reproduce images
- prepare your illustrations for print
- track the status of your manuscript through the production process
- return your corrections online
- purchase reprints through Rightslink[TM]
- register for article citation alerts
- take advantage of our i*OpenAccess* option
- access your article online
- benefit from rapid online publication via i*First*

See further information at:
www.informaworld.com/authors

or contact:
Author Services Manager, Taylor & Francis, 4 Park Square, Milton Park, Abingdon, Oxon OX14 4RN, UK, email: authorqueries@tandf.co.uk